41

Biblical Greek

Illustrated by Examples
by Maximilian Zerwick S.J.

Ninth Reprint

GREGORIAN & BIBLICAL PRESS

1963 – First Edition
1977 – First Reprint
1979 – Second Reprint
1985 – Third Reprint
1987 – Fourth Reprint
1990 – Fifth Reprint
1994 – Sixth Reprint
2001 – Seventh Reprint
2005 – Eight Reprint
2011 – Ninth Reprint

IMPRIMI POTEST
Romae die 18 oct. 1963
R.A.F. MacKenzie, sj
Rector Pont. Inst. Biblici

IMPRIMATUR
Vicariatus Urbis, die 21 oct. 1963
Aloysius, Card. Provicarius

Cover: Serena Aureli

© 2011 Gregorian & Biblical Press
Piazza della Pilotta 35, 00187 - Roma
www.gbpress.net - books@biblicum.com

ISBN 978-88-7653-554-3

Fr. Maximilian Zerwick, S.J., was a much revered professor of New Testament Greek at the Pontifical Biblical Institute for almost forty years until his death in 1975. During most of this time students who came to study at the Institute invariably had a background of classical Greek as part of their preparation for biblical studies. It was the task of Fr. Zerwick to help them make the transition from classical Greek to the "koine" Greek of the New Testament. He wrote in Latin (all students at the time knew Latin) "Graecitas Biblica" as a textbook for the course. The book consists of examples from the New Testament of how the Greek language functions in the text of the New Testament. "Graecitas Biblica" is thus the product of Fr. Zerwick's many years of experience and his knowledge not only of the Greek language but also of the text of the New Testament. As such it has considerable value for all those interested in discovering the nuances of the Greek of the New Testament. The Latin text of "Graecitas Biblica" was translated into English by Fr. Joseph Smith, S.J., a colleague of Fr. Zerwick at the Institute. It is this English translation which is here reprinted for the first time as part of the series "Subsidia Biblica".

James SWETNAM, S.J.
St. Louis, Missouri, U.S.A., 22 February 2011

FOREWORD

The success which attended the Latin « Graecitas Biblica » from its first (1944) to its revised and enlarged fourth edition (1960) suggested the advisability of an English translation. My colleague J. P. Smith (some of whose suggestions had already been incorporated in the fourth edition) has not only seen to the translation, but also contributed certain additions, notably in the chapters on the « tenses » and the « moods ».

The paragraph-numbers of the *third* edition are indicated in the margin because it is to that edition that reference is made in my *Analysis philologica Novi Testamenti graeci* of which 20,000 copies are in circulation.

Two works to which reference is frequently made are now likewise available in English translation, namely (Blass-) Debrunner's Grammar: *A Greek Grammar of the New Testament and Other Early Christian Literature. A Translation and Revision...*, by R. W. Funk (Cambridge – Chicago 1961) and Bauer's *Lexicon*: Arndt W. F. - Gingrich F. W., *A Greek-English Lexicon of the New Testament and...* (Cambridge – Chicago 1957).

In conclusion, it may be remarked that the purpose of the present treatise was not so much a purely scientific or philological one, as that of encouraging future ministers of the Word to have recourse to the original Greek text. This accounts for the multiplication of examples to illustrate the exegetical importance of the study of the κοινή, and also for the fact that attention has been given almost exclusively to points of syntax, morphology being relegated to a few remarks in the Conclusion.

Rome, the day of the election of Paul VI (21-6-1963)

M. ZERWICK S. J.

CONTENTS

Contents

Contents

XI

XII

Contents

Contents

I. GRAMMATICAL CONCORD (¹)

1) The Use of the Plural

1. **The indefinite plural** is a common enough usage, at least in those languages which lack a special form of indefinite subject pronoun such as the German « man » or the French « on ». It is used with especial frequency with verbs of telling: « they say » etc., cf. in Latin « dicunt, ferunt, tradunt ». Other verbs in the NT have perhaps been affected by the influence of the Aramaic tendency to avoid the use of the passive voice, e. g. Lk 12, 20 « Fool! This night your soul is required of you » ἄφρον, ταύτῃ τῇ νυκτὶ τὴν ψυχήν σου ἀ π α ι τ ο ῦ σ ι ν ἀπὸ σοῦ (WELLHAUSEN) (²).

2. It is however possible that here (Lk 12, 20) as elsewhere the indefinite plural is used as a circumlocution for the name of God. Thus Lk

---

(¹) Obviously, the sources used have been in the first place the principal grammars of Biblical Greek: F. M. ABEL, *Grammaire du grec biblique* 1927; A. DEBRUNNER, *Grammatik des ntl. Griechisch*, ed. 10, 1959; now in English: *A Greek Grammar of the N. T. and Other Early Chris.ian Literature*. Translated and edited by ROBERT W. FUNK. (hicago - London - Toronto 1961. L. RADERMACHER, *Neutest. Grammatik*, ed. 2, 1925; J. H. MOULTON and W. F. HOWARD, *Grammar of New Testament Greek*; A. T. ROBERTSON, *A Grammar of the Greek New Testament*. As for other works not normally cited explicitly in the text, I am indebted principally to: Gius. BONACCORSI, *Primi saggi di filologia neotestamentaria*; DANA and MANTEY, *A Manual Grammar of the Greek N. T.*; Ign. ERRANDONEA, *Epitome Grammaticae Graeco-Biblicae*; PAUL JOÜON, *L'Evangile de N. S. Jésus-Christ*; E. DE WITT BURTON, *Syntax of the Moods and Tenses in N. T. Greek*; J. HUMBERT, *Syntaxe grecque*, Paris, 1945. These last two authors were first used in the fourth Latin edition, the former for the treatment of the moods, the latter for that of the « tenses ».

(²) A certain Aramaic tendency to avoid the passive seems to be manifested in such expressions as ἀναβαίνειν « come up », used of a fish which is drawn up, Mt 17,27, or ἐξέρχεσθαι instead of ἐκβάλλεσθαι Lk 8,2; 4,41; cf. also ἀπελθεῖν εἰς τὴν γέενναν instead of βληθῆναι Mk 9,44.

I

12, 48 ᾧ παρέθεντο πολύ, περισσοτερον αἰτήσουσιν αὐτόν and Lk 6, 38; cf. also Lk 23, 31 (?). More often, however, this tendency to avoid the name of God results in what is called the « theological » passive (cf. 236).

2   3. The indefinite plural seems to be frequent in Aramaic (cf. *Dan.* 4,22. 28f and Ezra 4, 13). This is perhaps why it occurs with especial frequency in Mk, often, in parallel passages, « corrected » by Mt, and still oftener by Lk (³). In at least two places it has a certain exegetical importance, namely Mk 3,21 and 14,1, for:

3   4. in Mk (3,21) we read a text which seems offensive to the honour of the Mother of God: ἀκούσαντες οἱ παρ' αὐτοῦ ἐξῆλθον κρατῆσαι αὐτόν· ἔ λ ε γ ο ν γὰρ ὅτι ἐξέστη. These παρ' αὐτοῦ are later (v. 31) said to be « His mother and his brethren ». Were they necessarily the ones who thought Jesus was deranged? Not at all. The verb ἔλεγον may be taken as an indefinite plural: « they said », i. e. (« people said », « it was being said ») that He was deranged. It is moreover easier, with this interpretation, to understand why « His own » went forth; for the mere fact that the crowd pressed about Jesus does not explain their preoccupation or a notion on their part that He was deranged; their preoccupation is accounted for by the fact that « it was being said » that He was deranged. That the evangelist is in fact speaking of such a rumour is suggested by the fact that, by a ready association of ideas, he opposes to this popular rumour another one, put about by the scribes: καὶ οἱ γ ρ α μ μ α τ ε ῖ ς ἔλεγον ὅτι Βεελζεβοὺλ ἔχει. From what we know of Mark's manner of expressing himself (⁴) it may be taken as certain that the stress is on the subject οἱ γραμματεῖς as opposed to others; and here the only apt opposition to the scribes, with their view concerning Jesus, is to be found in the other rumour, the popular one (⁵).

4   5. In Mk 14,1 likewise, a certain awkwardness disappears and the state of affairs is clear, if ἔλεγον γάρ be understood as an indefinite plural. The text reads: « It was now two days before the Passover and the feast of the Unleavened Bread. And the chief priests and the scribes were seeking how to arrest him by stealth

---

(³) Cf. C. H. TURNER, *Marcan Usage*, in *J. Th. St.* 25 (1924) 377-386.
(⁴) Cf. M. ZERWICK, *Untersuchungen z. Markusstil*, Rom 1937, p. 90.
(⁵) Those who prefer to retain the identity of subject for ἐξῆλθον and ἔλεγον γάρ seek to explain the subject οἱ παρ' αὐτοῦ as other than « His mother and His brethren ».

and kill him; for they said (Ελεγον γάρ here Mt has δέ instead of γάρ), 'not during the feast, lest there be a tumult of the people'». Here Mark's γάρ indicates the reason for the deliberation how to take Him with guile, for it is here that the stress seems to lie. If however the verb has the same subject as the preceding one (« they deliberated ... for they said ... ») we would expect an opposition to « with guile », such as « Not openly ... » or « Not by force ... » instead of « Not on the feast-day ». The text is however readily understood if Ελεγον be taken as an indefinite plural expressing the objection raised by some member or members of the assembly: they deliberated how to take Him with guile « for it had been said » that He could not be taken on the feast-day for fear of a riot. Thus is removed that apparent awkwardness of the γάρ in Ελεγον γάρ, which seems to have accounted for the other reading δέ in Mt (*). There are however other places in which γάρ seems to be equivalent to δέ (473).

6. The indefinite plural has also been seen in the OT quotation in Mt 1,23, where the OT' s καλέσει becomes καλέσουσιν: ἰδοὺ ἡ παρθένος ἐν γαστρὶ ἕξει καὶ τέξεται υἱόν, καὶ καλέσουσιν τὸ ὄνομα αὐτοῦ 'Εμμανουήλ. This change, however, seems to have had for the evangelist a deeper sense, inasmuch as the whole context suggests that Joseph is here associated with Mary; for the writer insists three times on the legal paternity to be assumed and in fact assumed by Joseph, and this paternity is expressed in the phrase « thou shalt call his name ... »; cf. vv. 21, 25 (LÉON DUFOUR, see under 477).

7. What is called the generalizing or categorical plural has a certain affinity with the indefinite plural. It is often used in the NT, and consists in a plural referring in reality to a singular subject (class for individual), e. g. Mt 2, 20: (τελευτήσαντος δὲ τοῦ 'Ηρῴδου, v. 19, the angel says to Joseph) τεθνήκασιν γὰρ οἱ ζητοῦντες τὴν ψυχὴν τοῦ παιδίου. Mt 2,23: τὸ ῥηθὲν διὰ τῶν προφητῶν, referring in fact to Hosea alone (11,1). Many other examples are cited by Joüon (7). This is perhaps the explanation of Mt 27, 44, where it is said that the robbers crucified with Christ reviled Him, though in fact only one of them seems to have done so. Some see the same usage in Mt 28, 9f, where Jesus is said to have appeared to « the women », and so identify this apparition with that to Magdalene (Mk 16,9; Jo 20, 14-18).

(*) Cf. C. H. TURNER, loc. cit. p. 384f.
(7) Mt 14,9; 22,7. 24; 24,6; Mk 4,10; 7,37; Lk 5,21; 8,39; Jo 6,14. 26; 8,24; 9,3. 16. 34; 10,21; 13,4.

8. Another use of the plural for a single person is **the epistolary plural**, whereby the writer as it were associates himself with the reader. This plural seems to be rare in the Pauline letters, but it is found there, e. g. Rom 1,5; 1 Thes 2,18; and especially the alternation of singular and plural in 2 Cor 10,1 — 11,6, where Paul is certainly speaking of himself alone. For this reason it is rash to regard Paul's « we » as always referring to the apostle along with his associates. — Meecham, who drew attention to a similar alternation of singular and plural in the letter of Aristeas (⁸), regards the epistolary plural as the more formal, and the singular as rather a colloquial usage.

2) Indeclinables

9. In Php 2,1 St Paul introduces his admonition by a fourfold appeal: εἴ τις οὖν παράκλησις ἐν Χριστῷ

εἴ τι (l. v. τ ι ς) παραμύθιον ἀγάπης

εἴ τις κοινωνία πνεύματος

εἴ τ ι ς σπλάγχνα καὶ οἰκτιρμοί.

The question here arises, whether the defective concord of the fourth member, and of the variant to the second member, can be admitted, so as to read τις in all four members and take the sense as being « if there be any ... ». So far as Hellenistic Greek is concerned, we may answer: the neuter form τι is used indeclinably in papyri, i, e. without agreement in gender or number, e. g.: ἐπί τι (instead of τινα) μίαν τῶν... οἰκιῶν « on one of the houses » (P. Par. 15, 2nd cent. B. C.), or: ἐὰν δέ τι ἄλλα ἀπαιτηθῶμεν « if any other things be required of us » (P. Amh. II 85,11 of A. D. 78). Hence an indeclinable τις would be the less remarkable; but since we have no instances of such a use, some have preferred to read τι in all four of Paul's expressions, which is surely too great a modification of the text; this change would permit two interpretations, either understanding the verb « be » with an indeclinable Hellenistic τι, or understanding some other verb (e. g. δύναται) with τι as accusative

10. Since only the first four of the **numerals** 1-100 are declinable it is not surprising that there is a certain tendency to use even these four

---

(⁹) H. C. MEECHAM, *The Letter of Aristeas*, p. 102f.

indeclinably. Thus we have in Mk 14, 19 and Jo 8,9 the formula εἰς καθ' εἰς instead of εἰς καθ' ἕνα for « one at a time » (on the analogy of ἓν καθ' εν as Rev 4,8). Similarly τέσσαρες for the accusative τέσσαρας is frequently found in Septuagint MSS and papyri, though in the NT it occurs only in a variant to Rev 4,4.

6   11. Another word which can be shown to be used indeclinably from the second century BC onwards is πλήρης. This is a vulgarism, but it is to be found in the LXX, e. g. Job 21,24, and in several variants to the NT, namely Acts 6,3, 5; 19,28; Mk 4,28; 8,19; 2 Jo 8; while in Jo 1,14 we have: « And the Word became flesh and dwelt among us and we have beheld his glory (τὴν δόξαν αὐτοῦ), glory as of the only Son from the Father full of grace and truth (πλήρης χάριτος καὶ ἀληθείας) »; and here A. DEISSMANN, who regards πλήρης as indeclinable, sees in it a vulgarism in the Johannine prologue which he likens to a wild flower amid marble. Since therefore πλήρης here must be regarded as indeclinable if it is not referred to the subject of the sentence, one has the choice of referring it either to the accusative δόξαν or to the genitives αὐτοῦ or μονογενοῦς (rather than πατρός) (⁹).

7   12. Here may be mentioned also πᾶς, which is sometimes not regularly declined, and which in modern demotic Greek has become the indeclinable πᾶσα. This perhaps accounts for πᾶσα Ἱεροσόλυμα and for Mk 12, 28: ποία ἐστὶν ἐντολὴ πρώτη πάντων (instead of πασῶν), and finally for the use of πᾶν referring to persons: Jo 17,2: ἵνα πᾶν, ὃ δέδωκας αὐτῷ, δώσει αὐτοῖς ζωὴν αἰώνιον.

3) Lack of Concord in Appositions

8   13. In vulgar usage there is to be seen a tendency to neglect concord, both for gender and for case, in words used in apposition, and especially in participles so used. Thus in papyrus receipts we repeatedly find the formula: ἀπέχω παρ' αὐτοῦ τὸν ὁμολογοῦντα (instead of τοῦ ὁμολογοῦντος) (Pl Amh. II, 111-113 of A. D. 128), and from Ptolemaic times we have: ἀδικούμεθα ὑπὸ Ἀπολλωνίου ἐμβάλλων (instead of ἐμβάλλοντος) ἡμᾶς εἰς τὴν στερεὰν πέτραν (¹⁰). Incongruities of this kind in apposi-

---

(⁹) Cf. DEBR. 177, DEISSMANN LO⁴ p. 99f., MAYSER, Grammatik d. griech. Papyri . . . p. 63.

(¹⁰) Cited in PREISIGKE, Wörterbuch, under ἐμβάλλω as Petr II 4, 1, 2 (read 41,2).

tions, especially with participles, occur with remarkable frequency in the least literary of the NT books, Revelation, cf. 1,5; 2,13. 20; 3,12; 8,9; 14,12; 17,3; 20,2; such incongruities are especially frequent with the participles of λέγειν e. g. 2,20 : «But I have against you, that you tolerate the woman (τὴν γυναῖκα) Jez'ebel, who calls herself (ἡ λ έ γ ο υ σ α ἑαυτήν) a prophetess». Cf. also 3,12 ; 9,14 ; 11,15 ; 14,6; 19,20 etc.

14. The frequent lack of concord with the participle λέγων seems to be due to the influence of the invariable form *le'mor* used in Hebrew to introduce direct speech. Note how in Rev 11,1 λέγων is used as a mere particle introducing direct speech in a sentence in which there is no subject to which the participle, if regarded as such, can be referred.

Even Luke is not immune from such a tendency if, with most editors we are to read 20,27: ... τινες τῶν σαδδουκαίων οἱ ἀντιλέγοντες (instead of τῶν ἀντιλεγόντων) ἀνάστασιν μὴ εἶναι.

15. The exegesis of a passage is affected by this tendency in only one case, namely Mk 7,19, where we have, with reference to pure and impure foods: « And he said to them ... do you not see that whatever goes into a man from outside cannot defile him, since it enters, not his heart but his stomach, and so is evacuated (εἰς τὸν ἀφεδρῶνα ἐκπορεύεται) κ α- θ α ρ ί ζ ω ν πάντα τὰ βρώματα. Some refer the participle καθαρίζων to the subject of the whole sentence (Jesus), understanding « He said (this) .purifying = declaring pure all manner of food », the words καθαρίζων ... not being those of Our Lord, but an explanation added by the evangelist [11]. Others however take καθαρίζων as equivalent to καθαρίζοντα, referring to ἀφεδρῶνα, thus understanding «... into the privy which purifies all manner of food» [12]. As we have seen, this latter interpretation is linguistically possible, or at least, would be quite admissible, were the passage in the book of Revelation and not in St Mark, where such a usage seems exceedingly unusual [13].

---

[11] ORIGEN, JÜLICHER, A. SCHLATTER, most modern exegetes.

[12] ZORELL, KNABENBAUER (KLOSTERMANN, DEBR. 126,3; 137.3).

[13] Those who support this interpretation appeal to the accusative ὑποδεδεμένους in Mk 6,9, where one might expect a nominative, and to Mk 12,40, where οἱ κατεσθίοντες ... καὶ ... προσευχόμενοι is perhaps to be referred to the (very distant) genitive ἀπὸ τῶν γραμματέων (v. 38). — Moreover, a warning not to restrict lack of concord in participles too rigorously to vulgar usage is perhaps to be found in the Acts, and indeed in Paul's speech before Agrippa and Festus, where we read: 26,2f: ἥγημαι ἐμαυτὸν μακάριον ἐπὶ σοῦ μέλλων... ἀπολογεῖσθαι μάλιστα γνώστην ὄντα σε πάντων...

4) Relative Attraction

9   16. The attraction of the relative pronoun into the case of its antecedent is regular in Hellenistic and Biblical Greek, as it was in classical Greek. In Mt only three cases occur (18,19; 24,50; and 25,54: ὅθεν = ἐκεῖθεν οὗ) and in Mk only one (7,13), but in Lk the construction is very common.

10   17. In general, as in classical Greek, the relative is attracted from the a c c u s a t i v e into another oblique case (e. g. μνημονεύετε τοῦ λόγου οὗ ἐγὼ εἶπον ὑμῖν Jo 15, 20), but in Hellenistic usage the principle of attraction is often extended to a relative which otherwise would be in the (local, instrumental) dative, e. g. ἄχρι τῆς ἡμέρας ἧς (instead of ᾗ) ἀνελήμφθη, or in the common abbreviated formula μέχρις οὗ which means μέχρι τοῦ χρόνου ᾧ.

11   18. For the sake of greater elegance, the antecedent is sometimes transferred to the relative clause, e. g. Rom 4, 17: κατέναντι οὗ ἐπίστευσεν Θεοῦ = κατέναντι τοῦ Θεοῦ, ᾧ ἐπίστευσεν, or Acts 25, 18: οὐδεμίαν αἰτίαν ἔφερον ὧν ἐγὼ ὑπενόουν πονηρῶν = τῶν πονηρῶν ἃ ἐγὼ ὑπενόουν. A somewhat awkward example, in which the antecedent has to be attracted into the case of the relative instead of v i c e   v e r s a, is to be found in Acts 21,16: συνῆλθον... ἄγοντες παρ᾽ ᾧ ξενισθῶμεν Μνάσωνί τινι, « taking (us to) Mnason in whose house ... ».

12   19. The name « inverse relative attraction » is sometimes given to the usage whereby an antecedent is put into the case of the following relative, e. g. Mt 21,42 λίθον, ὃν ἀπεδοκίμασαν οἱ οἰκοδομοῦντες, οὗτος ἐγενήθη εἰς κεφαλὴν γωνίας, or in the canticle of Zachary Lk 1, 72f, where the accusative ὅρκον can be accounted for only by attraction to the following relative ὃν ὤμοσεν (the preceding verb being μνησθῆναι which requires the genitive). Cf. also Lk 12,48; 20,17; Acts 10,36; I Cor 10,16, In Sir 24,23 the same phenomenon misled the Latin translator into a false rendering of the enunciation of what is fundamental to the whole book, namely the identification of Wisdom with the Law of Moses: ταῦτα πάντα βίβλος διαθήκης... ν ό μ ο ν (instead of νόμος) ὃν ἐνετείλατο ἡμῖν Μωϋσῆς... for which᾽ the Vulgate has: haec omnia liber vitae... Legem mandavit Moyses ...

13   20. The difficulty is increased if, along with « inverse attraction », we have also the transfer of the antecedent into the relative clause. Thus the curious expression Heb 10,20 ἣν ἐνεκαίνισεν ἡμῖν ὁδόν is perhaps to be resolved into τῇ ὁδῷ ἣν ἐνεκαίνισεν ἡμῖν: « by the new way which opened for us ».

21. The close connection between antecedent and relative is further illustrated by the fact that a preposition governing the antecedent need not be repeated with the relative, e. g. Acts 13, 2 ... εἰς τὸ ἔργον ὃ (= εἰς ὃ) προσκέκλημαι αὐτούς; so too with ἀπό 13, 38.

II. THE CASES

1) Nominative

14 25. The pendent nominative (*nominativus pendens*; also called, in Latin, *nom. absolutus*, «absolute nominative», but note that the sense is quite different from that of «nominative absolute» in English grammar; also called *nom. relationis*, «nominative of relation» because expressing the notion of «with regard to...») is a form of anacoluthon frequent enough in vulgar Greek. It consists in the enunciation of the logical (not grammatical) subject at the beginning of the sentence, followed by a sentence in which that subject is taken up by a pronoun in the case required by the syntax, e. g. Acts 7,40: ὁ Μωϋσῆς οὗτος... οὐκ οἴδαμεν τί ἐγένετο αὐτῷ, or Rev. 2,26: ὁ νικῶν καὶ ὁ τηρῶν... τὰ ἔργα μου... δώσω αὐτῷ ἐξουσίαν.

15 26. In the same chapter we find also τῷ νικῶντι δώσω, but the pleonastic addition of αὐτῷ shows that the participle, although put in the dative, is in the author's mind «pendent», in accordance with the Semitic idiom of «nominal sentences» (pendent logical subject followed by sentence taking it up by means of a pronoun, cf. preceding paragraph).

16 27. Semitisms of this kind absent from the usual text of the synoptics are to be found in several places in that of Codex Bezae (D), e. g. Mt 10, 11 where the usual text has the correct and even elegant εἰς ἣν δ' ἂν πόλιν... εἰσέλθητε... D. has the very Semitic ἡ πόλις εἰς ἣν εἰσέλθητε εἰς αὐτήν... Cf. likewise D's variants to Mt 5,40; 17,14; Mk 1,34.

17 28. There are thus three possible constructions, all of which may be illustrated from the same passage Mt 5, 39-42: ὅστις σε ῥαπίζει... στρέψον αὐτῷ... (subject pendent even in correct Greek usage, being a relative clause, and may be called a pendent nominative, though the case is of course not indicated by the form) καὶ τῷ θέλοντι (D ὁ θέλων)... λαβεῖν ἄφες αὐτῷ (nominative in D, dative required by normal Greek syntax in usual text, but pleonastic αὐτῷ shows the dative to be «pendent») ...τῷ αἰτοῦντί σε δὸς καὶ τὸν θέλοντα... μὴ ἀποστραφῇς (classical syntax).

18   29. As is to be seen from the « pendent datives » of the examples already cited, the pendent nominative is merely the most frequent form of « pendent case », a case which may be genitive or dative or accusative. When the case is not that which normal Greek syntax would require, it may be determined by « inverse relative attraction ». For the accusative so determined see above (19) and note also the Pauline example, not obvious at first sight, 2 Cor 12,17 μή τινα ὧν ἀπέσταλκα πρὸς ὑμᾶς, δι' αὐτοῦ ἐπλεονέκτησα ὑμᾶς, where the accusative of τινα is determined by the accusative latent in ὧν standing for ἐκείνων οὕς. For the dative so determined cf. Lk 12,48 παντὶ δὲ ᾧ ἐδόθη πολύ, πολὺ ζητηθήσεται παρ' αὐτοῦ.

19   30. As may be seen from the examples cited, the pendent nominative (or other case) is especially frequent with participles or relative clauses. C. F. Burney ([1]) lists 27 pendent nominatives from the fourth gospel, and sees in this frequency a further argument in favour of his thesis that this gospe is a translation from an Aramaic original.

20   31. Others however admit Semitic influence only when the pendent word is πᾶς or used along with πᾶς, and hence, in Jo, only 6,39; 15,2; 17,2: ἔδωκας αὐτῷ ἐξουσίαν ἵνα πᾶν ὃ δέδωκας αὐτῷ, δώσει αὐτοῖς ζωήν. In fact pendent nominatives with « all, every » occur in Hebrew with especial frequency and (for those unaccustomed to the idiom) especial awkwardness; cf. e. g. 1 Sam 2,13 which, rendered literally into Greek, would read: πᾶς θύων θυσίαν, καὶ ἤρχετο ὁ παῖς τοῦ ἱερέως..., the sense being « whenever anyone offered sacrifice, the priest's servant would come... »

We have dwelt at some length on this point as an illustration of the Semitic mode of thought of the sacred writers, who are led by the influence of their mother-tongue into using with especial frequency a form of expression not unparallelled in Greek whether ancient or middle or modern or indeed in colloquial usage in most languages whose literary usage does not admit it.

21   32. In place of the predicate nominative we find, not indeed in contradiction with the spirit of Greek, but, in Biblical usage at least,

---

([1]) *The Aramaic Origins of the Fourth Gospel* 34. 63ff. 151.

fairly certainly owing to Semitic influence (Hebrew *le*), after γίνεσθαι and εἶναι (or rather, ἔσεσθαι, which is closer in sense to γίνεσθαι), εἰς with the accusative, and especially in O. T. quotations: ἔσονται οἱ δύο ε ἰ ς σάρκα μίαν, where Mt continues: ὥστε οὐκέτι εἰσὶν δύο ἀλλὰ σάρξ μία Mt 19,5f. Cf. also 21,42 the stone rejected by the builders ἐγενήθη ε ἰ ς κεφαλὴν γωνίας. With εἶναι not in the future tense we have in the NT only once a predicate with εἰς, 1 Jo 5,8 οἱ τρεῖς εἰς τὸ ἕν εἰσιν.

22 33. The Greek **nominative and vocative** are often identical in form, being distinguished only in the masculine and feminine singular, and not always there. Hence the tendency to eliminate the distinction even where the vocative has a form of its own, e. g. Jo 17,25: πατὴρ δίκαιε where the adjective shows that the author takes πατήρ as a vocative (instead of πάτερ). Moreover the nominative with the article is always used in appositions added to a vocative, e. g. Rev 15,3 Μεγάλα τὰ ἔργα σου, Κύριε ὁ Θεὸς ὁ παντοκράτωρ; 18,20: εὐφραίνου οὐρανὲ καὶ οἱ ἅγιοι καὶ οἱ ἀπόστολοι...

23 34. The nominative with the article is thus found for the vocative even in classical use; but where it occurs in the NT it is rather to be referred to Semitic influence, for in Hebrew the vocative is expressed exclusively by the nominative with the article, to which in Aramaic there corresponds the « emphatic » state, e. g. Mk 5,41, where the evangelist himself renders Ταλιθὰ κουμ literally: τὸ κοράσιον, ἔγειρε. Similarly 'Αββᾶ ὁ πατήρ Mk 14,36; Rom 8,15; Gal 4,6 etc. Moreover Elizabeth's ἡ πιστεύσασα in Lk 1,45 has a more vivid sense if it be taken as a vocative: μακαρία ἡ πιστεύσασα, rightly rendered in the Vulgate by the second person: « beata quae credidisti ». The Vulgate rightly continues, moreover, « quoniam perficientur ea quae dicta sunt tibi » although the Greek text has the third person τοῖς λελαλημένοις αὐτῇ.

2) Vocative

24 35. 'Ω with the vocative. In classical usage, the vocative is regularly introduced by the particle ὦ, whose omission constitutes an exception into whose reasons one may profitably inquire. In Hellenistic usage the contrary is the case: the omission of the particle has become the rule (and hence has no special significance), so that where ὦ is ex-

ceptionally used in the NT one is justified in supposing that there is some
reason for its use. In fact ὦ, apart from the Acts, occurs in contexts suggesting deep emotion on the part of the speaker. Thus Our Lord says
to the Canaanite woman, whose profound and somewhat unexpected
humility had moved him: ὦ γύναι, μεγάλη (note the emphatic position
of the adjective) σου ἡ πίστις Mt 15,28; with a different kind of emotion —
grief at the people's lack of faith — when the lunatic's father beseeched
Him to cure him, Our Lord exclaims: ὦ γενεὰ ἄπιστος, ἕως πότε πρὸς ὑμᾶς
ἔσομαι; ἕως πότε ἀνέξομαι ὑμᾶς; Mk 9,19 and parallels; cf. Lk 24,25. Note
likewise the indignant astonishment of St Paul manifested in his exclamation ὦ ἀνόητοι Γαλάται, τίς ὑμᾶς ἐβάσκανεν; Gal 3,1 (cf. Acts 13,10; 1 Tim
6,20; 6,11 [?]; Jas 2,20). This is but a little particle, but it casts such a light
on the state of mind of Our Lord and of His apostles, that no one, surely,
in reading the Scriptures, would wish to neglect its indications (²).

On the other hand it is not without a certain pleasure that we find
the learned writer Luke in the first chapter of the Acts addressing his friend
and patron ὦ Θεόφιλε, obviously without any special emphasis, but in con-
formity with the elegance of style which he has adopted as suitable to a
dedicatory formula (note also the position of the vocative, fairly late in
the sentence). This Attic unemphatic use of ὦ is to be found only in the
Acts (³). Thus Gallio addresses the Jews ὦ Ἰουδαῖοι, likewise, in completely classical manner, not at the beginning of the phrase, but after several
words, Acts 18,14.

3) Genitive.

25 36. The « general » genitive. Among the various usages into which
grammarians have classified the immense variety of the genitive, the
clearest and most useful are perhaps the two distinguished as « subjective » and « objective », inasmuch as such an expression as for example
ἡ ἀγάπη τοῦ πατρός may have two very different meanings: the love with
which the father loves his child (genitive denoting the subject of the verb

(²) In the LXX (except 4 Macc) the interjection ὦ is used only emphati-
cally, cf. M. JOHANNESSOHN, Der Gebrauch der Kasus... in der Septuaginta
(1910), p. 8-13.

(³) Cf. DEBR. 146, who refers to BRUGMANN-THUMB⁴ 432.

« love »), or the love with which the child loves its father (genitive denoting the object of love). In interpreting the sacred text, however, we must
beware lest we sacrifice to clarity of meaning part of the fulness of the
meaning. For example, in ἡ γὰρ ἀγάπη τοῦ Χριστοῦ συνέχει ἡμᾶς
(2 Cor 5,14), is Χριστοῦ an objective or a subjective genitive? We must
answer that neither of these alone corresponds fully to the sense of the
text; the objective genitive (Paul's love for Christ) does not suffice for, apart
from the fact that Paul usually renders the objective-genitive sense by εἰς
(cf. Col 1,4), the reason which he adds speaks of the love which Christ
manifested for us in dying for all men; nor is the subjective genitive (Christ's
love for us) fully satisfactory by itself, because the love in question is a
living force working in the spirit of the apostle. In other words, we cannot
simply classify this genitive under either heading without neglecting a
part of its value. It may also mean the love shown for us by Christ, in
His death and resurrection (cf. Rom 4,25!), inasmuch as known (and this
through the faith produced in the soul by Christ Himself) and so irresisti-
bly impelling the apostle to return that love.

26   **37.** So too, when Paul uses the expression εὐαγγέλιον τοῦ Χριστοῦ, this
genitive is to be classified neither as subjective nor as objective, because
it is both, and yet more. From the full sense of the expression one cannot
exclude any of the three or four ideas which follow: the « gospel of Christ »
is so called because (1) it is the good news brought and first preached by Christ
(subjective genitive); (2) it is the good news concerning Christ (objective genitive); (3) it is the good news preached by the apostle ἐν Χριστῷ i. e. by Christ's
commission and with Christ's presence and assistance working in preacher
and audience alike.

27   **38.** The like must be borne in mind also with regard to 2 Thess 3,5: ὁ
δὲ Κύριος κατευθύναι ὑμῶν τὰς καρδίας εἰς τὴν ἀγάπην τοῦ Θεοῦ καὶ εἰς τὴν ὑπο-
μονὴν τοῦ Χριστοῦ; for by « the patience of Christ » in the soul of the faithful
Paul means more than a patience inspired by the desire to imitate that of
Christ. Paul uses such expressions not only of patience but also of sufferings,
calling his own sufferings the « sufferings of Christ » (2 Cor 1,5). Why? Because
they are sufferings undergone for Christ's sake? Undoubtedly; but not for
that reason alone. Because they are undergone ἐν Χριστῷ, Christ Himself,
in the members of His mystical body, « fulfilling what is lacking » of the suf-
fering of the Head? Certainly, and perhaps even principally.

Similar considerations may be applied to « the circumcision of Christ »
Col 2,11, « the faith of Jesus Christ » Rom 3,22 and 26, « the obedience of faith »
Rom 1,5, « the love of God » Rom 5,5, διακονία πνεύματος 2 Cor 3,8, « the jus-
tice of God » Rom 10,3 etc.

28   39. It is clear that the genitive in Paul's οἱ τοῦ Χριστοῦ I Cor 15,23
expresses the kernel of his gospel, that mystical union of the faithful
with their Head, Christ, which in the very similar context I Thes 4,16
is expressed by Paul's more regular formula ἐν Χριστῷ. Hence the expression ‹mystical genitive› for this Pauline usage (A. DEISSMANN), and
an entire book published under the title « Union with Christ in St Paul
in the Light of his Use of the Genitive » (⁴) This book shows how the
grammarians' classification of the uses of the genitive, useful as it may
be, is inadequate and may become misleading. The author insists on
the fundamental force of the genitive, namely the indication of the
appurtenance of one notion to another. The exact nature of that appurtenance, of the relation between the notions, depends upon context
and subject matter, so that of itself the use of the genitive may have
as many varieties as there are ways in which two notions may be associated. Hence to the question, with regard to the expression « gospel of
Christ » and many others, whether the genitive is subjective or objective
or one of origin or the like, we must answer: it is not any of these
alone, but is a « general » genitive, a genitive used in general, indicating
simply the appurtenance of « gospel » to « Christ » etc. The nature and the
extent of the relation involved in this appurtenance is to be grasped by
a consideration not of grammatical usage but of the context, of St
Paul's whole theology of the « gospel of Christ » etc. Hence the title of
the book just referred to might well be not « Mystical Union in the Light
of the Genitive in St Paul », but « The Genitive in St Paul in the Light
of his Mystical Theology »: for it is the latter, and not the genitive,
which has light to cast upon the meaning (⁵).

29   40. The « Hebrew » genitive. Of the types of genitive commonly
listed by grammarians, the one which approaches most closely the « general » genitive is the « attributive » or « qualitative » one, also called the
« Hebrew » genitive, inasmuch as its scope and use in Biblical Greek
is extended, owing to Semitic influence, to many expressions in
which the Greeks used not a genitive but an adjective. Among the best-
known examples we have: ὁ οἰκονόμος τῆς ἀδικίας (= ἄδικος)... ὁ μα-

---

(⁴) « Die Christusgemeinschaft des Paulus im Lichte seines Genitivgebrauchs »
O. SCHMITZ, 1924.
(⁵) Cf. on this point also A. WIKENHAUSER, Die Christusmystik des
heiligen Paulus in Bibl. Zeitfr., XI, fasc. 8-10, p. 16ff.

μωνᾶς τῆς ἀδικίας «unjust gain», Lk 16,8f; ἀκροατὴς ἐπιλησμονῆς «a hearer of forgetfulness» = «a forgetful hearer» Jas 1,15. There is a danger that this manner of speaking may. mislead those unaccustomed to it into reading some recondite sense into a genitive which in reality corresponds to some quite ordinary adjective. Thus οἱ λόγοι τῆς χάριτος from the lips of Our Lord in Lk 4,22 are «attractive sayings»; πάθη ἀτιμίας Rom 1,26 are «base passions», σκεῦος ἐκλογῆς Acts 9,15 is «a chosen instrument»; but despite the external similarity, σκεύη ὀργῆς and ἐλέους Rom 9,22f are «vessels (full) of wrath, of mercy» (⁶).

30   **41.** This Semitic manner of speaking becomes even more alien to Greek idiom, if the possessive pronoun or a demonstrative which applies to the whole compound, and so to the qualified substantive, is put with the genitive that qualifies it, as for example «the sceptre of thy might» (Ps. 109,2) = «thy mighty sceptre», or «the throne of his glory» (Mt 19,28) = his glorious throne»; or Rom 7,24 «(who will deliver me from) the body of this death» = «this mortal body»; Php 3,21 «the body of our lowliness» = «our lowly body.»; Heb 1,3 «the word of his might» = «his mighty word»; Rev 13,3 «the wound of his death» = «his mortal wound» (⁷).

31   **42. A certain intimate relation** to a person or thing is expressed in a manner not indeed exclusively Semitic, but in our literature certainly prevalently so, by «son», υἱός, followed by a genitive.. This extended usage of the word «son» is more readily understood when it is a question of certain relationships to a person. Thus he who reproduces and expresses in his own way of life that of another is called a «son» of the latter; thus «sons of Abraham» Gal 3,7; «sons of the devil» Acts 13,10; Mt 13,38 (cf. Jo 8,39-44) and especially «sons of God» Mt 5,9 and 45.

(⁶) Cf. BL.–DEBR. 165 and the numerous examples collected by U. HOLZ-MEISTER in Z.f.k.Th. 41 (1917) 317-21, where however we find examples of genitives which do not belong to the same class, such as Rom 6,4 «walk in newness of life», which, if it were to be attributed to this class, would have to be interpreted «in lively newness», since in this class the genitive stands for an adjective. The use of a substantive for an emphatic adjective is not specifically Semitic, but belongs to the style of many languages: «newness of life» for «new life», «sublimity of speech» (1 Cor 2,1) for «sublime speech» might be cited as examples of Greek or Latin style.

(⁷) As a general rule, the Semitic languages add suffixes to the last member alone of compound expressions, even though they refer to the entire compound.

32   43. Such a usage becomes strange for many when υἱός is used with
the genitive of the name of a thing or an abstract notion. The relation which
is so expressed varies according to the subject matter. Thus in the OT
the strong are called « sons of strength », the contumacious « sons of con_
tumacy », those worthy of death « sons of death », those worthy to be beaten
« sons of stripes » Deut 25,2. The soldiers of the garrison are called the
« sons of the citadel » 1 Mac 4,2. Similarly in the NT those who are to rise
are called the « sons of the resurrection » Lk 20,36; he who merits peace
is called a « son of peace ». The « sons of this world » are contrasted with
the « sons of light » Lk 16,8; the « sons of light and sons of the day » 1 Thes
5,5 are those who belong to the realm of light and the risen sun, and show
this by the whole tenor of their lives. The friends of the bridegroom and
the wedding-guests are called υἱοὶ νυμφῶνος (i. e. of the house celebrating
the wedding; not « of the bridegroom » as the Vulgate renders it; that
would require νυμφίου) Mt 9,15. — Τέκνον is also used in the same
sense Eph 2,3; Gal 4,28; 1 Pet 1,14; 2 Pet 2,14; Lk 7,35 etc.

44. This is but one example of a wider usage proper to the Semitic languages, which, in the absence of an adjective which could be used substanti-
vally, express the meaning of the adjective by a genitive in the manner already
described (40) and supply the substantive « son » or some other, according to
circumstances, such as « man, mother daughter, father, lord »; e. g. « men of
name » = dignitaries; « man of discourses » = orator; « lord of hair » = hairy
person; « man of tongue » = calumniator; « lord of wrath » = irascible person; « mother of ways » = road-junction; « the son of my threshing-floor »
= my downtrodden people (Is 21,10); « son of fatness » = rich soil, etc. cf.
JOHANNESSOHN, *Der Gebrauch der Kasus* ... pp. 29-32.

33   45. Epexegetic genitive. From an exegetical point of view, especial
attention is to be paid to the « epexegetic » genitive or genitive of
apposition (i. e. in which the substantive added in the genitive is in
reality an apposition denoting the same person or thing as the substantive to which the genitive is attached, as in the English usage « city of
Rome », with which contrast the Latin *urbs Roma*) for it is comparatively
rare, and is not always immediately recognized as such, whence there
may arise apparent difficulties of interpretation. Of the many examples
collected by U. HOLZMEISTER from the NT ([8]) the following are some

_____

([8]) *Verb. Dom.* 25(1947), 112-117.

of the most important: the «sign of Jonah» Mt 12,39 is not a sign given
by or to Jonah or in any other way merely connected with him, but is
the sign which Jonah *was*, or Jonah himself, as a sign; «you will receive
the gift of the Holy Spirit» Acts 2,38 is not to be understood of a gift to
be given by the Holy Spirit, but of the Holy Spirit Himself to be received
as a gift; similarly 2 Cor 1,22 «the pledge of the Holy Spirit». Where Christ
is said to have descended εἰς τὰ κατώτερα μέρη τῆς γῆς Eph 4,9, the sense
seems to be not of a descent into the underworld, the «lower parts of the
earth», but of His coming into the world itself, called τὰ κατώτερα μέρη
with respect to heaven; in Col 1,18 κεφαλὴ τοῦ σώματος τῆς ἐκκλησίας
the second genitive is to be understood as an apposition: not «the body
of the church», but «the body, the church» (or, as the genitive is called
for by the syntax even in apposition: «of the body, of the church», with
a comma). The «crown of life» Rev 2,10 is the «crown» which consists
in eternal life. The «justification of life» Rom 5,18 seems to be the justification brought by life, consisting in life. The «vineyard of the earth»
Rev 14,18 is the earth metaphorically called a vineyard. Finally in Jo
8,44 τοῦ διαβόλου is clearly in apposition with τοῦ πατρὸς so that ὑμεῖς ἐκ
τοῦ πατρὸς τοῦ διαβόλου ἐστέ means «you are of the devil as father»
and not «of the father of the devil» (at the end of the same verse an apparent reference to the father of the devil is due to a curious use of αὐτοῦ
standing for «falsehood» although that substantive has not been used
in what precedes: ψεύστης ἐστὶν καὶ ὁ πατὴρ αὐτοῦ «he is false and
father of [it =] falsehood»).

46. Not unnaturally, there are doubtful cases, e. g. Eph 1,14, where the
Holy Ghost is called ἀρραβὼν τῆς κληρονομίας ἡμῶν εἰς ἀπολύτρωσιν τῆς περιποι-
ήσεως, and this last expression is by some understood as «for the redemption
which is acquisition» («epexegetic» genitive, whether the «acquisition» be
understood as God's acquisition of the redeemed or their acquisition of their
inheritance); others however take the genitive as objective, taking «acquisition» as meaning those acquired by God. So too Gal 5,5, out of faith we look
for ἐλπίδα δικαιοσύνης; if «hope» be taken in the concrete sense of what is
hoped for, the genitive may be taken as epexegetic: we look for our hope,
δικαιοσύνη = eternal life, but the genitive may also be taken as subjective:
we look for that which δικαιοσύνη (= οἱ δίκαιοι) hopes for. — Some moreover would understand the «sign of the Son of Man in the heavens» Mt 24,30
as the Son of Man Himself, as a sign, i. e. the glorification of the risen Christ,
an interpretation which is of no little value to the exegesis of the eschatological discourse (cf. FEUILLET in *Rev. Bib.* 56 [1949], 354).

17

47. Multiplicity of genitives. Where two genitives depend upon the same noun, Paul commonly puts one of them before and the other after that noun, e. g. 2 Cor 5, 1 ἡ ἐπίγειος ἡμῶν οἰκία τοῦ σκήνους (Debr. 168). Where, as often happens in Paul, several genitives follow one another, each commonly depends upon the preceding one, e. g. 2 Cor 4,4 τὸν φωτισμὸν τοῦ εὐαγγελίου τῆς δόξης (objective genitive) τοῦ Χριστοῦ. There are however exceptions, where the genitive is without the article and depends on a preposition, e. g. 2 Cor 3,18 where καθάπερ ἀπὸ Κυρίου πνεύματος may be rendered, as in the Vulgate « tamquam a Domini Spiritu »; cf. Mt 24,31 (DEBR. 168,2; 474,4).

34   **48. The genitive absolute** has a certain affinity with the « pendent » nominative and other « absolute » cases, inasmuch as it expresses some secondary determination of the main sentence in a syntactically independent form. In classical usage this construction is properly restricted to expressions whose subject does not occur in the main sentence, whether as subject or in any other function; if the subject of the subordinate phrase occurs in the principal sentence, the subordinate participle is simply put in agreement with the noun or pronoun of the main sentence to which it refers. Thus in Mt 5,1 instead of καθίσαντος αὐτοῦ προσῆλθον αὐτῷ it would have been more elegant to say καθίσαντι αὐτῷ προσῆλθον.

35   **49. The neglect of concordance** of the participle in favour of its absolute use is to be found in classical Greek, is fairly common in popular and Hellenistic Greek, and is still further extended in the Greek of the LXX and of the NT, where the general tendency of popular speech towards coordination instead of subordination is reinforced by the particular predilection of Semitic speech for juxtaposition of independent clauses in place of syntactical subordination.

The genitive absolute is indeed outwardly a form of subordination, but where it stands in place of the concordant participle, the subordination is comparatively incomplete. The use of the concordant participle supposes the conception of the entire sentence as one whole (« periodic » construction), while its neglect in favour of the absolute use is a result of the conception of the various elements of the sentence as juxtaposed, which is characteristic of the Semitic way of thought. Examples of this are abundant: Note Mt 1,18 μ ν η σ τ ε υ θ ε ί σ η ς τ ῆ ς μ η τ ρ ὸ ς αὐτοῦ Μαρίας τῷ 'Ιωσήφ... εὑρέθη ἐν γαστρὶ ἔχουσα where the absolute participle is used though its subject is identical with that of the main sentence, and Acts 22,17 where the two constructions (concordant and absolute participle) are strangely combined: ἐγένετο δέ μοι ὑποστρέ-ψαντι εἰς 'Ιερουσαλὴν καὶ προσευχομένου μου ἐν τῷ ἱερῷ γενέσθαι με ἐν ἐκστάσει («when I had returned... and was praying...»).

50. As occasionally in classical Greek and often in the papyri, so too in the NT genitive absolute participles are to be found with no expressed subject, e. g. Mt 17,14: καὶ ἐλθόντων πρὸς τὸν ὄχλον προσῆλθεν αὐτῷ ἄνθρωπος. Cf. Acts 21,31.

4) Dative

36   51. The later evolution of Greek was in the direction of the elimination of the dative. In modern demotic Greek the dative is found only in a «fossilized» form, its place being taken by the genitive-form or by a preposition with the accusative. Hellenistic and Biblical Greek offer slight traces of this evolution in its early stages. Thus we read Mk 8,18f: τοὺς πέντε ἄρτους ἔκλασα εἰς τοὺς πεντακισχιλίους... τοὺς ἑπτὰ εἰς τοὺς τετρακισχιλίους, and Acts 24,17: ἐλεημοσύνας ποιήσων εἰς τὸ ἔθνος μου; 1 Pet 1,4: κληρονομίαν τετηρημένην ἐν οὐρανοῖς εἰς ὑμᾶς.

This being so, attention is to be paid rather to the particular usages in which, against the general tendency, the dative takes the place, in Hellenistic Greek, of the classical accusative:

37   52. a) with verbs, e. g. προσκυνεῖν τινι (alongside the classical τινα) or καλῶς ποιεῖν τινι etc instead of classical τινα.

38   53. b) The dative of respect in place of the classical accusative is common, the accusative of respect being rare in the NT. An exception is Mt 27,57 ἄνθρωπος... τοὔνομα 'Ιωσήφ, whereas elsewhere we have always (τῷ) ὀνόματι, τῷ γένει etc. Occasionally this dative is to be found with verbs, e. g. στερεοῦσθαι τῇ πίστει Acts 16,5; περισσεύειν τῷ ἀριθμῷ ibid.; νη-πιάζειν τῇ κακίᾳ 1 Cor 14,20; παραβολευσάμενος τῇ ψυχῇ Php 2,30; most commonly however it is used with adjectives: πτωχὸς τῷ πνεύματι, καθαρὸς τῇ καρδίᾳ Mt 5,3, 8; somewhat more awkwardly, if the text is sound, ἁγνὸς τῷ πράγματι 2 Cor 7,11.

39   54. c) **The dative of time,** where the accusative was to be expected, inasmuch as «time how long» is expressed, is a Hellenistic usage. Hence no special nuance of meaning is to be sought in Rom 16,25 χρόνοις αἰωνίοις σεσιγημένου or Lk 8,29 πολλοῖς χρόνοις συνηρπάκει αὐτόν. Occasionally variant readings exist and so testify to the identity of sense, e. g. Jo 14,9: τοσοῦτον χρόνον and τοσούτῳ χρόνῳ μεθ᾽ ὑμῶν εἰμί or Acts 8,11: διὰ τὸ ἱκανῷ χρόνῳ and ἱκανὸν χρόνον ἐξεστακέναι αὐτούς. For Mk 8,2, indeed, three readings exist: ὅτι ἤδη ἡμέραι τρεῖς and ἡμέρας τρεῖς and ἡμέραις τρισὶν προσμένουσίν μοι.

40   55. **The dative of interest** *(dativus commodi)* is commonly recognized easily enough from the context, but occasionally this is not the case; thus in the well-known text καθὼς ἐλάλησεν πρὸς τοὺς πατέρας ἡμῶν, τῷ ᾽Αβραὰμ καὶ τῷ σπέρματι αὐτοῦ εἰς τὸν αἰῶνα, the second member τῷ ᾽Αβραὰμ etc. is commonly understood as parallelling πρὸς τοὺς πατέρας ἡμῶν, whereas it is rather to be understood as a dative of interest, giving the sense: «as He spoke to our fathers in favour of Abraham and his seed for ever» (Lk 1,55), all the more in that «to speak in favour» is a Hebrew circumlocution for «promise». Perhaps we have a dative of interest in Rev 8,4 also: ἀνέβη ὁ κάπνος ταῖς προσευχαῖς, but other interpretations exist.

41   56. The dative τῷ θεῷ is indeed often a dative of interest, and always when in conjunction with a verb as: ὁ δὲ ζῇ, ζῇ τῷ θεῷ Rom 6,10; perhaps also when used with an adjective as 2 Cor 10,4 τὰ ὅπλα... δυνατὰ τῷ θεῷ πρὸς..., but with an adjective τῷ θεῷ may also be a Hebraism giving the sense of an «elative» superlative, as Acts 7,20 ἀστεῖος τῷ θεῷ i. e. handsome even in God's estimation — «very handsome indeed»; cf. also Jonah 3,3 πόλις μεγάλη τῷ θεῷ.

42   57. **The dative of place** is said to be absent from the NT, with the exception of such adverbial expressions as κύκλῳ or πάντη, πανταχῇ. Some however in Acts 2,33 and 5,31 take the dative in τῇ δεξιᾷ τοῦ θεοῦ ὑψωθείς not as an instrumental but as a dative of place, «at the right hand of God».

58. **The dative of cause** in the NT indicates not only the instrument but sometimes also other causes, e. g. Gal 6,12 ἵνα τῷ σταυρῷ τοῦ Χριστοῦ μὴ διώκωνται «on account of the cross», or Rom 11,31 ἠπείθη-

σαν τῷ ὑμετέρῳ ἐλέει rendered by the Vulgate « in vestram misericordiam », the sense being, because God wished to have mercy on you (cf.
verses 20 and 30).

43 59. The dative of agent is a similar usage, but in the NT is commonly recognized only in Lk 23,15, where Pilate says « nothing worthy
of death ἐστὶν πεπραγμένον αὐτῷ (= ὑπ' αὐτοῦ) ». It may perhaps
however be admitted also for Jas 3,7 « every kind (φύσις may so be rendered here) of beast δεδάμασται τῇ φύσει ἀνθρωπίνῃ ». — The dative in
such expressions as γνωσθῆναί τινι, ὀφθῆναί τινι, θεαθῆναί τινι is not
conceived as a dative of agent, but as a simple dative object to a verb
with « deponent » sense (« appear » to someone, etc.).

44 60. To the dative of manner (e. g. παντὶ τρόπῳ, εἴτε προφάσει εἴτε
ἀληθείᾳ Php 1,18) belongs also the etymological figure used by the
LXX and the NT to render the Hebrew absolute infinitive (which however seems to have no Aramaic equivalent [Joὕον]). Thus in Gen 2,17
moth tamuth is rendered in the LXX θανάτῳ ἀποθανεῖσθε (cf. Mt 15,4).
The same emphatic reinforcement of the verbal notion is to be found in
ἐπιθυμίᾳ ἐπεθύμησα Lk 22,15; παραγγελίᾳ παρηγγείλαμεν Acts 5,28;
φίλος τοῦ νυμφίου χαρᾷ χαίρει Jo 3,29; cf. also Acts 2,17 from the LXX
and 4,17 (variant reading), 23,14 — both in the mouth of Jews —. and
Jas 5,17.

61. The same Hebrew construction (absolute infinitive) is elsewhere rendered by a participle, e. g. Heb 6,14 (= LXX) εὐλογῶν εὐλογήσω σε καὶ
πληθύνων πληθυνῶ σε. The two renderings are found together in Acts 28,26
(= LXX) ἀκοῇ ἀκούσετε... καὶ βλέποντες βλέψετε. In the NT the rendering with
the participle is confined to quotations from the LXX, but perhaps the same
idiom lies behind Eph 5,5 τοῦτο γὰρ ἴστε γινώσκοντες, though the verbs are
different ones.

45 62. This « internal » or « cognate » dative (so called because the noun
has the same root as the verb), although it is not entirely foreign to classical
usage, e. g. φυγῇ φεύγειν, γάμῳ γαμεῖν, nevertheless clearly rests in the
NT on a Semitic basis. This is however not necessarily the case if the noun
be accompanied by an adjective, e. g. ἐξέστησαν ἐκστάσει μεγά:η Mk
5,42; in this case however the internal accusative is almost always used,
e. g. ἐχάρησαν χαρὰν μεγάλην Mt 2,10.

63. The Semitic character of this etymological figure is clearly brought out by the frequency of its occurrence in the books of Maccabees: in the Hebraizing 1 Macc twenty-one times, in the other books, originally written in Greek: 2 Macc once, 3 Macc never, 4 Macc four times, but always with an added adjective (JOHANNESSOHN).

46   **64.** What is however most characteristic of Biblical Greek in the use of the dative is that this case, in most of its uses, is accompanied by the preposition ἐν, especially in the instrumental use, but also in the temporal, modal and causal ones (cf. 116-119). Sometimes too, other prepositions are used instead of the dative, namely εἰς (cf. 51 above) and μετά, e. g. μετὰ ὅρκου Mt 26,72 instead of ὅρκῳ as Heb 6,17; μετὰ φόβου 2 Cor 7,15 etc.; these prepositions are almost invariably used in modern demotic Greek.

65. Parables are often introduced by the formula ὁμοιωθήσεται, ὡμοιώθη, ὅμοιός ἐστιν with a following dative which however does not correspond, or corresponds only inexactly, to the term of the comparison. Thus « the kingdom of God » is not in reality « like unto a merchant », but is likened to the pearl of great price (Mt 13,45); nor is it « like unto ten virgins », but to the wedding (Mt 25,1), nor is it like the sower, but like the harvest (Mt 13,24). This looseness of expression is to be accounted for by the fact that the formulae ὅμοιός ἐστιν etc. are added in the Greek, the Aramaic using simply the preposition *le* corresponding to the dative; for the Jews were accustomed to introduce parables by a formula such as *Mashal*: *le* (*melek she . . .*), « Similitude: to (a king who . . .) » (for examples see Strack-Billerbeck II,8), this being an elliptical form of: « I will tell you a similitude. To what can the affair be likened? To (a king who...) »: cf. in the gospel a similar full formula with the question in Mt 11,6; Mk 4,30f; Lk (6,47); 7,31f; 13,18f. Clearly the Aramaic formula, and consequently also the Greek one used to render it, is not to be understood as « the kingdom of heaven is like a king », but « concerning the kingdom of heaven, it is as in the case of a king ». Though this interpretation is clearly enough called for in the examples cited above, this is less clear in others. Thus it is not so sure that we can maintain that the kingdom of heaven is really to be likened not to the grain of mustard-seed or the leaven, but to the tree wherein the birds nest and the leavened dough (J. JEREMIAS, *Die Gleichnisse Jesu*, ed. 5, 1956, p. 85f; and for the last-mentioned doubtful point cf. O. KUSS, *Zum Sinngehalt des Doppelgleich-*

nisses vom Senfkorn und Sauerteig, Biblica 40 [1959] 641-53, where it is shown that the idea of the evolution of the kingdom of heaven cannot be excluded from the parable).

5) Accusative

The original function of the accusative is to limit the extension of the verb. With « transitive » verbs, the extension is limited to the object. Thus is accounted for also the accusative « of respect », alongside which one may perhaps set the « adverbial » use of the accusative.

47 66. With regard to Hellenistic usage note the tendency to employ intransitive verbs transitively oftener than in classical Greek; e. g. ἐνεργεῖν, properly « act, operate » used absolutely, means also « effect », transitively. Both uses are to be found in Php 2,13 ὁ ἐνεργῶν ἐν ὑμῖν τὸ θέλειν καὶ τὸ ἐνεργεῖν. Hence for almost all the NT occurrences of ἐνερ- γεῖσθαι doubt may arise whether the voice is middle or passive, cf. e. g. 1 Thess 2,13 « you have received λόγον Θεοῦ ὃς καὶ ἐνεργεῖται in you », where some refer ὃς to λόγον and take ἐνεργεῖται as either passive « which is rendered effective by God » or middle « which operates ». It is clear that this text is of importance for the « theology of the word » so dear to Protestants.

Similary μαθητεύειν, properly, « to be a disciple » (Mt 27,57) is also used in the sense « to make a disciple » in Acts 14,21 and Mt 28,19: « going therefore make disciples of all nations »; for here μαθητεύσατε is not accurately rendered by « teach »: there immediately follows « teaching them to observe all things ». « Teaching » is therefore but one of the means whereby a person μαθητεύεται, i. e. is made a disciple of Christ (the other is the sacrament: βαπτίζοντες).

48 67. The same tendency towards the accusative is to be seen with verbs which in classical usage generally take a partitive genitive, perhaps because the partitive notion is sometimes not sufficiently in evidence to be grasped by the people in general and expressed in popular speech. E. g. ἐπιθυμεῖν γυναῖκα Mt 5,28; πεινᾶν, διψᾶν τὴν δικαιοσύνην Mt 5,6; κλη- ρονομεῖν τὴν γῆν Mt 5,5; ἐσθίειν τὴν σάρκα, πίνειν τὸ αἷμα Jo 6,53.

49   **68.** Where however the partitive sense is retained, it is often more clearly expressed by a preposition: ἐσθίειν ἀπὸ τῶν ψιχίων Mt 15,27; ἐκ τοῦ ἄρτου ἐσθιέτω καὶ ἐκ τοῦ ποτηρίου πινέτω 1 Cor 11,28. So too with pronouns: τίς ἐξ ὑμῶν instead of simply τίς ὑμῶν).

50   **69.** After ἀκούειν in classical usage the genitive is used of the person speaking, and the accusative of the thing (or person) of which one hears; the sound which one hears is classically in the genitive, in the NT vacillates between the two cases; «speech», λόγος is found even classically in both cases. So the grammarians, cf. DEBRUNNER 173. — J. SMITH suggests a simplification of this descriptive « rule », which renders more logical the distinction of case: the accusative represents what is directly grasped by the hearing (sound, news, what is said), and the genitive the source of what is heard, whether the person speaking or a voice conceived not as sound but as speaking, or the object making the noise which is heard. The attention to the source of what is said leads to the use of ἀκούειν not simply of the perception of sound, but with the notions « listen, attend, obey ».

For persons, cf. Mt 2,9 οἱ δὲ ἀκούσαντες τοῦ βασιλέως ἐπορεύθησαν or Mt 10,14. The matter is clearer when the object is φωνή: the accusative refers to physical perception of the sound, e. g. τὸ πνεῦμα ὅπου θέλει πνεῖ, καὶ τὴν φωνὴν αὐτοῦ ἀκούεις Jo 3,8 and similarly Jo 5,37. φωνή parallelled by εἶδος, and Rev 19,1; but the genitive is used if the « voice » be explicitly represented as speaking, e. g. Acts 11,7 ἤκουσα δὲ καὶ φωνῆς λεγούσης μοι; so too 22,7; Rev 11,12; or understood as such, inasmuch as the speaker's voice is represented as teaching, ordering or the like e. g. Jo 5,25: ἔρχεται ὥρα... ὅτε οἱ νεκροὶ ἀκούσουσιν τῆς φωνῆς τοῦ υἱοῦ τοῦ Θεοῦ; 10,3; 18,37.

Further confirmation is supplied by the use of λόγος or λόγοι as object of hearing. Here the accusative predominates and is for that reason perhaps not to be insisted upon (cf. Mt 10,14 where the rejection expressed in the context suggests understanding μηδὲ ἀκούσῃ τοὺς λόγους ὑμῶν in the sense of not even letting the apostles preach to them). The more normal the accusative, however, so much the more reason is there for supposing that the genitive is significant, e. g. Lk 6,47 has ὁ ἀκούων μου τῶν λόγων, where Mt 7,24 (completely parallel) has the accusative: ὅστις ἀκούει μου τοὺς λόγους τούτους: what both add, namely « and carries them out » renders clear the sense of the ἀκούειν, and this seems in Lk to have called forth the genitive, and in Mt to have allowed the accusative to stand. Cf. also Jo 19,8 with 19,13, where Pilate allows himself to be persuaded.

This seemingly fundamental distinction does not, however, resolve at once the difficulty of the apparent contradiction between:

Acts 9,7: Saul's companions ἀκούοντες μὲν τῆς φωνῆς μηδένα δὲ θεωροῦντες
Acts 22,9: Saul's companions τὸ μὲν φῶς ἐθεάσαντο, τὴν δὲ φωνὴν οὐκ ἤκουσαν τοῦ λαλοῦντός μοι

Here a distinction is commonly seen between hearing the voice and understanding it, the physical perception being expressed by the genitive and the understanding by the accusative, but this seems an arbitrary « ad hoc » distinction. The matter is perhaps rather to be expressed as follows: Saul's companions heard a sound (which he and Luke know to be a voice, that of the Lord, and so call it ἡ φωνή) but did not recognize it as the voice of a speaker. Thus in ἀκούοντες μὲν τῆς φωνῆς the genitive is used of the source of· the sound which they heard, in accordance with the explanation given above. In the second passage the genitive might once more have been expected for the same reason, but here the accusative is perhaps called for by the addition in the genitive of the source of the voice itself.

51   70. The general Hellenistic tendency to more explicit expression, reinforced sometimes for the NT by a certain Semitic influence, results in the use of prepositions instead of the simple accusative. Thus

a) as with γίνεσθαι, ἔσεσθαι the nominative predicate is replaced by εἰς with the accusative (cf. 32), so too εἰς is sometimes used with an accusative predicate, e. g. Mt 21,46: εἰς προφήτην αὐτὸν εἶχον or Acts 13,22: ἤγειρεν αὐτοῖς τὸν Δαυὶδ εἰς βασιλέα;

b) with verbs of fear and precaution, φοβεῖσθαι, φεύγειν, φυλάττεσθαι the accusative is found, but also ἀπό;

c) in place of the accusative of (spatial or temporal) extension we find ἐπί· (cf. 125) and (τό: ἐπὶ σάββατον τρία Acts 17,2; ἐπιποθίαν ἔχων ἀπὸ ἱκανῶν ἐτῶν Rom 15,23; ἦν δὲ ἡ Βηθανία ἐγγὺς τῶν Ἱεροσολύμων ὡς ἀπὸ σταδίων δεκαπέντε Jo 11,18.

71. One may perhaps mention in this connection the remarkable Hellenistic manner of indicating distance (in time or space) with the preposition (ἀπό, μετά, πρό) governing not the point from which the distance is measured, but the distance itself: instead of « six days before the Passover » we have πρὸ ἓξ ἡμερῶν τοῦ πάσχα Jo 12,1. Hence too, without the genitive of the point from which measurement is made, the preposition is used with the measure of distance in: (« the disciples were not far from land but ») ὡς ἀπὸ πηχῶν διακοσίων Jo 21,8; so too Jo 11,18; Rev 14,20.

52   **72.** Verbs which in the active can govern a double accusative retain in the passive, in Greek, the « accusative of the thing »: ἐν πνεῦμα ἐποτίσθημεν 1 Cor 12,13; ὁ κατηχούμενος τὸν λόγον Gal 6,6; δαρήσεται πολλάς (scl. πληγάς) Lk 12,47f. The same occurs where — as is admissible in Greek — the subject of the passive corresponds to a dative with the active, e. g. to πιστεύειν τινί τι « entrust somebody with something »: a passive is formed πιστεύεσθαί τι « be entrusted with something »: πεπίστευμαι τὸ εὐαγγέλιον Gal 2,7; 2 Cor 3,18. (Cf. in English « I am given a book » etc.).

53   **73.** This « accusative of the thing » is by analogy given a very extended use, so as to say, e. g. πεπληρωμένοι καρπὸν δικαιοσύνης Php 1,11; or τὴν αὐτὴν εἰκόνα μεταμορφούμεθα 2 Cor 3,18; and even τὴν ἅλυσιν περίκειμαι Acts 28,20.

74. The accusative « of respect », which on account of its frequency in classical usage is also sometimes called the « Greek » accusative, is rare in the NT (cf. 53), as in the κοινή in general. In the NT we find Mt 27,57 τοὔνομα Ἰωσήφ; Jo 6,10 τὸν ἀριθμὸν ὡς πεντακισχίλιοι; Heb 2,17. — Very similar is the **adverbial** use of the accusative: τὰ πολλά « to a great extent » Rom 15,22; τὸ πλεῖστον τρεῖς « three at most » 1 Cor 14,27; τὸ καθ' ἡμέραν Lk 11,3 and often; τὸ νῦν ἔχον Acts 24,25; τὰ νῦν Acts 17,30; τὸ τέλος « finally » 1 Pet 3,8; τὸ κατὰ σάρκα Rom 9,15; τὴν ἀρχήν « at all » Jo 8,25.

III. PREPOSITIONS

1) In General

54 78. For the better understanding of the language and of its evolution, note that prepositions were in origin adverbs, which did not «govern» cases, but rather were added to the cases for the clearer expression of the relationship between the verb and the noun, and later also between nouns. This adverbial character of prepositions is to be seen in the NT in such expressions as ἀνὰ εἷς Rev 21,21; καθ' εἷς Rom 12,5; ὑπὲρ ἐγώ 2 Cor 11,23.

55 79. On the other hand it is quite characteristic of Hellenistic usage that many adverbs have taken on a prepositional use. These adverbs may conveniently be distinguished from the older prepositions as « prepositions improperly so called ».

What is proper to Hellenistic usage in the matter of prepositions may be set forth approximately in the following rules:

56 80. a) The use of prepositional expressions instead of simple cases increases greatly (thanks to the analytical tendency whereby what was implicit in the case is explicitly expressed).

Cf. the usage proper to Luke, λέγειν πρός τινα instead of λέγειν τινι (in Lk 99 times and in Acts 52 times, as against Mt 0, Mk 5, Jo 19, Paul 2), and the frequency with which ἐκ and ἀπό are used instead of the partitive genitive alone, and even « absolutely », so that e. g. Jo 1,24 ἐκ τῶν φαρισαίων may be rendered, and perhaps ought to be rendered « (some) pharisees », as e. g. French « des pharisiens » (cf. 16,17; 2 Jo 4; Lk 11,16b etc.), i. e., of a different set of envoys from that of the priests of which the writer speaks in verse 19. See also 64, 68.

57 81. b) The number (or variety) of prepositions properly so called decreases: of the 19 prepositions of classical Greek, only seven survive in modern demotic Greek. In the NT the only ones completely extinct are ἀμφί and ὡς; but ἀνά and ἀντί are very restricted in use; as for the other prepositions, certain uses at any rate have either become rare or completely disappeared; for in general:

58   82. c) the variety in the use of individual prepositions likewise decreases. In the most ancient Greek most of the prepositions were used with several cases; in modern demotic Greek all the prepositions properly so called are used with the accusative only. In the NT three cases are still taken by ἐπί, παρά, πρός (once with the genitive); μετά, περί, ὑπό no longer take three cases, having lost the dative.

59   83. d) The use of prepositions « improperly so called » increases both in frequency and in variety. These adverbs are preferred to the old prepositions on account of the tendency to fuller expression (e. g. instead of πρό in the spatial sense we have ἔμπροσθεν, ἐνώπιον, κατενώπιον (Hebrew li/ne), and on account of the uniformity of construction (most of them with the genitive only).

     84. Hence also the frequency of the adverb ἐπάνω instead of ἐπί: ἐπάνω ὄρους Mt 21,7 and ἐπάνω αὐτῶν (scl. garments); so too with verbs: βάλλειν κάτω instead of καταβάλλειν Mt 4,6; βάλλειν ἔξω instead of ἐκβάλλειν Mt 5,13. Where — as often occurs — ἔξω is used instead of simple ἐκ there is perhaps the connotation of a certain idea of remaining outside, or of a place outside, e. g. Heb 13,13 ἐξερχώμεθα πρὸς αὐτὸν ἔξω τῆς παρεμβολῆς, i. e. to a place outside the enclosure; cf. Mt 10,14; 21,17 and 39; Mk 5,10 etc.

60   85. e) Above all a certain general law can be distinguished in the use of the prepositions, namely: those whose meaning is similar begin to be confused with each other in popular thought and so in popular speech; then, since they are no longer distinguished, the word which is phonetically stronger prevails over the other, and sometimes entirely supplants it. Thus in modern demotic Greek εἰς has supplanted ἐν, and ἀπό has taken the place of ἐξ, ὑπό, παρά.

61   86. In the NT some traces of this evolution are to be found here and there; hence it is well to know which are the prepositions on whose classical propriety of sense one can no longer insist.

2) Rival Prepositions

a) ἀπό = ἐκ

62   87. In 1 Thess 2,6 we read: οὔτε ζητοῦντες ἐ ξ ἀνθρώπων δόξαν οὔτε ἀφ' ὑμῶν οὔτε ἀ π' ἄλλων. The Vulgate rightly neglects the difference between the prepositions, translating by *ab* the ἐξ as well as the two ἀπό.

These two prepositions are used indifferently even in their·local sense, where the distinction would be more important; thus e. g. in Mt 3,16 we have βαπτισθεὶς δὲ ὁ ’Ιησοῦς εὐθὺς ἀνέβη ἀ π ὸ τοῦ ὕδατος, which might suggest that Jesus was baptized not in the Jordan but on its bank, since ἀπό means simply « from » and not « out of » which would be ἐκ; but it is certain that Mt with his ἀπό means the same thing as Mk 1,9f: ἐβαπτίσθη εἰς τὸν ’Ιορδάνην... καὶ εὐθὺς ἀναβαίνων ἐ κ τοῦ ὕδατος εἶδεν...

88. Hence ἐξέρχεσθαι (in the sense « come out, go out ») is often used with ἀπό, especially by Luke (thirteen times in the gospel, and never with ἐκ, in contrast with Mk who has ἐξέρχεσθαι with ἀπό once only (11,12) but ten times with ἐκ); on the other hand, ἐξέρχεσθαι is also used in the sense « go away » simply, as Lk 5,8, where Peter says Ἔξελθε ἀπ’ ἐμοῦ ὅτι ἀνὴρ ἁμαρτωλός εἰμι, Κύριε. This confusion of ἐκ and ἀπό is indeed common enough in Hellenistic Greek, but in the NT Hebrew influence is perhaps not entirely absent: in Hebrew and in Aramaic the same preposition *min* is used in both senses, although its opposition to « in » makes it closer to ἐκ, which perhaps accounts for the use in Rev of ἐκ more than a hundred times, as against about twenty occurrences of ἀπό.

89. The question has been raised whether at the end of the Lord's prayer in ῥῦσαι ἡμᾶς ἀπὸ τοῦ πονηροῦ (Mt 6,13) the words ἀπὸ τοῦ πονηροῦ are to be understood as referring to « evil » or to a personal « evil one » (the devil). Various reasons in favour of the latter sense are given by J.-B. BAUER in *Verb. Dom.* 34, 1956, 12-15, and one of them is the use of the preposition ἀπό instead of ἐκ after ῥύεσθαι, which is predominantly used with ἐκ when the reference is to deliverance from non-personal evils, and with ἀπό when the reference is to personal foes. In the NT (leaving out of consideration the text at present in question) ἀπό is twice found with a personal object and once with a non-personal one, while ἐκ is never found with a person but seven times with things. This is confirmed by the usage of the LXX: ἀπό with persons ten times, with things seven times; ἐκ with persons ten times, with things sixty times. This perhaps suggests, so far as this argument is concerned, that Mt 6,13 is to be understood as referring to the devil.

b) ἀπό = ὑπό and παρά

90. With the passive ἀπό begins to take the place of ὑπό, e. g. Acts 15,4 those who were said in the preceding verse to be προπεμφθέντες ὑ π ὸ τῆς ἐκκλησίας are now said to be received ἀ π ὸ τῆς ἐκκλησίας in the

29

Codex Vaticanus and in Ephrem rescriptus, though the usual text has
ὑπό; cf. 2 Cor. 7,13. Hence in Lk 1,26 where the angel is said to be sent
ἀ π ὸ τοῦ θεοῦ into a town of Galilee, it is possible to understand « from
God » instead of « by God », but it is not possible to insist on this sense
on the grounds that ἀπό is used and not ὑπό; and similarly
in Lk 1,45 where Mary is said to have believed what was said to her
π α ρ ὰ Κυρίου the sense may be simply « by God » although in classical
usage παρά would mean that the message came « from God », connoting
the transmission by the angel as in Lk 1,26f (unless one prefers to
take παρὰ Κυρίου with ἔσται τελείωσις rather than with τοῖς λελαλημένοις αὐτῇ).

c) ὑπέρ = ἀντί.

64   91. Ὑπέρ generally means « for » in the sense « in favour of », but
not rarely covers also « for » in the sense « in place of », e. g. Jo 11,50
συμφέρει ὑμῖν ἵνα εἷς ἄνθρωπος ἀποθάνῃ ὑπὲρ τοῦ λαοῦ which Caiaphas
certainly did not mean « for the good of » the people; he immediately
adds καὶ μὴ ὅλον τὸ ἔθνος ἀπόληται; or Gal 3,13 Christ redeemed us
from the curse becoming ὑπὲρ ἡμῶν κατάρα (so too 2 Cor 5,14. 15. 21; 1 Tim
2,6 (cf. Mk 10,45!); Tit 2,14), Mere substitution is expressed by ὑπέρ in
Phm 13: to minister to me in your stead: ὑπὲρ σοῦ (cf. also 1 Cor 15,29).

65   92. On the other hand ἀντί (« for » = « in place of ») also seems to
have extended its scope. Its original sense « (set) over against » connotes
a certain equivalence to its object, with consequent possibility of substitution, or the equivalence of price and what is acquired in exchange
or buying (δοῦναι τὴν ψυχὴν λύτρον ἀντὶ πολλῶν Mt 20,28), or the equivalence of merit and its reward or punishment: κακὸν ἀντὶ κακοῦ Rom
12,17, or the common ἀνθ᾽ ὧν (= ἀντὶ τούτων ὅτι) as in ἔσῃ σιωπῶν ἀνθ᾽
ὧν οὐκ ἐπίστευσας Lk 1,20; so too ἀντὶ τούτου « therefore »; and finally
true substitution: ἀντὶ ἰχθύος ὄφιν Lk 11,11.

66   93. It seems however that ἀντί may drop the original notion of
equivalent and take on simply the sense of ὑπέρ: « take the stater and give
it to them ἀντὶ ἐμοῦ καὶ σοῦ » Mt 17,27.

67   94. Hence the question may at least be raised, whether δοῦναι τὴν ψυχὴν λύτρον ἀντὶ πολλῶν Mt 20,28 necessarily has a connotation of substitution, or can be taken simply with the sense of ὑπέρ, as with ἀντίλυτρον

in 1 Tim 2,6. From a linguistic point of view the question cannot be satis-
factorily answered; for as we have seen, ὑπέρ itself may have the notion of substitution. Thanks to the same confusion between ὑπέρ and
ἀντί the already obscure problem of baptism ὑπέρ τῶν νεκρῶν (1 Cor 15,29)
becomes even more so.

68   95. Similarly for Jo 1,16 : «of His fulness we have all received καὶ
χάριν ἀντὶ χάριτος» the question arises whether there is sufficient justification for the opinion which insists, on account of the use of ἀντί, on the
sense of substitution of a new grace in place of the old grace which is abol-
ished, e. g. of the Holy Spirit instead of the presence of Christ (D'ALÈS)
or of the presence of God in Christ instead of the divine presence in the
shekinah (D. FRANGIPANE); for perhaps ἀντί may signify rather the succession of grace « one grace after another ». For such a sense Philo (de po-
steritate Caini 145) is usually cited: χάριτας... ἑτέρας ἀντ' ἐκείνων καὶ
ἀεὶ νέας ἀντὶ παλαιοτέρων (where however the context shows that real
substitution is meant); so too Martyrium Petri et Pauli 136,13: ἄλλα
ἀντι ἄλλων ψευσάμενοι. It is to be noted that among the few old prepositions that survive in modern demotic Greek we have ἀντίς with precisely
the sense of substitution which some have suspected of becoming restricted in the NT.

d) ὑπέρ = περί

69   96. In Eph 6,18f we read: προσευχόμενοι π ε ρ ὶ πάντων τῶν ἀγίων καὶ
ὑ π έ ρ ἐμοῦ; the Vulgate rightly neglects the difference of preposition and
uses pro in both cases. Moreover, just as here περί is used with the same
concrete sense as ὑπέρ, so too ὑπέρ is found where one might have expected περί. Hence one must not look for any recondite sense where the
Baptist says, Jo, 1,30: οὗτός ἐστιν ὑ π ὲ ρ οὗ ἐγὼ εἶπον... Although the
Precursor does in fact testify « for » Christ, here it is correct to translate
« This is He of whom I said... » The affinity of sense which gives rise
to the confusion is clear enough in e. g. Jo 17,9.

Other examples: περί instead of ὑπέρ, see Mt 26,28; Rom 8,3; Heb 5.3;
10,6. 8. 18. 26; 13,11 etc. ; ὑπέρ instead iof περί, which n Hellenistic usage
is much commoner than περί instead of ὑπέρ, is in the NT practically
restricted to Paul: Rom 9,27; 1 Cor 4,6; 2 Cor 5,12; 7,14; 8,23; 9,2; 12,5 etc.
This Pauline preference is perhaps to be explained in part from the agreement
with the use of the Hebrew preposition 'al (= upon = ὑπέρ) in the sense
« about » (= περί).

e) εἰς = πρός

70   97. A confusion corresponding somewhat to that between ἀπό and ἐκ is to be found likewise between πρός and εἰς, inasmuch as εἰς is no longer restricted to the sense «into» but may mean simply «to» or «towards». E. g. Mk 5,38f we read καὶ ἔρχονται ε ἰ ς τὸν οἶκον, but what follows: καὶ ε ἰ σ ε λ θ ὼ ν λέγει αὐτοῖς might suggest that the εἰς stands for πρός. Similarly where Jesus is said to have betaken Himself κατ᾽ ἰδίαν εἰς πόλιν καλουμένην Βηθσαϊδά (Lk 9,10), the sense must be «to the neighbourhood of...» (Cf. also Mt 21,1; Mk 11,1; Lk 18,35; 19,29; Jo 4,5).

So too Jo 20,3 demands, owing to the context, the rendering «Peter and John were going to the tomb», though the text has ἤρχοντο ε ἰ ς τὸ μνημεῖον; for the account continues: «the two of them were running together and... (John).... came first to the tomb (again εἰς τὸ μνη- μεῖον)... but did not go in (οὐ μέντοι εἰσῆλθεν)... So Simon Peter came up and went into the tomb (εἰσῆλθεν εἰς τὸ μνημεῖον)... Then therefore the other disciple also entered, who had come first to the tomb (ὁ ἐλθὼν πρῶτος ε ἰ ς τὸ μνημεῖον). This description in its Greek form (not in the Vulgate, which distinguishes between «in» and «ad», verses 4, 6, 8) seems at first sight to agree admirably with archaeological data, which show in such tombs a distinction between the antechamber and the tomb itself, so that it would be possible to go «into» the tomb in one sense without «entering» it in the other. Since however εἰς τὸ μνημεῖον in verse 3 seems to mean simply «to the tomb» (which it would more certainly mean if the aorist had been used instead of the imperfect), εἰς may well be taken in the same sense in verses 4 and 8 (as the Vulgate takes it). It thus follows that the mere use of εἰς in this text does not prove that Our Lord's tomb had an antechamber ([1]).

98. In the metaphorical sense also εἰς and πρός are used indifferently, not only, as is obvious, with great frequency to indicate the end in view, but also in rarer uses, e. g. causally «on account of »: for just as the Ninivites are said to have done penance εἰς τὸ κήρυγμα Ἰωνᾶ (Mt 12,41), and a prophet to be received εἰς ὄνομα προφήτου (Mt 10,41), so also (Mk 10,5) Moses is said to have permitted divorce πρὸς τὴν σκληροκαρδίαν ὑμῶν.

([1]) Cf. *Verb. Dom* 21 (1941) p. 76 n. 4.

f) εἰς = ἐν

71   99. In Hellenistic usage the distinction between rest and motion
begins to be neglected, and this is especially clear in the use of εἰς instead of ἐν. In classical usage εἰς is found with verbs of rest, but with
a connotation of preceding motion, e. g. παρεῖναι εἰς τὴν πόλιν (just as
ἐν is found with verbs of motion, with the connotation of following rest):
the so-called « pregnant construction ». If F. - M. ABEL is right (²), it is
this that led εἰς, in Hellenistic usage, to make further inroads into the
province of ἐν, to be confused with ἐν, and finally to supplant it, so
that in modern demotic Greek, ἐν (along with the dative) having disappeared except in some set phrases, εἰς alone is used of « in(to) » whether of rest or of motion.

72   100. Not a few traces of this evolution in its early stages are to be
found already in the NT. Thus in Lk 9,61 ἀποτάξασθαι τοῖς εἰς τὸν
οἶκόν μου (say farewell to those at my home), or 11,7 τὰ παιδία μου...
εἰς τὴν κοίτην εἰσίν (« in bed »). There is no point in seeking a latent
idea of motion in these cases.

73   101. Not only in the local sense, but also in metaphorical ones εἰς
may be used in place of ἐν. Unless this be borne in mind, a text such as
Acts 7,53 : ἐλάβετε τὸν νόμον εἰς διαταγὰς ἀγγέλων is extremely
puzzling; substitute however ἐν for εἰς, and take it in the (Semitic) instrumental sense, and the mystery disappears; there is no idea whatever
of motion involved. Cf. also Acts 19,3, where Paul asks εἰς τί οὖν ἐβαπ-
τίσθητε, and receives the answer εἰς τὸ Ἰωάννου βάπτισμα, showing that
εἰς is taken as instrumental ἐν in the question also.

74   ·102. One must thus beware of insisting overmuch on the use of εἰς
in contexts where a connotation of motion would be welcome to the theo-
logian. E. g. though in Jo 1,18 Jesus is called the Only-begotten ὁ ὢν
εἰς τὸν κόλπον τοῦ πατρός, it would be an exaggeration to ascribe to the
evangelist the intention of expressing by the use of εἰς the trinitarian
relation of « esse ad » whereby the second divine Person is said to be constituted. Nor can one place any great confidence in the confirmation of
such an exegesis by recourse to 1,1: καὶ ὁ λόγος ἦν πρὸς τὸν θεόν (where

(²) Grammaire du grec biblique, p. 216; § 48c.

one might have expected παρὰ τῷ θεῷ), because the Hellenistic neglect
of the distinction between rest and motion causes a confusion, similar
to that between εἰς and ἐν, between the accusative and the dative with
πρός; it is true, however, that elsewhere in John πρός seems always
(about 100 times!) to be used in a dynamic sense, (which in our case
may be understood as one of personal relationship) while the sense « with
someone» is always rendered by παρά with the dative, 1,39; 4,40; 8,38; 14,17
23,25; 17,5; or by μετά with the genitive (about 20 times).

75   103. A further argument in favour of the view that a special meaning is to be attached to the use of εἰς in 1,18 and of πρός in 1,1 can be
found in the fact that the fourth gospel offers scarcely any other example
(20,7?) to suggest a neglect of the distinction between εἰς and ἐν. As
for ἔστη εἰς τὸ μέσον Jo 20,19 and 26, the verb is, as in classical usage,
regarded as one of motion (so too 21,4?); Jo 9,7 ὕπαγε νίψαι εἰς τὴν κο-
λυμβήθραν shows εἰς influenced by the verb of motion ὕπαγε. One might
perhaps suspect ἐν of standing for εἰς in Io 3,35; 5,4; but one of
these texts is of doubtful reading, and both can be accounted for as
« pregnant constructions» (99). — Finally it is noteworthy that even the
book of Revelation, whose language is more vulgar than that of any other
book of the NT, and which can certainly be attributed to John himself
even as regards its form, does not confuse εἰς and ἐν. — So much for
the sense of εἰς in Jo 1,18.

104. Those however who maintain that in John εἰς in the local sense
is always dynamic must give serious consideration to 19,13: Pilate led Jesus
forth καὶ ἐκάθισεν ἐπὶ βήματος, εἰς τόπον λεγόμενον Λιθόστρωτον. Here, even
if εἰς τόπον be explained as due to the verb of motion in « led forth »,
it is not easy to understand ἐκάθισεν ἐπὶ βήματος as meaning that Pilate
sat « in the judgement seat ». The expression is more readily understood as
meaning that Pilate led Jesus forth and made Him sit on the magistrate's
dais, saying to the Jews « Behold your king! ». This may seem a strange interpretation, but it is not a new one, and weighty arguments in its favour are adduced by I. DE LA POTTERIE in Bib 41(1960), 217-47.

105. Hence too ἐν is perhaps to be taken in its full sense in 1 Jo
4,16: we have known and believed τὴν ἀγάπην ἣν ἔχει ὁ θεὸς ἐν ἡμῖν.
This does not seem to mean ἣν ἔχει... εἰς ἡμᾶς, nor does it seem sufficient to understand it of the love which is manifested ἐν ἡμῖν i. e. among
us, namely the mission and ministry of the Son; but in St John's theology

the sense seems perhaps to be the communication of divine love whereby we are constituted not only its object but also in a certain wise its subject (cf. Rom. 5,5).

76   106. **Immunity** from this confusion of εἰς and ἐν (in the local sense) is usually ascribed to Mt and all the epistles of the NT (except for 1 Pet 5,12): a point of importance for exegetes, in that, apart from Mk Lk Acts, where it may stand for ἐν, the presumption is that εἰς is to be taken in its full sense.

Thus for example Matthew's manner of expressing himself allows and even suggests taking εἰς in its strict sense where he reports the command to baptize in the words: «... baptizing them εἰς τὸ ὄνομα of the Father...» (28,19). The use of εἰς seems to suggest the end and effect of baptism, a special relation to the Holy Trinity assumed by the person baptized (³).

Mt 10,41 cannot be urged as an objection as if εἰς ὄνομα were the equivalent of ἐν ὀνόματι in the expression «receive a just man εἰς ὄνομα δικαίου»; for the sense here called for is a causal one, for which the preposition εἰς is suitable, just as the Semitic equivalent *le* admits not only a final but also a causal sense, as here in *leshem* «in view of» (cf. the English use of «in view of» loosely in a causal as well as a final sense); cf. also e. g. Mt 12,41, the Ninivites do penance εἰς τὸ κήρυγμα Ἰωνᾶ (cf. 99).

77   107. **Let us now come to Paul.** In Php 1,5 Paul gives thanks to God and expresses his joy ἐπὶ τῇ κοινωνίᾳ ὑμῶν εἰς τὸ εὐαγγέλιον, which the Vulgate renders «super communicatione vestra in Evangelio» and not «... in Evangelium». So far as Hellenistic usage is concerned this version could stand, and the resulting sense would be quite Pauline: the thanksgiving would be for the fact that the Philippians, having received the Gospel, were giving proof of their possession of it in their lives and behaviour. But since we are not justified in taking a Pauline εἰς as standing for ἐν, the Vulgate's rendering must be rejected and κοινωνία εἰς τὸ εὐαγγέλιον is to be understood as cooperation in the spread of the gospel. Hence this text is a fine Biblical testimony to the lay apostolate.

_____

(³) Cf. STRACK-BILLERBECK I, p. 1045t.

78   **108.** There is yet another text in the same epistle, where the Vulgate, by a similarly incorrect version, has misled many into an erroneous interpretation: Php 2,11: « that at the name of Jesus every knee be bent...

and every tongue confess *quia Dominus Jesus Christus in gloria est Dei Patris* »; which can only mean « that the Lord Jesus Christ is in the glory of God the Father », as the fulfilment of Christ's petition to the Father to be glorified with Him in the glory He had with Him before the world was made (Jo 17,5). The Greek text, however, does not admit this sense, for it has ὅτι Κύριος Ἰησοῦς Χριστὸς ε ἰ ς δόξαν θεοῦ πατρός, where εἰς δόξαν... means « to (not: in) the glory... », so that the real sense is: « that... every tongue confess that Jesus Christ (is) the Lord (= God), to the glory of God the Father ».

79   **109.** The Vulgate's neglect of the distinction between εἰς and ἐν has however its greatest theological importance in Col 1,16: τὰ πάντα δι' αὐτοῦ καὶ εἰς αὐτὸν ἔκτισται, where the Vulgate renders *in ipso* instead of *in ipsum*. Here the difference between εἰς and ἐν alters the entire outlook on the universe, for Christ is said to have been not only the efficient cause of creation, but also its final cause. All things converge upon Him, are directed to Him; He is not only the First but also the Last, not only the beginning of all things but also their end (Rev 22,13). The investigation of the depths of this mystery is the affair of theologians. I call it a mystery, for if Christ as beginning is « the Word », He is certainly here said to be the end as the incarnate Word.

80   **110.** The Vulgate, which in all these examples has treated εἰς as equivalent to ἐν, nevertheless renders the strict sense of εἰς in the one passage in which one might suspect Paul of having used it in place of ἐν, in Eph 3,16:«... I bend the knee to the Father... that He may give you... δυνάμει κραταιωθῆναι εἰς τὸν ἔσω ἄνθρωπον. There are in fact modern versions which translate as if the text were ἐν τῷ ἔσω ἀνθρώπῳ.(⁴)

Paul's style, however, justifies the attempt to retain the strict sense of εἰς, as in Huby's rendering (⁵).

(⁴) « Am inwendigen Menschen » M. DIBELIUS, « am inneren Menschen » C. RÖSCH, O. KARRER.

(⁵) «... D'être puissamment fortifiés... pour le progrès en vous de l'homme intérieur ». Similarly *La Bible de Jérusalem*: «... pour que se fortifie en vous l'homme intérieur ».

It is perhaps possible to insist further on the article τόν, so as to understand « *the* inner man » as not only an object of the strengthening action of the Holy Spirit, but as the end in view: κραταιωθῆναι εἰς τὸν ἔσω ἄνθρωπον = be strengthened so as to produce « the inner man », this being so understood as the state of the perfect Christian (this is especially suggested by the use of the aorist).

This will perhaps not be admitted, on account of the analogous expression in Rom 7,22 and 2 Cor 4,16; but it serves to show to what practically useful considerations one may be led by attention to a detail of style, namely that in the epistles the distinction between εἰς and ἐν is observed.

81   III. An exception to this rule may be admitted for 1 Pet 5,12: ἔγραψα... ἐπιμαρτυρῶν ταύτην εἶναι ἀληθῆ χάριν τοῦ θεοῦ, ε ἰ ς ἣν στῆτε. There is an « easier reading » εἰς ἣν ἐστήκατε which corresponds to the Vulgate's « in qua statis »; as for the more difficult reading στῆτε, its sense (« enter upon » the grace of God) seems to rule it out, unless it be taken as meaning « remain » (*). Here, therefore, if we exclude the proper sense of στῆτε and also the « pregnant » use of εἰς (cf. 99), we have almost certainly εἰς instead of ἐν. But is not this example of popular usage, exceptional and indeed unique in the epistles, one which may be welcome and valuable, as confirming in moving fashion the opinion, probable on other grounds, that this clause of the epistle, and this one alone, was written by St Peter with his own hand, perhaps in letters as awkward as the expression. This vestige of the hand of the first Pope may arouse in us much the same emotion as that expressed in a famous papyrus letter written to his father by a young man serving in the navy: γράψον μοι ἐπιστόλιον... ἵνα σου π ρ ο σ κ υ ν ή σ ω τ ὴ ν χ έ ρ α ν, ὅτι με ἐπαίδευσας καλῶς (BGU II, 423).

3) Some Individual Prepositions

a) Διά

82   112. The causal use of διά with the accusative, « on account of », is extended to the final cause, e. g. Mk 2,27 διὰ τὸν ἄνθρωπον = τοῦ ἀνθρώπου ἕνεκα (Mt 24,22; Jo 11,42; Rom 4,25; 11,28 etc. and cf. the formula διὰ τοῦτο... ἵνα Rom 4,16; 1 Tim 1,16; Phm 15) and so διά is on the way to the meaning « for » which it has in modern Greek.

(*) For examples see U. Holzmeister, *Epistula prima S. Petri*, p. 441.

83 113. The causal sense with the genitive, which of itself expresses only intermediary or instrumental causality (« through »), e. g. God speaks διὰ τοῦ προφήτου, may cover also the principal cause, e. g. Rom 11,36 where it is said of the Creator that ἐξ αὐτοῦ καὶ δι᾽ αὐτοῦ καὶ εἰς αὐτὸν τὰ πάντα. So too 1 Cor 1,9; 12,8; Heb 2,10; 13,11; 1 Pet 2,14 etc. Hence to much stress must not be laid on the use of the preposition διά with the genitive as expressing the role of mediator, where it is used of Christ's (the Word's) action as creator (Jo 1,3. 10; Col 1,16) or redeemer (Rom 5,9).

84 114. The same tendency towards the extension of the field of a preposition is to be seen where διά with the genitive is used of the manner of acting. The means whereby a thing is done is already in a certain sense a manner in which it is done, e. g. διὰ λόγου « orally » Acts 15,27 as opposed to διὰ τῆς ἐπιστολῆς 2 Cor 10,11. From this starting point the use is extended to manners which are not means but mere circumstances: ἔγραψα ὑμῖν διὰ πολλῶν δακρύων 2 Cor 2,4 (cf. Rom 4,11; 14,20; 2 Cor 3,11; 6,8), even a circumstance which hinders the action, so that one might almost render « in spite of »: ὁ διὰ γράμματος καὶ περιτομῆς παραβάτης Rom 2,27. — Some derive this usage rather from the notion of a circumstance through which one passes and so, in which one acts: we walk διὰ πίστεως οὐ διὰ εἴδους 2 Cor 5,7.

85 115. Διά with the genitive in the temporal sense means not only, as in classifical usage, duration (διὰ ὅλης νυκτός) or lapse of time after which something happens: δι᾽ ἡμερῶν « after some days » Mk 2,1, but also, which is not classical, the space of time within which something happens; in Mt 26,61 Christ can rebuild the temple διὰ τριῶν ἡμερῶν, which the Vulgate renders « post triduum », but Jo 2,19 has τρισὶν ἡμέραις. So too Acts 1,3; 16,9; 17,10; 23,31.

b) Ἐν

86 116. **Sociative use.** The preposition ἐν, thanks in part at least to the influence of Semitic be, increases its scope to a very great extent. In Biblical usage the value of ἐν seems to be very ill defined, and often to be very far indeed from the local sense. Thus where Mk 5,2 speaks of a man ἐν πνεύματι ἀκαθάρτῳ one might feel that it would be more logical to say the spirit was in the man rather than the man in the spirit, and one might explain the preposition as meaning that man was in the power of the spirit. Later however in the same chapter (5,25) such an explanation will not avail, for the woman with the flux of bood is said to have been ἐν ῥύσει αἵματος.

87   **117.** The question has a certain importance when one wishes to understand what Paul means by saying sometimes that we are in Christ, or in the Spirit, and at others that Christ, or the Spirit, is in us. Indeed the distinction in Paul's mind between the two notions seems to be so small, not to say non-existent, that he explains and as it were defines the one by the other: Rom 8,9: «you are not in the flesh but in the Spirit, if the Spirit of God dwells in you». So he is «in the Spirit», in whom the Spirit is, or as the apostle goes on to say, who «has the Spirit»: «but if anyone have not the Spirit of Christ, the same is not of Him». In John also the dwelling of God (Christ) in us and our dwelling in God (Christ) are two correlative and inseparable aspects of the same reality, cf. 1 Jo 4,13. 15. 16; Jo 6,56; 15, 4f; in Jo 8,44 it is said of Satan that he is not in the truth because the truth is not in him. Thus ἐν (not without Semitic influence) is practically reduced to the expression of a general notion of association or accompaniment, which would be rendered in English by «with»: a man with an unclean spirit, a woman with a flux of blood.

To this usage belong also such examples as: to be ἐν περιτομῇ or ἐν ἀκροβυστίᾳ Rom 4,10; to come ἐν πληρώματι εὐλογίας Rom 15,29; the priest enters ἐν αἵματι = bringing blood with him Heb 9,25; to come ἐν ῥάβδῳ 1 Cor 4,21; or Lk 14,31 the king reflects whether he can with (ἐν) ten thousand stand up to one who · comes against· him with (μετά) twenty thousand; and in general where ἐν is used of an instrument: propitiation ἐν αἵματι Rom 3,25; or of the manner in which something is done: ἐν τάχει Lk 18,8 ; ἐν δικαιοσύνῃ = δικαίως Acts 17,31; ἐν δόλῳ Mk 14,1.

88   **118.** Some may perhaps be apprehensive lest we reduce to banality certain Pauline formulae which are dear to us and full of boundless depths of meaning, by putting ἐν Χριστῷ, ἐν πνεύματι and the like in the same class, philologically, with ἐν πνεύματι ἀκαθάρτῳ, ἐν ῥύσει αἵματος, and even with ἐν ῥάβδῳ and ἐν τάχει. Such apprehension is unfounded; for here again we must repeat what was said in dealing with the genitive (39): we must beware of the notion that words and grammatical usage have of themselves a certain definite and invariable content of meaning. They are in reality conventional signs whose sense is usually fairly general, the exact meaning being in each case determined by usage and above all by the subject matter. Just as the genitive of itself indicates merely an appurtenance of one thing to another, and for this reason may, according to the subject matter, express even the most exalted mystical union between Christ and those who are « Christ's », so too ἐν, indicating of itself merely association or concomitance, may represent, according to the subject matter, connections of utterly different kinds, from that between an action and its rapidity (ἐν τάχει) to that between Christ and those who are «in Christ». Hence the nature of this connection is to be sought in divine revelation, and not in the sense of the word ἐν. It would be waste of time and energy to collect from profane literature all the occurrences of ἐν with a noun standing for a person, in the hope of arriving at a deeper understanding of the mystery which Paul intended to express by the words ἐν Χριστῷ.

89   **119. The instrumental use.** As is well known, the NT uses ἐν with almost Semitic frequency instead of the instrumental dative, e. g. Rev 6,8 ἀποκτεῖναι ἐν ῥομφαίᾳ καὶ ἐν λιμῷ καὶ ἐν θανάτῳ. This is perhaps the reason why ἐν is occasionally used for other causes than the instrumental one, and may be rendered « because of ». This is clearly the sense in e. g. Acts 7,29 where Moses flees ἐν τῷ λόγῳ τούτῳ (i e. because the man said to him «who has set thee up to be a judge over us? ») or Mt 6,7 the heathens think they will be heard ἐν τῇ πολυλογίᾳ αὐτῶν. Hence ἐν τούτῳ (Jo 16,30) may mean «therefore» and ἐν ᾧ (Heb 2,18) «because». — Unless this usage be taken into account, how is one to understand Paul when he says, of the hope of resurrection, Acts 24,16: ἐν τούτῳ (= «therefore») καὶ αὐτὸς ἀσκῶ ἀπρόσκοπον συνείδησιν ἔχειν..., or Rom 8,3 τὸ γὰρ ἀδύνατον τοῦ νόμου ἐν ᾧ ἠσθένει διὰ τῆς σαρκός, where the only reasonable sense for ἐν ᾧ is «in that» = «because».

90   **120. Use as dative.** The great extension of the use of ἐν in the evolution of Hellenistic Greek goes so far as its addition, without any special significance, to the simple dative. It is questionable whether any traces of this pleonastic use are to be found in the NT. The chief example in favour of an affirmative answer is I Cor 14,11, where we have a dative without ἐν and one with ἐν with complete parallelism of sense. Speaking

of the vanity of «speaking with tongues» (unless accompanied by interpretation) Paul says ἐὰν οὖν μὴ εἰδῶ τὴν δύναμιν τῆς φωνῆς, ἔσομαι τῷ
λαλοῦντι βάρβαρος καὶ ὁ λαλῶν ἐν ἐμοὶ βάρβαρος. Whatever may be
alleged to account for the addition of ἐν (which is lacking in not a few
MSS), whether that it is added lest ἐμοὶ be taken with λαλῶν, or that
ἐν ἐμοὶ means more or less «in my view» as occasionally in Attic poetry
(cf. DEBR. 220,1), the fact remains that the complete parallelism does
not allow ἐν ἐμοὶ to be taken in a different sense from τῷ λαλοῦντι. On the
basis of this clear case one may perhaps be justified in neglecting the ἐν
in several other texts, if the context suggests this. So. e. g. Gal 1,16: it
pleased God to reveal His Son ἐν ἐμοὶ that I might preach Him ἐν τοῖς
ἔθνεσιν. Cf also 2 Cor 4,3; 8,1; Rom 1,19; and perhaps 1 Jo 4,9; Lk 2,14.

91   121. A. FRIDRICHSEN invokes this pleonastic use of ἐν with the dative in favour of a new interpretation of what Paul said to Agrippa Acts
26,29: «I would to God καὶ ἐν ὀλίγῳ καὶ ἐν μεγάλῳ that not only you,
but all those who today hear me, should become such as I am». Fridrichsen renders the expression «concerning both small and great» (dative of interest) (').

He brings forward in favour of this interpretation the following points:
1) Paul takes up Agrippa's ἐν ὀλίγῳ, and playing on the expression,
gives it another meaning which, owing to the added contrast ἐν μεγάλῳ
(a not obscure reference to the king) seems to be «concerning the small».
2) Moreover, what is more important, the order of words leads him to take
καὶ ἐν ὀλίγῳ καὶ ἐν μεγάλῳ with εὐξαίμην ἄν rather than with the following γενέσθαι. Whatever be the degree of probability of this interpretation, we have an example of the importance which the pleonastic
use of ἐν with the dative may have for exegesis.

c) Ἐπί

92   122. Ἐπί is the one preposition which is still to be found in the NT
in frequent use with all three cases, although here too there is to be seen
a confusion of the cases with a general tendency towards the accusative.

(') «I would to God, concerning both small and great». *Coniectanea*
Neotestamentica III (1938), p. 15.

93   123. In its **local use** ἐπί was used classically with the accusative for the connotation of motion or extension only, rest at a point being expressed with the dative or the genitive. Cf. the triple classical use in Acts 27,43f, where those who can swim are bidden ἐπὶ τὴν γῆν ἐξιέναι, and the rest seek salvation ἐπὶ σανίσιν and ἐπὶ τινων τῶν ἀπὸ τοῦ πλοίου. Often however, though with variant readings, ἐπί with the accusative answers the question « where? » (not « whither? ») e. g. Lk 2,25: πνεῦμα ἦν ἅγιον ἐπ' αὐτόν or περιπατεῖν ἐπὶ τὴν θάλασσαν Mt 14,25. Cf. also the frequent formula ἐπὶ τὸ αὐτό « together » and in Rev a promiscuous use of all three cases but with a great predominance of the accusative, in the expression « sit upon the throne ».

94   124. Contrariwise, ἐπί with the genitive is found, as in classical usage, where there is a notion of « aiming at » or « hitting » an object: βάλλειν, πίπτειν ἐπὶ τῆς γῆς. The accusative and the genitive are found together and in a quite similar sense in Mt 25,21: « because thou wast faithful over little (ἐπὶ ὀλίγα) I will set thee over much (ἐπὶ πολλῶν) ». This example, however, belongs to the **metaphorical use**, where e. g. of rule « over » we find in the NT, alongside the classical genitive, the accusative as in βασιλεύσει ἐπὶ τὸν οἶκον 'Ιακώβ Lk 1,33.

125. 'Επί is often added to the **accusative of measure**, especially in the temporal sense (in Acts thirteen times, in Lk three times), e. g. ἐπὶ χρόνον for χρόνον τινά simply, and in like manner also ἐφ' ὅσον, ἐπὶ πολύ, ἐπὶ πλεῖον, ἐπὶ σάββατα τρία (Acts 17,2). 'Επί with an accusative of measure in a non-temporal sense is found in Mt 25,40 and 45: ἐφ' ὅσον (οὐκ) ἐποιήσατε ... where the Vulgate renders « quamdiu » although the sense is « in so far as », or better (as direct object) « (so much as =) whatever », (« What you have [not] done to one of these little ones, you have [not] done to Me »).

95   126. 'Επί **with the dative** is generally used to indicate the basis or grounds for an action: ἐπὶ δὲ τῷ ῥήματί σου χαλάσω τὰ δίκτυα Lk 5,5. Hence it is used with the verbs πιστεύειν, ἐλπίζειν, and in general to denote the grounds for emotional or other reactions, with such verbs as εὐχαριστεῖν, χαίρειν, λυπεῖσθαι etc.

96   127. This **causal sense** must be adverted to in the formula ἐφ' ᾧ = « inasmuch as », lest one render obscurely and ambiguously (as does the Vulgate) «and so death has come upon all men ἐφ' ᾧ (Vulgate: *in quo*) all have sinned» Rom 5,12, a rendering which has led some to take the previously mentioned «Adam» as antecedent of «quo», whereas ἐφ' ᾧ simply means «inasmuch as». Similarly Php 3,12: «I pursue that perchance I may take hold, ἐφ' ᾧ (Vulgate: in quo) I have been taken hold upon by Christ Jesus» (cf. also Php 4,10 and 2 Cor 5,4); but see 129.

97   128. Ἐπί with the dative may also have the sense of addition. In the examples alleged this is usually clear: «Herod added this too ἐπὶ πᾶσιν» Lk 3,20; or ἐπὶ πᾶσιν δὲ τούτοις τὴν ἀγάπην Col 3,14. Hence ἐπί takes on the sense «in addition to» and even «apart from», a sense which, has been applied to Mt 19,9, as a solution to the difficulty concerning divorce (⁸).

98   129. Ἐπί with the dative in the final sense is found in the NT as it was in classical usage (e. g. ἐπὶ βλάβῃ); thus Paul writes «created in Christ... ἐπὶ ἔργοις ἀγαθοῖς» Eph 2,10; ἐπ' ἐλευθερίᾳ ἐκλήθητε Gal 5,13; and «for God has not called us ἐπὶ ἀκαθαρσίᾳ ἀλλ' ἐν ἁγιασμῷ» 1 Thess 4,7 where however the ἐν in the phrase which follows may perhaps suggest a «pregnant construction» (cf. 99) for the ἐπί. Some put also under this heading the double ἐφ' ᾧ in Php 3,12 (cf. 127) and 4,10. — The same usage is very frequent in Flavius Josephus.

d) Κατά

99   130. As regards the other prepositions, one may note especially the common Hellenistic usage of κατά with the accusative in place of the sim-

----

(⁸) Cf. M. BRUNEC in *Verbum Domini* 27 (1949), 8-16. The same author solves in a similar manner the difficulty in the parallel text Mt 5,31, where he also takes παρεκτός in an additive sense instead of an exceptive one, rendering: «whoever repudiates his wife, in addition to the defilement (for which he repudiates her) causes her to be defiled by adultery », i. e. the repudiation has for sole effect that the wife, in addition to the defilement for which she is repudiated, is subjected to a further and still greater defilement, namely that of adultery, since she remains bound in marriage (*ibid.*, p. 5-8). A more obvious interpretation of the phrases in question is however the one which in παρεκτός λόγου πορνείας and μὴ ἐπὶ πορνείᾳ (in a conditional clause equivalent to «except in case of πορνεία ») sees a real exception, and understands πορνεία as the Hebrew legal term *zenut* meaning a marriage (in accordance with Lev 18) unlawful because incestuous. Cf. *Verb. Dom.* 38 (1960), 193-212.

ple subjective or possessive genitive, or its use with a personal pronoun instead of the possessive one alone, so that e. g. ἡ καθ' ὑμᾶς πίστις means simply «your faith», Eph 1,15; τὸ κατ' ἐμὲ πρόθυμον «my readiness», Rom 1,15; οἱ καθ' ὑμᾶς ποιηταί «your poets», Acts 17,28; τὸ κατὰ τὸν Παῦλον «the affair of Paul», Acts 25,14; ἡ κατ' ἐκλογὴν πρόθεσις τοῦ θεοῦ «God's design of choosing» (whom He will), Rom 9,11. Perhaps (?) the otherwise obscure text Eph. 4,22 ἀποθέσθαι... κατὰ τὴν προτέραν ἀναστροφὴν τὸν παλαιὸν ἄνθρωπον may be rendered: «put off the old man of former ways». This usage, common enough in Hellenistic Greek, is derived from the local sense «(looking) towards» which becomes in the metaphorical use «regarding» and so «pertaining to», and so takes on the value of the simple genitive.

100   131. Hence the question may also be raised, whether in the titles of the gospels the κατὰ Ματθαῖον is to be understood simply as «of Matthew», or whether there is an underlying idea of a single gospel appearing in four forms, «according to Matthew» etc. This latter view has been the common one (⁹) but the former is not to be excluded, since the same expression (κατά instead of the genitive to indicate authorship) is to be found for books by other authors, where there is no suggestion of other works on the same subject (¹⁰).

NB. In either case, the author is indicated; what is in question is only whether or not the use of κατά necessarily connotes other authors on the same subject. We state explicitly that the author is indicated, because some have maintained, on the gounds of the use of κατά, that the titles indicate not the authors of the gospel, but the preachers «according to» whom others composed the gospels. If this had been the case, however, when the titles were given in the second century, our gospel of Mark would

---

(⁹) This opinion finds a powerful confirmation in the Muratorian fragment, which lists the third gospel as «tertium evangelii... librum secundum Lucam».

(¹⁰) E. g. 2 Macc 2,13 has: ἐν τοῖς ὑπομνηματισμοῖς τοῖς κατὰ Νεεμίαν; Jos. Flavius, c. Ap. 1,3 writes that Thucydides seems to have been most accurate in composing τὴν καθ' αὐτὸν ἱστορίαν; Epiphanius has: ἡ κατὰ Μωϋσέα πεντάτευχος. Cf. HÖPFL-GUT, Introductio III, p. 6.

have been given the title, according to the tradition of the time, κατὰ Πέτρον, and that of Luke κατὰ Παῦλον. (Cf. HÖPFL-GUT, loc cit.).

e) 'Από

101   132. With regard to the preposition ἀπό we may note its perfective force in verbs compounded with it (cf. the like force of the like adverb « off » in English : « round off, finish off, pay off » etc.). Though the primitive sense of ἀπό is that of separation, this notion may be, in the literal local sense, entirely absent; e. g. ἀφικνοῦμαι « arrive », ἀποτελῶ « complete » (¹¹). The connotation of restitution to a prior (and proper) state is often present, e. g. ἀποκαθίστημι restore, ἀποκαταλλάσσω reconcile, ἀποδίδωμι return, restore (a debt etc.), ἀπέχω « I have received » (payment of a debt etc.).

102   133. Hence even the verb ἀπέρχομαι seems to be used not in the sense « go away » but rather with the sense of going to a place where one is called or ought to go, e. g. Mk 3,13 « and He called to Himself those whom He Himself wished καὶ ἀπῆλθον πρὸς αὐτόν ». Similarly perhaps Mt 2,22; Mk 16,13; Lk 17,23. Hence too it seems hardly justifiable to conclude from the verb ἀπῆεσαν (εἰς τὴν συναγωγήν) Acts 17,10 that the synagogue was outside the city; the verb may suggest the notion of going where they were accustomed to go. So too ἀποστρέφω means rather « convert » (= restore to the proper place) than « avert », Mt 26,52; 27,3.

f) 'Εκ

103   134. An important usage, especially in Paul, is that described by Zorell in the following manner: as we use the ending « -ist » to denote a member of a certain class or party or sect or school of thought (« socialist, idealist, pessimist » etc), so Paul uses for the same purpose ὁ ἐκ...., οἱ ἐκ... etc., with the genitive of what is the characteristic of the class in question: ὁ ἐκ πίστεως Ἰησοῦ Rom 3,26; οἱ ἐκ πίστεως = « the faithful » Gal 3,7 9; παντὶ τῷ σπέρματι οὐ τῷ ἐκ τοῦ νόμου μόνον ἀλλὰ καὶ τῷ ἐκ πίστεως Ἀβραάμ Rom 4,6; οἱ ἐκ νόμου Rom 4,14; so too with the verb « be »: ὅσοι ἐξ ἔργων νόμου εἰσιν Gal 3,10. Cf. 1 Jo 3,19; Jo 8,23; and

(¹¹) Chrysostom distinguishes λύτρωσις from ἀπολύτρωσις and takes the latter as full and complete redemption: on Rom 3,24: PG 60,444; on Rom 8,23: PG 60,531; cf. Verb. Dom. 30 (1952), 20.

45

in general the Johannine expressions ἐκ θεοῦ, ἐκ τοῦ διαβόλου, ἐκ τοῦ κόσμου τούτου etc.: Jo 8,44; 15,19; 17,14; 1 Jo 3,8 10 12.

135. These examples perhaps suggest the origin of this kind of expression: ἐκ indicates origin, and the character of a person or thing is determined by origin and upbringing. So in classical usage this type of expression (οἱ ἐξ Ἀκαδημίας etc.) denoted schools of thought by indicating the school whence came the manner of thinking characteristic of them.

IV. THE ADJECTIVE

104   140. The neuter adjective with the article is used, in completely Greek fashion, especially by Paul, in a sense analogous to that of the abstract substantive: τὸ μωρὸν τοῦ Θεοῦ σοφώτερον τῶν ἀνθρώπων ἐστὶν καὶ τὸ ἀσθενὲς τοῦ θεοῦ ἰσχυρότερον 1 Cor 1,25; but the Vulgate is right in rendering, not «stultitia» and «infirmitas» but concretely «quod stultum est Dei», «quod infirmum est Dei». The difference between such expressions and abstract substantives is to be seen likewise in Rom 2,4: τοῦ πλούτου τῆς χρηστότητος αὐτοῦ... καταφρονεῖς, ἀγνοῶν ὅτι τὸ χρηστὸν τοῦ Θεοῦ εἰς μετάνοιάν σε ἄγει; Here χρηστότης is the divine property, and τὸ χρηστόν its concrete application in God's dealing with the sinner. Php 3,8: τὸ ὑπερέχον τῆς γνώσεως Χριστοῦ, either the «surpassing good» which *is* the knowledge of Christ (γνώσεως as epexegetic genitive) or the excellence of Christ which passes understanding (γνώσεως genitive of comparison); Php 4,5: τὸ ἐπιεικὲς ὑμῶν. Cf. Rom 9,22; 1 Cor 7,35; Heb 6,17; 7,18.

105   141. This neuter is used also of persons, if the emphasis is on the quality, e. g. Heb 7,7 τὸ ἔλαττον ὑπὸ τοῦ κρείττονος εὐλογεῖται. Cf. also Jo 3,6: τὸ γεγεννημένον ἐκ τῆς σαρκὸς σάρξ ἐστιν καὶ τὸ γεγεννημένον ἐκ τοῦ πνεύματος πνεῦμά ἐστιν, where it is true that the expression is primarily understood of persons, but the use of the neuter lays down an absolute and universal principle based on the distinction and separateness, each in its own sphere, of the natural and supernatural orders.

106   142. The verbal adjective in - τος has usually, but not always 1) a passive sense, as ἀγαπητός «beloved»; often however it has 2) an active sense as συνετός «intelligent», ἀρεστός «pleasing», ἄψευστος «truthful», ἄβλαπτος «harmless», ἀγέλαστος «not laughing». Not seldom the same verbal adjective is used in both active and passive sense, e. g. δυνατός «powerful» (active) and «possible» (passive), αὐθαίρετος «of one's own accord» (active) and «self-appointed» (passive), ἀναντίρρητος «uncontesting» (active) Acts 10,29 but «incontestable» (passive) Acts 19,36;

παράκλητος in active sense «consoler», in passive «advocate»; ἀπαρά-
βατος in active sense «everlasting» (lit. = «not-passing»), in passive sense
«inviolable» (lit. «not to be passed = transgressed»); ἀνεπαίσχυντος
which in the passive sense means «unabashed» either as «having nothing
to be ashamed of» or as «not timid» = «energetic», is used in an active
one «not causing shame to (the Church)» in 2 Tim 2,15. So too e. g. ἄσωτος
passively «beyond salvation», or actively «unable to save» i. e. prodigal; so too θεόπνευστος 2 Tim 3,16, which is used as an argument for the
inspiration of the Scriptures, cannot be said to be unambiguous in itself,
for the word might mean «breathing God» as well as «inspired by God».

107   143. The use of comparative forms in Biblical Greek undergoes
modification owing to two influences: the Semitic one, and that of popular speech in general.

108   144. a) Semitic influence. As Hebrew and Aramaic lack a comparative form, so too in Biblical usage the sense of the comparative or superlative is sometimes rendered by expressions using the positive:

109   145. α) Positive for comparative. The comparative sense of an adjective may be recognized from a following ἤ «than» or (often in the LXX)
παρά, ὑπέρ («beyond»), ἀπό (Hebrew min), e. g. Mk 9,45: καλόν ἐστιν ... ἤ
= «it is better to enter life lame than ...».
     Similarly after a substantive, as Lk 13,2: ἁμαρτωλοὶ παρὰ πάντας
or 15,7 χαρά... ἔσται ἐπὶ ἑνὶ ἁμαρτωλῷ... ἤ ἐπὶ ἐνενήκοντα ἐννέα
δικαίοις; and even after a verb μᾶλλον is sometimes omitted, as 1 Cor
14,19: θέλω πέντε λόγους ... λαλῆσαι ... ἤ μυρίους. In Lk 18,14 the
publican is said to have left the temple δεδικαιωμένος παρ᾽ ἐκεῖνον = «more
justified than he», which here means in fact «justified whereas the other
was not», as Ps 45 (44), 8 ἔχρισέν σε θεὸς ... παρὰ τοὺς μετόχους σου.

110   Without ἤ, we have e. g. «συμφέρει σοι that one of thy members
perish καὶ μὴ the whole body be cast into Gehenna», where the sense is
certainly «it is better for thee... than that ...»; cf. Jo 11,50.

111   146. β) The positive is used Semitically for the superlative in speaking of a group or class; thus Elizabeth's greeting to Mary, εὐλογημένη
σὺ ἐν γυναιξίν means «Most blessed art thou of women» Lk 1,42, just
as in the Song of Songs 1,8 ἡ καλὴ ἐν γυναιξίν means «most beautiful of
women». So too ἐντολὴ μεγάλη ἐν τῷ νόμῳ is the greatest commandment,

Mt 22,36. Again, the class (namely, the parts) being « understood », ἡ ἀγα-θὴ μερίς is the best part, Lk 10,42. Similarly with the comparative form Lk 9,48: ὁ μικρότερος ἐν πᾶσιν ὑμῖν ὑπάρχων οὗτός ἐστιν μέγας which means « the least ... is the greatest ». Cf. Also 1 Cor 12,23; Heb 8,11; 4 Kings 10,3; 1 Sam 15,9; Amos 2,16; Mic 7,4.

112   147. b) A different modification results from the general evolution of popular speech which tends to abolish the distinction between duality and plurality, which in certain uses forms the only distinction between comparative and superlative, namely in such expressions as « the bigger of the two » but « the biggest of (three or more) ». English usage tends towards the superlative in both cases (« the biggest of the two »), whereas in Greek the general tendency was towards the use of the comparative form; moreover, the comparative form tended to supplant the superlative in its elative sense also (« very big »).

113   148. Hence it is not astonishing that Paul writes 1 Cor 13,13 « there remains faith, hope and charity, these three; μείζων δὲ τούτων ἡ ἀγάπη ». Here we have the comparative used for the « true » or « relative » superlative (« greatest »); for the elative (« very ... »); cf. Acts 17,22 where Paul calls the Athenians δεισιδαιμονεστέρους, which may · be rendered « very pious »; or Acts 24,22 where Felix is said to have put off judgement ἀ κ ρ ι β έ σ τ ε ρ ο ν εἰδὼς τὰ περὶ τῆς ὁδοῦ, which the Vulgate renders « certissime sciens ... » and which may perhaps be better rendered simply « knowing for certain ».

149. Thus too ὕστερος « latter » is used in the sense « last », 1 Tim 4,1, and the adverb ὕστερον is found not only in comparative sense « later », Mt 4,2; 21,30. 32; but also in superlative sense « lastly », 21,37; 26,60. — In the obscure verse Mt 17,11b: ὁ μικρότερος in the kingdom of heaven is greater than (John the Baptist), this can be understood as meaning « the least in the kingdom of heaven ... », with all the difficulties involved by such an interpretation. It is perhaps better, however, to keep the comparative sense and explain the meaning of the verse as St Augustine does: the lesser = the junior = Christ. Cf. M. BRUNEC in Verb. Dom. 35(1957), 262-70.

150. The comparative (perhaps by way of the elative) seems to be used in a weakened sense instead of the simple positive. Thus τάχιον may stand for « quickly » as well as for « very quickly » where Our Lord says

to Judas «what thou doest, do τάχιον» Jo 13,27. So too 1 Tim 3,14 τάχιον means simply «soon ». Similarly in Acts 17,21 the Athenians are said to be ever eager ἀκούειν τι καινότερον, where the comparative seems to have the force of the simple positive (unless one prefer to regard it as a superlative «the latest news»). Hence too Lk 11,53 περὶ πλειόνων is rightly rendered by the Vulgate «de multis».

114   151. Although in general the comparative form took the place of the superlative one, the opposite was the case for two adjectives, whose superlative form supplanted the comparative one: πρῶτος is used instead of πρότερος and ἔσχατος instead of ὕστερος (cf. e. g. Mt 21,28. 31; 27,64; but on the contrary Mt 21,37; Mk 16,14; Lk 20,32). The use of πρῶτος in the sense «former, prior» is of a certain exegetical importance, for if this use were not taken into account, and the canons of classical usage were applied, it would follow from the prologue to the Acts that Luke wrote, or at least intended to write, not merely the gospel and the Acts but at least one other book of the same series (¹); for he begins, referring to his gospel: τὸν μὲν πρῶτον (not πρότερον) λόγον ἐποιησάμην, and the superlative πρῶτος would in classical usage suppose plurality and not duality, for which πρότερος would have to be used.

115   152. Again, only one sense could be given, according to literary usage, to the puzzling expression of Luke (2,2): αὕτη ἡ ἀπογραφὴ πρώτη ἐγένετο ἡγεμονεύοντος Κυρηνίου; it would mean that the census was the first of a series of at least three, and was made under Quirinus. When Hellenistic usage is taken into account, however, complications arise; for the sense may be that the census was the former of two only, and was made under Quirinus, or else that it was prior to (a well-known one) made under Quirinus (by elliptical expression; so LAGRANGE) (²).

───────────

(¹) This is in fact the contention of Th. ZAHN (*Apostelgeschichte* [1919] p. 16-18), who well knows that the distinction between πρῶτος and πρότερος was neglected in popular speech, but does not admit that Luke, with his erudition, would have used so colloquial a form in his prooemium.

(²) There is finally, the interpretation of the expression as meaning the beginning of the census, on the grounds of Herod. 7,92: ἀφ' ἧς ὁ χειμὼν ὁ πρῶτος ἐγένετο « whence the storm first started », and Thucyd. 1,55; 2,22. Also 1 Sam 14,14 καὶ ἐγενήθη ἡ πληγὴ ἡ πρώτη has been rendered « and the beginning of the massacre was that Jonathan smote ... twenty men » (TALVACCHIA).

116   **153.** The obsolescence in Hellenistic Greek of the category of duality results also in the use of ἕτερος for ἄλλος and vice versa τίς for πότερος; and the confusion even goes so far as to allow ἀμφότεροι to be used of a plurality with the meaning « all ». This use was recognized for Byzantine Greek, but it is to be found in papyri so early as the third and second centuries, so that some authors (e. g. RADERMACHER, K. LAKE) even in Acts 19,16 take κατακυριεύσας ἀμφοτέρων as referring to all seven of the sons of Scephas, the Jewish exorcists mentioned in verse 14. One may compare Acts 27,8, where τὰ ἀμφότερα refers to *three* doctrines there listed: the resurrection, angels, the spirit.

V. THE NUMERALS

117   154. As in Hebrew the days of the month were denoted by the cardinal numbers, so too in the NT the first day of the week (Sunday) is μία σαββάτων (Mt 28,1: εἰς μίαν σαββάτων). A similar Hebraism is to be found in Rev 9,12: ἡ οὐαὶ ἡ μία ἀπῆλθεν = « the first woe...».

118   155. Already in the NT, owing to a development shared by Greek with other languages, the numeral εἷς takes the places of τις and becomes a sort of indefinite article (for the NT there was also a Semitic influence, that of Hebrew 'echad and Aramaic had): εἷς γραμματεύς Mt 8,19; ἐπερωτήσω ὑμᾶς ἕνα λόγον Mk 11,29 etc.; the two words are also found together: εἷς τις Lk 22,50.

119   156. Owing to the neglect of duality (ὁ) εἷς stands for ὁ ἕτερος: οἱ δύο υἱοί μου, εἷς ἐκ δεξιῶν καὶ εἷς ἐξ εὐωνύμων Mt 20,21 (Gal 4,24; Acts 23,6).

120   157. In the distributive sense we have, instead of ἀνὰ δύο the expression δύο δύο Mk 6,7, in the same way as συμπόσια συμπόσια Mk 6,39; this is characteristic of popular speech in Greek no less than in Hebrew, Aramaic, Coptic etc., whence in the NT it is rather to be attributed to Semitic influence. — For εἷς καθ' εἷς cf. 10.

158. In Mk 4,8 we read: « and other (seed) ... fructified ... and bore εἰς τριάκοντα καὶ ἐν ἑξήκοντα καὶ ἐν ἑκατόν». On this reading (εἰς... ἐν... ἐν, as in Codex Vaticanus, Klostermann says that the variation is pointless and the reading of Codex Sinaiticus, εἰς... εἰς.... εἰς is a correction of it; one should read with Codex Alexandrinus, Codex Bezae, the Washington (Freer) Codex, and Q ἐν... ἐν... ἐν, and aspirate ἐν... ἐν... ἐν (so too in verse 20), taking ἐν as a sign of multiplication (an Aramaism: Wellhausen) so that e. g. ἐν ἑκατόν = ἑκατονταπλασίονα « a hundredfold ».

121   159. (Ἕως) ἑβδομηκοντάκις ἑπτά (Mt 18,22) is not « seventy times seven», but « seventy seven times» (= ἑβδομηκοντάκις ἑπτάκις) as the Vulgate rightly translates it here and in Gen 4,24, where the LXX has the same imperfect expression. Since the Genesis text deals with vengeance, and Matthew's with forgiveness, it is very probable that the Gospel text intentionally alludes to the OT one (MOULTON)..

VI. THE ARTICLE

122   165. The function of the article is to point out (it was in origin a demonstrative), to determine, to set apart from others, to identify as *this* or *these* and not simply «such». We can therefore always be sure that the use of the article shows the thing spoken of to have been in the author's mind (or in that of those whose speech-habits established current usage) determinate and familiar; but the sense in which it was such for the author is not always clear to his readers, although the matter may at times be quite important for the exegesis.

123   166. E. g. in Lk 16,15 we read that Our Lord said to the Pharisees: ὑμεῖς ἐστε οἱ δικαιοῦντες ἑαυτοὺς ἐνώπιον τῶν ἀνθρώπων. Here the predicate has the article because it is a participle meaning «those who ...» (ἐστὲ δικαιοῦντες would be un-Greek and equivalent to Greek δικαιοῦτε), and so suggests a class of «self-justifiers» known to the people; probably those who in Israel went by the name of «holy ones», but whom Our Lord calls not «holy» or «just», but skilful in passing themselves off before men as such. Some however, take the article as «anaphoric», i. e. referring to what precedes, especially to the parable of the unjust steward, whose application and «key» would thus be found in ὑμεῖς ἐστε οἱ δικαιοῦντες ἑαυτούς, in the same way as the «Thou art the man» with which the prophet Nathan explained his parable. If however the article is to be understood in this manner, as indicating the application of the parable, the latter would have to be interpreted in an entirely new fashion (¹). Whatever be the value of this new interpretation, we have here in any case an illustration of the great importance and frequent ambiguity of the use of the article.

124   167. Another example: what is the meaning of the article, where Our Lord before the Sermon on the Mount is said to have gone up εἰς τὸ ὄρος Mt 5,1? It *may* indicate that at the time of the evangelist one of Our Lord's sermons was well-known as having been delivered on a mountain, or on a particular mountain; but the article is also explained by

---

(¹) R. Pautrel, cf. *Verb. Dom.* 25 (1947), 54-56; 172-76.

taking τὸ ὄρος as meaning simply the hilly ring which almost entirely surrounds the Lake of Gennesareth, so that from any part of the shore one went up εἰς τὸ ὄρος. In that case the article might suppose in the writer's mind a clear picture of the region about the lake, and would e-voke that picture in the minds of those of his readers who knew the region. However, as Jesus is always (nine times) said, on leaving the crowd, to go up εἰς τὸ ὄρος (with the article), we seem to have here a stereotyped phrase like the English « into the mountains», « into the country », « to the seaside ».

125   168. Again, a knowledge of the custom which then existed in Palestine for the invitation of guests is reflected in the writer's spontaneous use of the article in « he sent τὸν δοῦλον αὐτοῦ at the hour of the dinner » Lk 14,17. This article might of itself suggest that the master had but the one servant, but this seems unlikely in the context, so that the article is rather to be understood as meaning « the » servant whom it was customary to send just before the banquet, and who was for that reason known in Latin as the « vocator ».

126   169. For Paul ὁ Κύριος is Christ, Κύριος Yahweh; yet in the much-discussed text 2 Cor 3,17: ὁ δὲ Κύριος τὸ πνεῦμά ἐστιν, it would seem from the context that ὁ Κύριος means God; for verse 17 explains (δέ, cf. 467) verse 16, where the LXX is cited concerning the « conversion (of the Jews) to the Lord (πρὸς Κύριον) ». Taking up this Κύριον Paul uses the anaphoric article in continuing ὁ δὲ Κύριος (i. e. the « Lord » of the quotation) τὸ πνεῦμά ἐστιν. The article with the predicate τὸ πνεῦμα seems likewise to be anaphorical, indicating that spirit repeatedly spoken of in the preceding context. This is *one* of the interpretations of this verse.

127   170. How eloquent and full of meaning the article can be is seen also in Php 2,2f; Paul bids the Philippians to be τὸ ἓν φρονοῦντες and τῇ ταπεινοφροσύνῃ ἀλλήλους ·ἡγούμενοι ὑπερέχοντας ἑαυτῶν. The article in τὸ ἓν may simply correspond to that in « the same », which is the meaning; but since one might also have written ἓν φρονοῦντες without the article, it seems that Paul is thinking of some definite « one thing » known to him and to the Philippians, filling the minds and hearts of all and effecting a unity of spirit; the article in τῇ ταπεινοφροσύνῃ suggests that humility proper tu Christians which Paul has so often inculcated and on which he is about to insist once móre, appealing to the example of God incarnate. — Where Abraham, bidden to sacrifice his son, is said not to have wavered τῇ ἀπιστίᾳ (Rom 4,20), the article connotes that well-known diffidence which may in adversity lead to refusal of faith. Such examples are legion.

171. The **omission** of the article shows that the speaker regards the person or thing not so much as this or that person or thing, but rather as *such* a person or thing, i. e. regards not the individual but rather its nature or quality.

128   **172.** Hence it is sometimes stated as a ‹ rule › that ‹ the article is not used with the predicate ›. In fact, predicates commonly lack the article, but this is not in virtue of any ‹ rule › about predicates in particular, but in virtue of the universal rule; for in the nature of things, the predicate commonly refers not to an individual or individuals as such, but to the class to which the subject belongs, to the nature or quality predicated of the subject; e. g.· Jo 1,1 καὶ Θεὸς ἦν ὁ Λόγος, which attributes to the Word the divine *nature* (ὁ Θεὸς ἦν ὁ Λόγος, at least in NT usage, would signify personal identity of the Word with the Father, since the latter is ὁ Θεός).

129   **173.** Where Paul writes Php 1,21: ἐμοὶ γὰρ τὸ ζῆν Χριστός, the article suggests that τὸ ζῆν is subject (2) and Χριστός predicate (and not, as is often supposed, vice versa). This is a point of great importance, because the sense is entirely different according as τὸ ζῆν is taken as subject or predicate: taking it as predicate, ‹ for me Christ is life › suggests the idea of Christ dwelling in Paul as the principle of supernatural life; whereas, taking it as subject, as it should be taken, ‹ for me living is Christ ›, inverts the causal order to give the sense ‹ the fruit of my life is Christ ›. It is in fact in this sense that the context which follows explains Paul's thought, for he takes up τὸ ζῆν Χριστός by saying εἰ δὲ (the illative δέ) τὸ ζῆν ἐν σαρκί, τοῦτό μοι καρπὸς ἔργου... The fruit of Paul's life can be said to be ‹ Christ › because Paul's life-work is the ‹ building up of the body of

---

(²) What the article does no more than suggest becomes certain from the parallelism with what follows: καὶ τὸ ἀποθανεῖν κέρδος, where τὸ ἀποθανεῖν is certainly the subject.

Christ ». Indeed, the whole context demands an interpretation not in terms of a principle of life but in terms of the effect attained by a way of life; for the question under discussion is, whether life or death is to be preferred, and Paul hesitates because both have the same effect: μεγαλυνθήσεται Χριστός... εἴτε διὰ ζωῆς εἴτε διὰ θανάτου (verse 20). How διὰ ζωῆς? Because τὸ ζῆν Χριστός.

130   174. This example shows how far, and with what profit, the exegete may be led by a consideration of the article in distinguishing subject from predicate, inasmuch as the latter may be detected by the absence of the article. I say « often », because the article may be found with the predicate for more than one reason, e. g. where the predicate instead of indicating the class or nature or quality (of greater extension than the subject) indicates an individual or individuals identical with the subject (so that the proposition is convertible) e. g. οὐκ εἰμὶ ὁ Χριστός Jo 1,20; or ἐγώ εἰμι ἡ ὁδὸς καὶ ἡ ἀλήθεια καὶ ἡ ζωή Jo 14,6; ὑμεῖς ἐστε τὸ ἅλας τῆς γῆς Mt 5,13 etc. Hence even in the example Php 1,21 (preceding paragraph) τὸ ζῆν might (outside the context) be understood as a predicate (« *the* life for me is Christ », i. e. my only true life, as in ἐγώ εἰμι... ἡ ζωή).

175. The use of the article in the predicate was carefully investigated by E. C. COLWELL in *J. B. L.* 52(1933), 12-21. This author maintains that the use or omission of the article with *determinate* nouns depends very much on the position of the predicate noun before or after the verb: before the verb the article is commonly omitted (even when the noun is certainly determinate), but after the verb it is commonly used. There are not a few very persuasive examples of this: Jo 1,49 σὺ εἶ ὁ υἱὸς τοῦ θεοῦ, σὺ βασιλεὺς εἶ τοῦ Ἰσραήλ, or Jo 19,21 « write not ὁ βασιλεὺς τῶν Ἰουδαίων but that he said βασιλεὺς εἰμι τῶν Ἰουδαίων. The same title with the article after the verb is found in Mt 27,11. 37; Mk 15,2; Lk 23,3. 37; Jo 18,33. Similarly the title « Son of God » in the predicate: thirteen times with the article, always after the verb, ten times without the article, of which nine cases before the verb. For other good examples see Mt 13,37-39; 23,8-10. The consequence of this for exegesis would be: a noun preceding the verb and lacking the article should not be regarded as « qualitative » on the mere grounds of the absence of the article (e. g. Jo 1,1 καὶ θεὸς ἦν ὁ Λόγος); a noun following the verb and lacking the article should *a fortiori* be taken as « qualitative ». The theory has its appeal, but it is not easy to admit that the reason for the use of the article is to be found in a circumstance (order of words) which seems to belong to an altogether different category (*).

_____

(*) Even less convincing the attempt made by Eugène LEMOINE in his booklet *Théorie de l'emphase grecque classique et biblique*, Paris 1954, Paul Geuthner (12, rue Vavin). His theory is built on the distinction of two kinds of enunciations which the Author calls ἐμφάσεις and ἐννοήσεις respectively.

131   **176.** As we have said, the absence of the article draws attention to the nature or quality as distinct from the individual. Hence w i t h a b s t r a c t   n o u n s, which of themselves express qualities, attention is to be paid to the presence of the article, which gives to the quality a determined concrete application. Note for example how great a difference of meaning there is between χάρις with the article and the same noun without the article in Eph 2,8 and 5. In verse 8: τῇ γὰρ χάριτί ἐστε σεσωσμένοι διὰ πίστεως, the apostle understands by ἡ χάρις the entire work of redemption, that concrete historical fact, which inasmuch as it is due to the mercy and liberality of God is called χάρις; while in verse 5: χάριτί ἐστε σεσωσμένοι attention is called to the manner of our redemption as being salvation by divine grace and not by our works.

177. Further, how great is the difference of meaning and doctrine, according to the use or omission of the article, where Paul speaks of (ὁ) νόμος. In the epistle to the Galatians alone the word νόμος occurs ten times with the article and 21 times without it. Although each case is to be judged on its own merits (182), we may say in general that ὁ νόμος is the Mosaic Law, while νόμος is simply « law » as such (though in the context the law in question may be the Mosaic one). Cf. Rom 3,20; 5,13.

132   **178.** Or consider the implications of the article where John (or Our Lord as reported by John) speaks of ἡ ἀλήθεια, τὸ φῶς, ἡ ζωή. Here the article expresses something of that exuberance and power of conviction, thanks to which all other forms of truth or light or life pale into insignificance and as it were lose their title to be called by those names, before that Truth and Light and Life which Christ is. Similarly of an opposite notion: ἐκεῖ ἔσται ὁ κλαυθμὸς καὶ ὁ βρυγμὸς τῶν ὀδόντων, where the article suggests that consummate grief which moreover already exists, though it is fully known to none but Our Lord who here speaks of it (Mt 8,12 and parallels; 13,42).

133   **179.** Thus with abstract nouns attention is to be paid to the presence of the article. On the other hand, w i t h   c o n c r e t e   n o u n s it is the absence of the article which calls for attention, where, that is to say, the article was of itself to be expected or could stand in the context; for in such cases attention is called to the nature and quality of what is expressed by the noun, and this may sometimes have a considerable effect on the sense. An example is Heb 12,7 τίς γὰρ υἱός, ὃν οὐ παιδεύει πατήρ. Here the omission of the article with both υἱός and πατήρ brings out the force of the argument as drawn from the very notions « son » and

« father », from the nature of things, as if the apostle meant: what true son is there (as opposed to νόθοι of verse 8) who is not disciplined by a father worthy of the name.

134   **180.** Lk 10,21 « I confess to thee, Father, because thou hast hidden these things ἀπὸ σοφῶν καὶ συνετῶν and revealed them νηπίοις » expresses the qualities wisdom, intelligence, simplicity, and may be interpreted as suggesting a causal connection between the qualities and the corresponding actions of the Father. — Where Paul says « I wish to be found in Christ μὴ ἔχων ἐμὴν δικαιοσύνην τὴν ἐκ νόμου ... the absence of the article with ἐμὴν δικαιοσύνην insists strongly on the quality of that righteousness, so that one might almost render « not having a righteousness of my own », namely that given by the observance of the Law, as opposed to the righteousness which comes from God (Php 3,9).

135   **181.** So too, where St Paul describes his inner experience in the preaching of the gospel to the Thessalonians by saying « our preaching to you was not carried out in word alone ἀλλὰ καὶ ἐν δυνάμει καὶ ἐν πνεύματι ἁγίῳ καὶ ἐν πληροφορίᾳ πολλῇ ... », 1 Thess 1,5, the omission of the article with ἐν πνεύματι ἁγίῳ seems to mean that Paul is speaking not so much of the third person of the Trinity as of His activity, i. e. of a certain divine inspiration experienced by the preacher, and rightly put by him on the same level with δύναμις and πληροφορία which are likewise divine gifts belonging to the psychological order (*).

136   **182.** In this last example, however, we insist on the absence of the article only because the resultant sense is supported by the context, for we do not deny that in a different context the prepositional phrase ἐν πνεύματι ἁγίῳ might be equivalent to ἐν τῷ Ἁγίῳ Πνεύματι, and that for two reasons. In the first place, there here arises the difficult and obscure question of the use of the article with proper names; and in the second place, in prepositional phrases the lack of the article (ἐν οἴκῳ, ἐπὶ γῆς etc), when the sense is merely adverbial (« at home, on earth »), i. e. where the substantive is not determined (e. g. ἐν τῷ οἴκῳ τοῦ πατρὸς αὐτοῦ) is — on account of that sense — normal, and unremarkable even in classical usage, while in Hellenistic Greek there is an even stronger tendency to omit the article in prepositional phrases. In Biblical Greek, moreover, the lack of the article may occasionally be overlooked even when a determination

---

(*) Similar considerations apply to Luke's use of πνεῦμα ἅγιον without the article e. g. 1,15. 35. 41. 67; 2,25 (where πνεῦμα twice follows with anaphoric article, verses 26 and 27) etc.

follows and even without a preposition, in such set phrases as ἄγγελος Κυρίου, δόξα Κυρίου etc., because in Semitic usage the substantive would be in the « construct » state and so without the article.

137   183. There are thus three cases in which the absence of the article with a concrete and determinate substantive cannot be insisted upon: proper names, prepositional phrases, and nouns with a following genitive (i. e. where influence of the Semitic construct state is possible). We may add what is almost a grammatical rule: if the noun used with a following genitive is itself without the article, the article is generally omitted, by a sort of assimilation, with the genitive also, especially, it would seem, in such formulae as Πνεῦμα Θεοῦ Rom 8,9, τὸ Πνεῦμα τοῦ Θεοῦ 1 Cor 3,16 etc.; λόγος Θεοῦ 1 Thess 2,13, ὁ λόγος τοῦ Θεοῦ 1,8: similarly (ἡ) ἀνάστασις (τῶν) νεκρῶν, (ἡ) ἡμέρα (τοῦ) Κυρίου.

138   184. The **repetition** of the article distinguishes two coordinated notions, while on the contrary the use of but one article before a number of nouns indicates that they are conceived as forming a certain unity, if not as identical. Thus 1 Thess 1,7f « you are become a model for all ἐν τῇ Μακεδονίᾳ καὶ ἐν τῇ ᾿Αχαίᾳ » distinguishes . the two provinces, while immediately afterwards the apostle goes on to say « for the word of the Lord has been spread by you not only ἐν τῇ Μακεδονίᾳ καὶ ᾿Αχαίᾳ, ἀλλ᾿ ἐν παντὶ τόπῳ », where the same two provinces are taken together as opposed to « everywhere (else) ». — The letter of the council of Jerusalem, by joining under the same article the three regions to which it was addressed (Acts 15,23) may perhaps be said rather to discourage a wider promulgation of its contents, a point which would be important. — In Php 1,19 οἶδα γὰρ ὅτι τοῦτό μοι ἀποβήσεται εἰς σωτηρίαν διὰ τῆς ὑμῶν δεήσεως καὶ ἐπιχορηγίας τοῦ πνεύματος ᾿Ιησοῦ Χριστοῦ, the use of but one article shows that in the writer's mind the prayers of the faithful and the ἐπιχορηγία τοῦ πνεύματος ᾿Ιησοῦ Χριστοῦ were intimately connected; indeed one might even be tempted to regard the prayers of the faithful as being the ἐπιχορηγία τοῦ πνεύματος ᾿Ιησοῦ Χριστοῦ (the genitive being an « objective » one). — In 1 Thess 2,12 God « has called you εἰς τὴν ἑαυτοῦ βασιλείαν καὶ δόξαν », where the single article joining « kingdom » and « glory » suggests that the former as well as the latter is to be taken in the eschatological sense, i. e. of that sharing of kingship with Christ and God to which we are called (cf. 1 Cor 4,8). —

In Acts 20,21 the object of the apostle's preaching is well said to be « conversion to God and faith in Christ », but under the one article, so that one may almost understand « conversion to God by faith in Christ ». — In Php 2,17 ἡ θυσία καὶ λειτουργία is « sacrificial service ». — In Php 1,25 εἰς τὴν ὑμῶν προκοπὴν καὶ χαρὰν πίστεως is « for your advance in the joy of the faith ». — In Heb 5,2 τοῖς ἀγνοοῦσιν καὶ πλανωμένοις = « those who err through ignorance ». — On the other hand, we are perhaps warned not to insist too far by such examples as 2 Cor 8,4. 19. 24; 9,13; 1 Pet 4,14.

139 185. Sometimes the use of but one article with more than one noun seems even to suppose and express the divinity of Christ, e. g. Eph 5,5 ἡ βασιλεία τοῦ Χριστοῦ καὶ θεοῦ or Tit 2,13 « awaiting the coming of the glory τοῦ μεγάλου θεοῦ καὶ σωτῆρος Ἰησοῦ Χριστοῦ »; cf. also 2 Pet 1,1; 1,11; 2,20; 3,18. One must however say that such examples « seem to suggest » the divinity of Christ, and not that they are proofs of it, since the unity of article would be sufficiently accounted for by any conjunction, in the writer's mind, of the notions expressed.

140 186. The distinction between the **attributive** and the **predicative** use of adjectives is chiefly manifested by the presence with the attributive adjective, of the substantive's article, either because the adjective is put between the article and the substantive, or because the article is repeated before the adjective set after the substantive, while the predicative adjective has no such article, e. g. Jo 5,36 ἔχω τὴν μαρτυρίαν μείζω, which is equivalent to ἡ μαρτυρία ἣν ἔχω μείζων ἐστίν, or rather, ἔχω μαρτυρίαν ἡ μείζων ἐστίν.

141 187. As is seen from the example, an adjective in predicative use is sometimes equivalent to a relative clause of the type which in English is preceded by a comma; this suggests a solution of the difficulty encountered by exegetes in Heb 9,1, where we have: « the preceding (covenant) had indeed also δικαιώματα λατρείας τό τε ἅγιον κοσμικόν », which might suggest that the new covenant likewise has a terrestrial sanctuary. The adjective κοσμικόν is however in predicative position, and we may render « . . .(its) sanctuary, which (however) was a terrestrial one », in opposition, that is, to the sanctuary of the new covenant, which is a heavenly one (cf. 8,5) not made by hands (cf. 9,11). Note however that the predicative adjective can not always be correctly rendered by such a relative clause; e. g. in 1 Thess 3,13 εἰς τὸ στηρίξαι ὑμῶν τὰς καρδίας ἀμέμπτους the sense is precisely *not* «your hearts, which are blameless», but the adjective, being predicative, is to be joined with its noun through the verb (στηρίξαι): to strengthen your hearts (so as to be) blameless . . .

142   188. The attributive or predicative use of the adjective πᾶς distinguishes between different senses. In attributive position (the noun having the article) it denotes that the thing or class named is «taken as a whole», e. g. ἦσαν οἱ πάντες ἄνδρες ὡσεὶ δώδεκα «twelve in all» Acts 19,7 (cf. 27,37); ὁ πᾶς νόμος «the law in its entirety» Gal 5,14. In predicative position (the noun having the article) it means «all (the) . . .» e. g. πᾶς ὁ νόμος «the entire law (without exception of any precept)», πάντες οἱ ἄνδρες «all the men» without exception. In the same sense, however, if the substantive has no article, the meaning will be «all» (without «the»), «every», e. g. πᾶς νόμος «all law», «every law», the article being omitted because the reference is not to individuals as such but to the nature or class; as often with πάντες ἄνθρωποι (thirteen times in Paul; but he has also «the least πάντων ἁγίων» Eph 3,8, and πάντες ἄγγελοι Heb 1,6). Thus in the singular πᾶς without the article means «every» in a distributive sense: πᾶς ἄνθρωπος «every man»; πᾶσα χαρά «whatever can be called joy» Jas 1,2; μετὰ πάσης παρρησίας «with full liberty» Acts 4,29, while with the article it means «the whole» (⁴).

189. Hence in πᾶσα γραφὴ θεόπνευστος 2 Tim 3,16 it is correct to insist on the absence of the article as showing that inspiration belongs to Scripture *as such* («all Scripture . . . .»), whereas with the article («all the Scripture . . .») it would simply register the fact that the existing Scripture was inspired, without establishing a formal principle.

143   190. It must however be noted that in Hellenistic Greek πᾶς is used even without the article in the sense «(the) whole (of)», especially with (geographical) proper names: πᾶσα Ἱεροσόλυμα = the whole city Mt 2,3; πᾶς Ἰσραήλ Rom 11,26 (so often in the LXX), and in Biblical usage also

---

(⁴) It is to be noted that the use or omission of the article with πᾶς is in the last analysis based on the considerations exposed above (**165, 171**): cf. J. M. BOVER in *Biblica* (1932) 411-34.

πᾶς οἶκος 'Ισραήλ Acts 2,36; in Christ πᾶσα οἰκοδομή ... αὔξει εἰς ναὸν ἅγιον Eph 2,21 certainly means « all *the* edifice » and not (as classically) « every edifice ». (Cf. πάντες = « all » without the article 188).

144   191. This irregularity may obviously sometimes render Biblical texts ambiguous. In Acts 17,26 we read « from one (man) God made πᾶν ἔθνος ἀνθρώπων dwell ἐπὶ παντὸς προσώπου .τῆς γῆς ». If πᾶν ἔθνος here means « the whole race » we have a simple allusion to the creation of ˙man and the unity of the human race, a notion which was also a favourite one of the Stoic philosophers who formed part of Paul's audience on the Areopagus. If however πᾶν ἔθνος ἀνθρώπων is to be taken, as in classical usage, to mean « every people of mankind » set by God each in its own place and for its own time, we have a totally different idea, namely that of God as lord of history and supreme ruler of peoples and nations, a « theology of history » which was then proper to Israel alone. Note that in the same verse the Semitic ἐπὶ παντὸς προσώπου τῆς γῆς, where the meaning is clearly, despite the absence of the article, « the whole face of the earth », serves to commend the interpretation of πᾶν ἔθνος also as « the whole race ».

145   192. A further characteristic of Hellenistic Greek is the frequency with which a substantive without the article is followed by an adjective with the article, i. e. where the substantive is first used indefinitely or generically, and then taken up as determined by an adjective, e. g. Acts 7,35 « God sent Moses σὺν χειρὶ ἀγγέλου τοῦ ὀφθέντος αὐτῷ ἐν τῇ βάτῳ » = by the hand of an angel, the one who appeared ... »; or εἰρήνην ἀφίημι ὑμῖν, εἰρήνην τὴν ἐμὴν δίδωμι ὑμῖν « ... peace, a peace namely My own » Jo 14,27; ταχὺ ἐξενέγκατε στολὴν τὴν πρώτην Lk 15,22 and frequently: Lk 7,32; 18,9; Acts 11,21; 25,23 etc.

VII. THE PRONOUN

146   **195.** With regard to pronouns two points are especially to be noted: their very frequent and pleonastic use, and the loss of the finer distinctions between them. Both of these are points which must be taken into account in order to interpret correctly the Biblical text, or at least, points to which it is necessary to draw the attention of those prone to apply to Biblical Greek the canons of classical and literary usage.

1) Great Frequency

147   **196.** The great frequency with which pronouns are used is due to what may be called the « analytic » tendency of any living spontaneous popular speech, a tendency that is to express explicitly what is already contained implicitly in the expression used or in the nature of the subject matter; and the usage of the Biblical writers is rather to be regarded as a colloquial one.

If the frequency of pleonastically added pronouns is even greater in Biblical Greek than in the ordinary Greek of the time, this may perhaps be accounted for by the influence of Semitic usage, where the ease with which suffix-pronouns may be added favours their abundant use.

148   **197.** Hence in **oblique cases** the emphasis which would usually be supposed to be intended in classical Greek (so as not to admit a pleonastic use) is scarcely ever to be suspected in Biblical Greek. E. g. « and when he finds (the sheep) he puts it εἰς τοὺς ὤμους α ὐ τ ο ῦ » Lk 15,5 (the pronoun being ordinarily omitted in Greek especially with parts of the body) or in verse 20 of the same chapter the prodigal son went πρὸς τὸν πατέρα ἑ α υ τ ο ῦ.

149   **198.** In the **nominative**, for personal pronouns, there are more grounds for suspecting a certain emphasis, but even here the emphasis should not be too readily insisted upon, where the context does not favour it. In Mk 6,31, Our Lord says to the apostles: δεῦτε ὑ μ ε ῖ ς α ὐ τ ο ὶ

κατ' ἰδίαν..., where the αὐτοί added to ὑμεῖς is perhaps to be neglected as in the Latin versions (1). Similarly Lk 9,44 θέσθε ὑ μ ε ῖ ς εἰς τὰ
ὦτα ὑμῶν where we are scarcely to understand any opposition of the disciples to whom the admonition is given and the crowd that « wondered
at all that He did ». Cf. also Jo 15,16 ἔθηκα ὑμᾶς, ἵνα ὑ μ ε ῖ ς ὑπάγητε...;
in this text emphasis would have the effect of inducing a change of the sense
(opposition to Jesus); similarly in Jo 5,39.

150

199. Luke in particular makes frequent use of αὐτός (in the nominative) not in its proper intensive sense (« himself ») but simply as a third-
person pronoun with only the slightest emphasis or none at all, e. g., without any change of subject even, Lk 16,23 has: «... the rich man ...
was buried in hell; and lifting up his eyes ... he saw Abraham ... and
Lazarus ... καὶ α ὐ τ ὸ ς φωνήσας εἶπεν· πάτερ 'Αβραάμ ... ». It may here
be noted that the use of the pronoun tends even to confuse the sense,
since at first sight it might seem to indicate Abraham or Lazarus. This
practice of beginning a fresh sentence with καὶ αὐτός, although very
common in the gospel of Luke (about forty places), is however not to be
found in the same author's Acts, or at least, not without emphasis (²).

200. Entirely analogous considerations apply to the use in Jo of the
pronoun ἐκεῖνος, which is frequent, even in the nominative, without any
emphasis, as a simple third-person pronoun.

(¹) Modern translators admit this pronoun as emphatic and render « you
alone » or the like (as Jo 6,15 has in a parallel passage αὐτὸς μόνος) indicating
the separation of the disciples from the crowd. Others render « vous autres »
(J. Huby), « vous aussi » (M. - J. Lagrange) and so suppose an opposition
to Jesus Himself, who had previously been κατ' ἰδίαν, For the use of αὐτός here
cf. the corresponding English use: « by yourselves ».

(²) For details see W. Michaelis, Das unbetonte καὶ αὐτός bei Lukas,
in Studia Theologica 4 (1951), against Eduard Schweizer's article in Theol.
Zeitschrift 6 (1950), 161-85. But cf. also M. Black, An Aramaic Approach...,
1954, p. 64. This author suspects an underlying Aramaic circumstantial proposition (waw + pronoun + verb: cf. the Irish idiom « and he calling out »
or the like) and points to the frequency with which Codex Beza (D) corrects
Luke's καὶ αὐτός into idiomatic Greek, e. g. Lk 5,1 καὶ αὐτὸς ἦν ἑστώς (D:
ἑστῶτος αὐτοῦ); so too 5,17; 7,12; 17,16; 19,2. Clearly the writer of D regarded Luke's way of expressing himself as un-Greek.

151   201. The use of a **pronoun repeating the relative** (e. g. γυνὴ ἧς εἶχεν τὸ θυγάτριον αὐτῆς πνεῦμα ἀκάθαρτον Mk 7,25) is very frequent in Semitic languages, where it is often necessary to the sense; for the Hebrew relative particle *asher* or the Aramaic one *di* is indeclinable and hence its determination in gender, number and case requires (save when it belongs to the verb) an added pronoun. In the NT this phenomenon is a rare one, almost limited to Mk and Rev. Another example from Mk is John the Baptist's statement (1,7) to be found in the same Semitic form also in Lk 3,16: ... οὗ οὐκ εἰμὶ ἱκανὸς λῦσαι τὸν ἱμάντα τῶν ὑποδημάτων α ὐ τ ο ῦ ; cf. Mt 3,12 = Lk 3,17; Jo 13,26. Examples are more numerous in Rev: 3,8; 7,29; 13,8; 20,8. Acts 15,17 is a quotation from the LXX.

152   202. To the same idiom belong also the cases in which οἷα is taken up by τοιαύτη Mk 13,19; οἷος by τηλικοῦτος Rev 16,18; οἷα by οὕτως Mk 9,3; ὅπου by ἐκεῖ Rev 12,6 14 or by ἐπ' αὐτῶν 17,9.

153   203. In the NT this phenomenon can certainly be regarded as a Semitism, although similar usages are to be found in classical Greek, very rarely, and in modern Greek very frequently, as well as in popular usage in other languages.

154   204. The **proleptic use** of pronouns (*), i. e. their use to « introduce » a noun which follows (cf. the examples at the end of the paragraph) is a pure Aramaism, and has been almost entirely eliminated from the usual text, but Codex Bezae (D) has preserved several clear cases which have escaped correction and suggest what may have been the style of the first servile versions of the Aramaic tradition. We may cite as examples (from D) Mt 12,45 « and the last state of him (i. e.) of that man (α ὐ τ ο ῦ τοῦ ἀνθρώπου ἐκείνου) becomes worse than the first », and Mk 5,15 καὶ θεωροῦσιν α ὐ τ ὸ ν τὸν δαιμονιζόμενον ... διηγήσαντο δὲ πῶς ἐγένετο α ὐ τ ῷ τῷ δαιμονιζομένῳ.

155   205. Even in the usual text there seem to remain at least some traces of this Aramaism, whose recognition as such solves the problem set by certain pronouns otherwise difficult to explain in an intensive sense,

---

(*) Cf. M. BLACK, *An Aramaic Approach to the Gospels and Acts*, Oxford 1946, pp. 70-74.

e. g. Mt 3,4 α ὐ τ ὸ ς δὲ ὁ Ἰωάννης εἶχεν τὸ ἔνδυμα αὐτοῦ ἀπὸ τριχῶν καμήλου. Similarly Mk 6,17. 22 α ὐ τ ὸ ς δὲ ὁ Ἡρῴδης ... εἰσελθούσης τῆς θυγατρὸς α ὐ τ ῆ ς τῆς Ἡρῳδιάδος ...; Mk 12,36f αὐτὸς Δαυίδ ...; Lk 10,7 ἐν α ὐ τ ῇ δὲ τῇ οἰκίᾳ. From Jo cf. 9,13 and 18. Perhaps an Aramaic original literally ὅταν ἔλθῃ ἐν τῇ δόξῃ α ὐ τ ο ῦ τοῦ πατρὸς (αὐτοῦ) may explain why Mk 8,38 has ἐν τῇ δόξῃ τοῦ πατρὸς αὐτοῦ, while Lk 9,26 has ἐν τῇ δόξῃ αὐτοῦ καὶ τοῦ πατρός.

206. A certain pronominal prolepsis, also redolent of Semitism, is to be found where the subject of a relative clause is anticipated by a pronoun in the main clause, as Lk 2,30 « my eyes have seen *thy* salvation, which thou hast prepared ... »; Jo 2,23 « seeing *His* signs which He did »; so too 7,3 τὰ ἔργα σου, ἃ ποιεῖς; cf. 17,24. This idiom recalls those of the OT such as « ... abandoned the counsel *of the elders*, which they had given him » 3 Kings 12,8 or « in all the sins *of Jeroboam* which he committed », 4 Kings 17,22.

207. In other places the subject of a subordinate clause is anticipated in the main clause as its object: Jo 5,42: ... ἔγνω ὑμᾶς ὅτι τὴν ἀγάπην ... οὐκ ἔχετε; Jo 11,31: ἰδόντες Μαριὰμ ὅτι ταχέως ἀνέστη ... So too 4,35; 6,7; 7,17; cf. Mt 25,24.

156   208. The great frequency of use characteristic of pronouns in Hellenistic Greek is not shared by the **reflexive** pronoun. This is indeed almost always used where it immediately follows its verb as direct object (e. g. κρίνοντες ἑαυτούς), but in all other cases it is for the most part neglected, especially in the possessive genitive (*), the ordinary (non-reflexive) forms being used instead. This neglect, which is also Hellenistic, is perhaps favoured in Biblical usage by the fact that Hebrew and Aramaic suffix-pronouns do not distinguish reflexive from non-reflexive.

157   209. As regards the form of these pronouns, the third-person form of the reflexive (ἑαυτοῦ) often takes the place of the first or second person forms in the singular, and always does so in the plural (with the single

---

(*) Only Luke has the possessive genitives ἑαυτοῦ, ἑαυτῶν with any frequency; he uses them, indeed, seemingly without emphasis or any other reason; cf. Lk 15,20: the prodigal son ἦλθεν πρὸς τὸν πατέρα ἑαυτοῦ; Acts 14,14.

exception ὑμῶν αὐτῶν in a quotation 1 Cor 5,13), e. g. 2 Cor 3,5 «not that we are capable of thinking something of ourselves (ἀφ' ἑαυτῶν) as from ourselves (ὡς ἐξ ἑαυτῶν) »; cf. also 1 Cor 11,31; Acts 23,14 etc. This lack of distinction between the first and the third person pronoun in the difficult passage 2 Cor 10,12 renders possible a variant reading ascribing to the apostle what the usual reading understands of his adversaries.

158   210. It is further to be noted that the contracted form αὐτοῦ for ἑαυτοῦ is scarcely ever — if indeed·at all — to be found in the NT. Hence there is scarce justification for reading αὐτοῦ where the uncials have unaspirated AYTOY. Merk's edition of the Greek NT has αὐτόν, αὐτούς at least in Jo 2,24; Lk 23,12; Acts 14,17; but in Php 3,21 αὐτῷ (though the sense is certainly reflexive) along with all recent editions: ὑποτάξαι α ὐ τ ῷ τὰ πάντα. It is remarkable that commentators make no remark on this· very rare use (non-reflexive form though the pronoun immediately follows its verb, cf. 208), although here the apostle ascribes to Christ what in 1 Cor 15,25-28 (ps 8,7) he ascribes to God.

159   211. Since then αὐτοῦ is to be found with reflexive sense, ambiguity may sometimes arise. Thus Eph 2,16 has «... to reconcile both in the one body to God διὰ τοῦ σταυροῦ, ἀποκτείνας τὴν ἔχθραν ἐ ν α ὐ τ ῷ », where ἐν αὐτῷ can mean «in Himself» (so the Vulgate, and such was the sense previously in the same chapter, verse 5), or it can refer to the cross; cf. also Col 1,20; 1 Jo 5,10; Jas 5,20.

160   212. Instead of the reflexive pronoun the NT also uses after the Semitic fashion ψυχή, cf. Lk 9,24 with the following verse: « he who wishes to save τὴν ψυχὴν αὐτοῦ shall lose it, and he who loses τὴν ψυχὴν αὐτοῦ ... shall save it. For what does it profit a man to gain the whole world, but bring himself (ἑαυτόν) to loss? ».

2) Neglect of Distinctions

The finer shades of distinction between various pronouns are neglected. Thus:

a) οὗτος, ὅδε

161   213. Οὗτος is no longer used, as in classical Greek, exclusively to refer to something which precedes, but may refer to something which follows, in which case ὅδε was used classically. Thus 1 Cor 11,17 Τοῦτο (δὲ παραγγέλλων οὐκ ἐπαινῶ) ὅτι... seems to mean « this, namely ».

b) Οὗτος, ἐκεῖνος

162   **214.** Οὗτος for a proximate and ἐκεῖνος for a remote antecedent are indeed distinguished, but in vivid speech the proximateness or remoteness may be not grammatical, according to the order of mention, but psychological.

Thus e. g. Peter before the Sanhedrin after the cure of the lame man, having spoken of Christ « whom God has raised from the dead », goes on: « ἐν τούτῳ οὗτος stands before you cured. Οὗτος is the stone that was rejected... » (Acts 4,10 f). This last οὗτος here refers back to the same antecedent as ἐν τούτῳ, i. e. Christ, an antecedent remote in the grammatical sense but proximate in the speaker's mind as being the subject of the whole discourse. It has been justly observed that in the LXX, a translation which in the nature of things lacks the vivacity of speech, the distinction between οὗτος and ἐκεῖνος is observed on a strict grammatical basis, although it has no equivalent in the Hebrew text.

c) Ὅς, ὅστις

163   **215.** The relative pronouns ὅς and ὅστις are classically used to refer respectively to an antecedent regarded, for the relative clause, as determinate (ὅς = «..., the one who » etc.) or indeterminate (ὅστις = «..., one who » etc.), so that ὅστις either shares the indeterminate status of its antecedent or, if the antecedent is itself determinate, regards it not as individual but as of such a nature. In this latter case ὅστις may easily have a causal sense (« inasmuch as ») or a consecutive one (« such as »). The distinction is therefore one which affects the sense, and does so in much the same way as the presence or absence of the article (171 ff).

164   **216.** In Hellenistic and Biblical Greek, however, this distinction between ὅς and ὅστις is often neglected, especially by Luke, ὅστις being used instead of ὅς, e. g. Lk 2,4 « Joseph went up... εἰς πόλιν Δαυίδ, ἥτις καλεῖται Βηθλεέμ ». Here the sense is clearly simply the determinate « (the one) which is called Bethlehem », and not any indeterminate one such as « inasmuch as it is called Bethlehem » (a sense which would have fitted a text εἰς Β., ἥτις καλεῖται πόλις Δαυίδ).

165   217. In not a few cases, however, ὅστις may retain its proper sense,
e. g. with generic antecedent Mt 7,15 προσέχετε ἀπὸ τῶν ψευδοπροφητῶν
οἵτινες (« inasmuch as they ») ἔρχονται ... ἐν ἐνδύμασι προβάτων;
with a completely determinate one Jo 8,53 « art thou greater than our
father Abraham, ὅ σ τ ι ς ἀπέθανεν », where ὅστις is used because Abraham
is not regarded in the relative clause as a particular person who is in fact
dead, but as *such* a person as to be dead, i. e. as mortal (⁵). So too in Acts
17,1 « having traversed Amphipolis and Apollonia they came to Thessa-
lonica, where (ὅπου, not οὗ) there was a synagogue », one may well suspect a causal sense and conclude that Paul did not stop at Amphipolis
or Apollonia because there was no synagogue there; but especially in Luke
ὅπου may well stand for simple οὗ. So too in Jo 7,42 the sense « inasmuch
as ... there » for ὅπου fits very well: ἀπὸ Βηθλεέμ..., ὅπου ἦν Δαυίδ,
ἔρχεται ὁ Χριστός.

218. Ὅστις seems to bear sometimes the sense « who, as such », instead
of the one with inverse causal order « such a one as », e. g. Gal 4,24 referring
to the two covenants: μία... εἰς δουλείαν γεννῶσα, ἥτις ἐστιν ᾿Αγάρ = which,
as such, is represented by Hagar; i. e. the quality connoted is not (as with « inasmuch as ») the one expressed in the relative clause, but the one expressed
in that of the antecedent. — So too, perhaps, Gal 2,4; 2 Thess 1,9; and frequently in parables: « ... is like a wise man ὅστις (who, as such, i. e. because
he was wise) built... » Mt 7,24 26. Cf. also Lk 10,42 « Mary has chosen the
better part, ἥτις (which for that reason) shall not be taken from her » (LA-
GRANGE).

166   219. Finally, as at least one example of the consecutive sense, we
may cite Mt 2,6: « for from thee shall come a leader (ἡγούμενος without
article) ὅ σ τ ι ς ποιμανεῖ τὸν λαόν μου » where the Vulgate rightly uses
the subjunctive « qui regat » and not as in Greek the future (« qui reget »),
for the sense can be roughly « a leader such as to lead ». Cf. 1 Cor 5,1. —
One may perhaps understand a concessive sense in Lk 1,20: « ...because
thou hast believed my words, οἵτινες will be fulfilled in their season »,
almost = « though they are such as ... » (German: *die doch*); cf. Heb 12,5.

220. It must however be admitted that all these fine distinctions remain
somewhat doubtful. C. C. CADBURY (*J. B. L.* [1923], 150-57) regards the distinction between ὅς and ὅστις (at least in Luke) as practically extinct; their

(⁵) In German I would render this: « der doch auch gestorben ist ».

221-223   The Pronoun

use now depends not on the sense, but on the form: in the oblique cases the simple relative, but in the nominative the forms ὅς ἥτις ὅ, οἵτινες αἵτινες ἅ. This evolution is perhaps to be accounted for also by the tendency to avoid confusion with the article.

d) Τίς, ὅς

167   221. There is a great affinity between relative clauses and indirect questions after verbs of saying, knowing etc. (⁶). Hence it comes about that in Hellenistic Greek τί may be used in place of the relative, e. g. Mk 14,36 ἀλλ' οὐ τί ἐγὼ θέλω, ἀλλὰ τί σύ (⁷), or the relative instead of the interrogative, Mt 6,8 οἶδεν γὰρ ὁ πατὴρ ὧν (instead of τίνων) χρείαν ἔχετε.

168   222. It is however matter for dispute whether the relative may be used in place of τίς in a direct question. In favour of an affirmative solution we have such texts as Mk 9,11 and 28 where ὅτι (indeterminate relative?) seems to stand for τί = διὰ τί «why?». The disciples ask, Mk 9,28: ὅτι ἡμεῖς οὐκ ἐδυνήθημεν ἐκβαλεῖν αὐτό; Some however explain this as an elliptical expression for τί (ἐστιν) ὅτι...

Here must be mentioned also the obscure reply given by Jesus to those who asked him: σὺ τίς εἶ; Jesus said to them: τὴν ἀρχὴν ὅτι (ὅ τι) καὶ λαλῶ ὑμῖν Jo 8,25, which is still commonly rendered, as it was of old, « why do I speak to you at all? », or « d'abord, pourquoi donc (καί) est-ce que je vous parle? » (Joüon), i. e. « you do not deserve an answer ». Those who understand ὅτι as a relative are left with the more difficult rendering «(I am) just what I tell you».

169   223. Finally we have Mt 26,50, where Jesus says to Judas: « Friend, whereto art thou come? » a generally accepted rendering which supposes

---

(⁶) The affinity between the relative and the interrogative is to be seen also from the fact that exclamations of astonishment, classically expressed with relative forms, are in Hellenistic Greek and in the NT expressed with interrogative ones, e. g. πόσοι (instead of ὅσοι) μίσθιοι Lk 15,17. Hence Mt 6,28: « consider the lilies of the field πῶς αὐξάνουσιν » would classically be an indirect question, but in NT usage *may* be understood as an exclamation.

(⁷) Hence Jo 2,4 τί ἐμοὶ καὶ σοί might so far as Hellenistic Greek is concerned be rendered, as has been suggested, « what is mine is thine », but this interpretation is entirely lacking in probability on account of the Semitic expression which certainly underlies the Greek.

70

Neglect of Distinctions

that the relative may stand for the interrogative in a direct question, for the Greek has ἑταῖρε, ἐφ' ὃ πάρει; (a reading which is certain and supported by ancient versions).

Those — and they are many — who do not admit ὅς = τίς must explain this saying of Our Lord's as elliptical, supplying ποίησον (« do that for which thou art come ») or τοῦτ' ἔστι or the like.

Other examples similar to our text are to be found, but they do not solve the problem, as they may be regarded as favouring either opinion (*). Thus on drinking-cups (thought to be of the first century A. D.) such inscriptions are to be found as εὐφραίνου ἐφ' ὃ πάρει, or ἑταῖρε, ἐφ' ὃ πάρει, εὐφραίνου and some take ὃ not as relative (« rejoice, which is what you are here for ») but as interrogative (« rejoice; what are you here for? ») (DEISSMANN). — In the « Sayings of the Fathers » (Migne PG 65,105 c) Abbot Arsenius is said to have often urged himself to fervour by saying to himself: 'Αρσένιε, δι' ὃ ἐξῆλθες. The sense is however obscure : is this a question, or an elliptical expression, or does it not simply mean « This is what you left the world for » (Διὸ ...)? — In the Acts of the Martyrs, Agathonica is said to have replied to those who called to her, as she went forth to her martyrdom, to have pity on her child, that God would· look after him, ἐγὼ δὲ ἐφ' ὃ πάρειμι, which Harnack rendered « what am I here for? » but E. C. Owen prefers « I (emphatic contrasted with my son) must do that for which I am here ».

These examples, so widely separated from one another in time and in circumstances, and yet agreeing in the choice of words, suggest that the expression was a fairly frequent colloquial (proverbial?) one, and leave our question unanswered.

(*). Cf. ZORELL, V. D. 9 (1929) 112-116; E. C. E. OWEN, Journ. Th. Stud. 29 (1927-8) 384-6; DEISSMANN, Licht v. Osten, ed. 4, 100-105.

VIII. VOICE (OF VERBS)

170   225. The «voice» of a verb expresses the relationship between its grammatical subject and the action: Greek distinguished an «active» voice, representing the subject as simply acting (or being), a «passive» voice representing the subject of the verb as the object of the action, «middle» voice representing the subject as acting (or causing another to act) with respect to himself (the subject). At an early stage in the evolution of Greek there existed only the active and middle voices, whereas the term of the evolution has been to leave only active and passive. Thus the middle voice, as a distinct form (and it is only in the aorist and future forms that it has a form distinct from that of the passive) has lost ground and become obsolete. Several traces of this evolution are to be found in Hellenistic and NT Greek:

171   226. The active verbs which (for a reason not readily obvious) in classical Greek took on middle form in the future (only) tend to assimilate the future to the rest of the verb, i. e. to give it the active endings: ἁμαρτήσω, ἁρπάσω, γελάσω, κλαύσω, κράξω etc. Ἀκούσομαι remains however alongside ἀκούσω, and ζήσομαι alongside ζήσω: Luke in the Acts always uses the middle form ἀκούσομαι (four times: 3,22; 17,32; 21,22; 28,38) except in a quotation from the LXX, (28,26), whereas in the gospels the middle form is not found, but only the active (Mt 12,19; 13,14; Jo 5,25; 5,28; 10,16). John has ζήσω four times, ζήσομαι once (11,25). Paul also has ζήσω where it is himself who speaks (Rom 6,2; 2 Cor 13,4; Heb 12,9) while in quotations from the LXX he keeps the middle form (Rom 1,17 = Gal 3,11 = Heb 10,38; Rom 10,5 = Gal 3,12); similarly Mt 4,4 = Lk 4,4. Apart from this ζήσομαι is found only Mt 9,18; Lk 10,28.

172   227. The verb ποιεῖν is in classical usage put in the middle voice where it has for object a noun denoting action, with which it forms a periphrasis equivalent to a simple verb, e. g. (for the NT also) πορείαν ποιεῖσθαι for πορεύεσθαι, μνείαν ποιεῖσθαι for μεμνῆσθαι, ἀναβολὴν ποιεῖσθαι for ἀναβάλλειν, δέησιν ποιεῖσθαι « to pray » as distinct from δέησιν ποιεῖν, which would mean « compose a prayer » (object independent of verb).

It is said that this distinction between simple action (middle voice) and action resulting in production of the object (active voice) is no longer strictly observed in the NT (cf. DEBRUNNER 310,1 along with the « Nachtrag ») and many examples are alleged with ποιεῖν where (it is said) ποιεῖσθαι was to be expected. On careful examination, however, the use of the active can generally be accounted for, and this is especially true for Luke. Thus the middle voice˙ is regularly used in Lk 5,33; 13,22; in Acts 1,1 τὸν μὲν πρῶτον λόγον ἐποιησάμην (hence not « I composed the former discourse » which would have the active, but « I discoursed on the former occasion »); 15,3 ἐποίουν χαράν is « gave rise to joy » (and not « made merry »!) so that the active is correct; so too 23,12 ποιήσαντες συστροφήν, not « rioted » but « stirred up a riot », whereas just after this we have (23,13) οἱ τὴν συνωμοσίαν ποιησάμενοι i. e. not « instituted a conspiracy » but « conspired ». So too 24,12 Paul says he has not been found ἐπίστασιν ποιοῦντα ὄχλου i. e. « stirring up... » and 25,3 ἐνέδραν ποιοῦντες does not mean « lying in wait » but « installing an ambush »; and again the middle regularly used 27,18.

228. All this suggests that Luke found it natural to distinguish the voices in such expressions, and since Luke's Greek is a truly κοινή vernacular (cf. its confusion between εἰς and ἐν), it would seem that in the Greek of which it is representative the distinction was still observed, which makes it likely a fortiori that it was still observed in the rest of the NT in general. In fact, an examination made by J. Smith, and too long to be reported here in full, of all the revelant texts, shows that the distinction can practically always be supposed to have been observed, with the exception of πόλεμον ποιεῖν (four times in Rev: 11,7; 12,17; 13,7; 19,19) and leaving out of consideration the difficult text Mk 2,23: «... His disciples began ὁδὸν ποιεῖν τίλλοντες τοὺς στάχυας » (¹).

(¹) The variant readings show that this text caused difficulties from the beginning. Ὁδὸν ποιεῖν according to the rule given above should mean not « make their way = go forward » (which would have the middle voice) but, with independent verb and object, « make a path », a sense which of itself seems unlikely both because such a path is hardly made by « plucking the

173   229. Just as the active took the place of the middle in the future of active verbs, so too the middle loses ground, but in favour of the passive, in «deponent» verbs. The commonest example of this in the NT is the aorist ἀπεκρίθη (195 times) instead of ἀπεκρίνατο, which is found only four times in the synoptic gospels, οὐδὲν ἀπεκρίνατο being said of Jesus three times in non-parallel passages (Mt 27,12; Mk 14,61; Lk 23,9), to which must be added Lk 3,16; Jo 5,17. 19; Acts 3,12; nor is the middle form found elsewhere in the NT. This seems to confirm Moulton-Milligan's observation that the form ἀποκρίνασθαι was an especially «solemn» one in Hellenistic usage. — For the formula in question cf. 366.

174   230. On account of this Hellenistic tendency to use passive forms in «deponent» sense, one must beware of insisting on a passive sense for them. Thus e. g. where Paul writes to the Thessalonians (I, 1,5) οἴδατε οἶοι ἐγενήθημεν ἐν ὑμῖν δι' ὑμᾶς the Vulgate is right in rendering «quales fuerimus», however much the context may suggest the passive sense (Paul's «being made» such as he was by the action of God); ἐγενήθη occurs three other times in the same chapter. In 1 Cor 1,30 however (ὃς ἐγενήθη σοφία ἡμῖν ἀπὸ Θεοῦ) one may render, instead of the deponent «become», the passive «be made».

175   231. For the same reason one must not insist too much on the difference between ἠγέρθη ἐκ νεκρῶν and ἀνέστη, as if the passive form ἠγέρθη always and necessarily connoted the action of God the Father, for it may simply mean «arose» and is rightly so rendered («surrexit»)

---

ears» and also because Jesus in his answer does not speak of work forbidden on the Sabbath, but of eating what is forbidden; such a sense can however perhaps not be entirely excluded owing to the incertitude shown by Mt and Lk and the manuscript tradition concerning what is said to be forbidden by the Pharisees: «to pluck and eat» (Mt), «to pluck and eat, rubbing (the ears) with their hands» (Lk), «to make their way plucking» or rather, as has just been said «to make a path by plucking» (Mk). It is further to be noted that the sense «make a path» accounts for the fact that the principal verb is «began (ὁδὸν ποιεῖν)» and «plucking» is expressed by a participle: «began to make a path (by) plucking the ears», whereas if the sense were «make their way» one would have expected «began to pluck the ears as they made their way» rather than «began to make their way plucking the ears», though the expression of the principal action by a participle and a concomitant one by a main verb, unusual as it is, is not impossible (cf. **376**).

by the Vulgate in e. g. Mk 14,28; 16,6; Mt 27,64 etc. This may perhaps partly account for the remarkable fact that while the substantive ἀνάστασις (νεκρῶν, 'Ιησοῦ) occurs frequently, the verb ἀναστῆναι is found for Christ's resurrection only once in the epistles (1 Thess 4,14; but it it occurs seven times in the gospels and twice in Acts) as against thirteen cases where Christ is said ἐγερθῆναι. (Note however that the resuscitation [ἐγείρειν] of Christ is in many places explicitly attributed to the Father).

So too σταθείς and ἐστάθη often mean simply στάς and ἔστη; thus where Paul speaks σταθείς ἐν μέσῳ τοῦ 'Αρείου πάγου the passive form does not imply that someone had « set » him there (Acts 17,22). Cf. also Mt 18,16; Lk 18,11; Acts 5,20; Rom 14,4; Col 4,12.

176   232. Despite these traces of the obsolescence of the middle voice, middle forms still retain a wide field of usage in the NT for all the senses for which they are found in classical use: a « direct » middle (i. e. with reflexive sense) is found e. g. in Mt 27,5 ἀπήγξατο (Judas) « hanged himself » and 2 Pet 2,22 ἡ λουσαμένη and Mk 14,54 θερμαινόμενος; for the causative and permissive sense cf. Acts 22,16 βάπτισαι καὶ ἀπόλουσαι τὰς ἁμαρτίας σου « have thyself baptized and cleansed ... »; Gal 5,12 ἀποκόψονται.

177   233. The Hellenistic tendency to greater explicitness often results indeed in the use of the active voice with a pronoun (reflexive or not in form) or the addition of such a pronoun to the middle verb, e. g. ἄλειψαί σ ο υ τὴν κεφαλήν Mt 6,17; διεμερίσαντο τὰ ἱμάτιά μου ἑ α υ τ ο ῖ ς Jo 19,24 (= LXX).

178   234. The « indirect » use of the middle voice, indicating that the subject acts of itself, is also not rare in the NT, and it is this use which especially shows the writers to have retained a feeling for even the finer distinctions between the sense of active and middle forms; e. g. Rom 3,9 προέχεσθαι, whether this be understood as excelling *by one's virtues* or in that of proferring an excuse or a defence *of oneself*; Acts 9,39 the widows bewailing their benefactress Tabitha are described as ἐπιδεικνύμεναι to Peter the garments she had made, the middle voice indicating as it were how they so showed the garments they were actually wearing; in Acts 12,4 Herod arrested Peter and ἔθετο ἐν φυλακῇ ... βουλόμενος ... ἀναγαγεῖν αὐτὸν τῷ λαῷ, where the middle ἔθετο connotes the intention of keeping him for the end proposed.

This difference between the middle and the active is especially clear when the same verb is used in the same context in both voices. E. g. it is scarcely to be ascribed to chance that Mk 6,23f makes a quite classical distinction between αἰτῶ (simply « ask ») and αἰτοῦμαι (avail oneself of one's right to ask); for Herod says to Herodias's daughter αἴτησον and ὅτι ἐὰν αἰτήσῃς, whereupon the daughter says to her mother τί αἰτήσωμαι: So too Jas 4,2f seems to make a deliberate distinction between the two forms of this same verb: οὐκ ἔχετε διὰ τὸ μὴ αἰτεῖσθαι ὑμᾶς· αἰτεῖτε καὶ οὐ λαμβάνετε, διότι κακῶς αἰτεῖσθε. Cf. also 1 Jo 5,15f.

Some authors however speak here of the writers' arbitrary and uncertain use of the middle voice.

179   235. Finally, as is commonly the case when a distinction begins to be neglected, there are examples of **usages contrary to the general trend**, where in the NT and in Hellenistic Greek in general verbs are used in the middle voice whereas classical Greek used the active, e. g. περιβλέπεσθαι (Mk 9,8 etc.) for the Attic περιβλέπειν; ἀπεκδύεσθαι for stripping not oneself but another, Col 2,15; φυλάττεσθαι Mk 10,20 for φυλάττειν etc.

236. The « **theological passive** » is a name given to the passive used in order to avoid directly naming God as agent, e. g. four times in the Beatitudes, Mt 5,5 « they shall be comforted », 5,6 « they shall be filled », 5,7 ἐλεηθήσονται, 5,9 « they shall be called . . . ». Hence Mk 2,5 « thy sins are forgiven thee » seems to connote God as final source of the forgiveness of sins, from whom « the Son of Man has the power to forgive sins ». — This usage occurs so often in the sayings of Jesus that J. JE-REMIAS puts it among the signs indicating that the « ipsissima verba Jesu » are being reported (Festschrift WIKENHAUSER p. 93). STRACK-BILLER-BECK 1,443 list from Mt alone: 3,10; 5,5-9; 5,25. 29; 6,7. 9. 10. 33; 7,1. 2. 19; 10,19. 30 etc., and add that in rabbinic literature this passive construction is relatively rare, its place being more frequently taken by the indefinite plural as in Lk 16,9 (cf. 2). Cf. however for a contrary opinion H. SCHÜRMANN, *Das Gebet des Herrn*, note 88.

IX. THE « TENSES »

1) Aspect

240. In the title of this chapter the word « tenses » is put in inverted commas because the forms to be treated of are but inaccurately called « tenses ». The « future » and the « present » do connote time so far as the name is concerned, but not even the names of the other « tenses » express the notion of time: the name « imperfect » connotes incompleted action and « perfect » completed, while « aorist » (privative α and ὁρίζω « define, determine ») connotes simply the action without further determination. Hence the very names of the « tenses » warn us to distinguish carefully between the notion of the time of an action and of the manner in which the action is regarded, its « aspect ». In fact, « aspect » is an essential element of the Greek « tenses » (leaving out of account the future) and hence is always distinguished by the form, whereas the time of the actions is expressed in the indicative only, and in the other moods is either lacking or secondary. Moreover the time expressed is only « absolute » time and not « relative » time, i. e. the relationship of simultaneity or anteriority with respect to (e. g.) the principal verb's time: « relative » time is never expressed in Greek by the verbal form of itself, but can be gathered only from the sense in the context.

241. Three « aspects » can be distinguished, according as the action of the verb is presented by the speaker:

1) as a simple realization (e. g. in the indicative for the mere statement of historical fact) without reference to continuation or repetition, but simply « globally »: the « aorist »;

2) as a nature or kind of activity in progress or habitual (repeated) or simply as this *kind* of activity or activity tending to a given end: the « present » or « imperfect »;

3) as a completed act resulting in a « state of affairs » which is predicated by the verb as holding for the present time: the « perfect »

(but outside the indicative the notion of time is absent); or for the past time in question: the « pluperfect ».

NB: The aspects, as was said above, *present* the action *as* a simple fact, etc.; the use of the « tenses » is determined not so much by the objective reality (which commonly admits all three aspects according to what the speaker wishes to express) as by the speaker's needs: he will use the aorist for an action which objectively lasted a long time or was repeated, if what he wishes to express is simply the fact that the action took place; or the present for an action which is of its nature momentary, if what he wishes to express is the nature or kind of action as distinct from its concrete realization.

It is obvious that the distinction of aspect is of no little importance for the accurate interpretation of the text; it will therefore be well to illustrate this distinction at some length by means of examples.

2) The Aorist

181   **242.** The distinction between a simply posited and a continued act is spontaneously observed by the NT writers accustomed to Greek, as may be shown from the parallel text of the Lord's prayer: Mt 6,11 has « give us this day our daily bread » and hence, since he wishes to express simply a definite petition, uses the aorist: δ ό ς ἡμῖν σήμερον, whereas Lk 11,3, wishing to express the notion of the continual assistance of providence day by day, uses the present: ... δ ί δ ο υ ἡμῖν τὸ καθ' ἡμέραν (¹). Cf. also Mt 5,10 χαίρετε « be joyful », of a state of mind, with Lk 6,23 χάρητε of a particular reaction of joy.

(¹) On the other hand Lk 9,23 has, along with Mt and Mk: « if anyone wishes to come after Me, ἀρνησάσθω ἑαυτὸν καὶ ἀράτω τὸν σταυρὸν αὐτοῦ καὶ ἀκολουθείτω μοι where the aorists can be understood of a definitive self-denial and assumption of the cross once for all; Lk however, alone, adds here too καθ' ἡμέραν, a strange expression in such a context. Note however that this addition is very uncertain for it is lacking in many MSS and would be all the more strange in that it is elsewhere in Lk, where it is very frequent, accompanied always by the present, as is natural. Perhaps this strange addition of the notion of repetition to the aorist aspect of the verb shows that καθ' ἡμέραν was an insertion made after the composition of the rest of the Greek text, or was inserted by Luke himself into the preexistent text of his source.

Other examples: in Lk 8,50 (B) Our Lord exhorts Jairus to confidence, after he has heard of his daughter's death, with the words μὴ φοβοῦ, μόνον πίστευσον, while in Mk 5,36 we have μὴ φοβοῦ, μόνον πίστευε. Mark's present expresses the idea of a kind of attitude to be kept up, and so may perhaps be rendered « do not lose faith » (retain the faith you have had so far), whereas Luke's aorist expresses an act to be posited, and so may perhaps be rendered « make an act of faith » (conceive faith greater than you had before hearing of the girl's death). — « Καταμάθετε the lilies of the field » Mt 6,28 is an exhortation to consider them here and now (as it were « here are the lilies, look at them! ») or to learn definitively their lesson, while Lk 11,9 « αἰτεῖτε and you shall receive, ζητεῖτε and you shall find, κρούετε and it shall be opened to you » is on the other hand a general exhortation to a manner of acting, and in the context (the importunate friend) clearly refers to perseverance in asking etc. Similarly note the distinction between γρηγορεῖτε (Acts 20,3) « be vigilant », γρηγορήσατε (1 Pet 5,8) « watch out! » (or: « wake up! »); as for γίνου γρηγορῶν (Rev 3,2) it seems to be meant to mean « be (always) wakeful ».

243. A present imperative may express the notion of an action to be continued, or a general principle to be followed as occasion arises in the future.

244. Sometimes the present expresses the notion of « setting about » an activity, of occupying oneself about something, and thus several verbs which of their nature refer in the concrete to a definite act to be posited are used in the present form, e. g. ἔγειρε (« get up! ») φέρε, ὕπαγε, πορεύου (this latter form twenty times in the gospels against five aorists).

245. The first epistle of Peter shows a remarkable preference for the aorist imperative: 1,13. 15. 17. 22; 2,2. 13. 17; 3,10. 11. 14. 15; 4,7; 5,2. 5. 6. 8. 9, as against only nine present imperatives (BIGG). It is not however to be concluded that the author did not accurately distinguish the aspects, but only that it suited him to express those commands with that aspect. *Aorist has prohibition in absolute*

182 246. Especially in prohibitions it commonly happens that μή with the present imperative is used to forbid the continuation of an act, and μή with the aorist subjunctive to forbid a future one (with an absolute prohibition, as distinct from the prohibition « in principle » conveyed by the present; but the aorist may be used simply because it is more vivid and absolute, or regarding a general case as a particular one: Mt 5,42; 6,2f 7; Jo 5 9 etc.). Examples are: μὴ φοβοῦ «fear no more» Lk 1,13; 1,30; 2,10 and often, against μὴ φοβηθῆτε αὐτούς Mt 10,26 of future persecutors; in the profaned temple: μὴ ποιεῖτε «cease to make» My father's house a house of commerce Jo 2,16; μὴ γράφε to Pilate Jo 19,21 in the sense «do not leave written».

Exceptions usually cited for the NT are Jo 3,7; Mt 1,20; 1 Tim 4,14, but the only one which must be admitted as such is Jo 3,7 μὴ θαυμάσῃς said to the already astonished Nidodemus (W. Bauer with Moulton: «hier kommt eine gewisse Ungeduld zum Ausdruck». See also 254). Mt 1,20 may be explained by putting the stress on παραλαβεῖν (which refers to the future); the angel says to the anxious and hesitant Joseph: μὴ φοβηθῆς παραλαβεῖν Μαριάμ = take Mary without fearing. As for Paul's admonition to Timothy μὴ ἀμέλει ἐν σοὶ χαρίσματος 1 Tim 4,14, there is no reason for not taking it as referring to the present, like the admonition to «revive the grace of God» (ἀναζωπυρεῖν) 2 Tim 1,6.

247. The distinction between aorist and present has acquired a certain notoriety in the interpretation of Our Lord's words to Magdalene μή μου ἅπτου Jo 20,17. Why should she not touch Him? Is He not the same Lord who not only allowed the penitent woman to touch Him, but praised her for it (Lk 7,38) and who, when Mary the sister of Lazarus touched Him to anoint Him, rewarded her by saying that wherever the gospel was preached her deed would be commemorated (Mk 14,9)? Why then should not the faithful Magdalene touch the feet of her Lord? As for the reason given, «for I am not yet ascended to my Father», it only increases the obscurity. A solution is offered by the aspect used in the prohibition, namely not the aorist of simple prohibition, μή μου ἅψῃ, but the present μή μου ἅπτου, which refers to continued action and means in effect «you have no need to cling to me», as if the Lord were saying «That will do, let go of me, you will see me again, for I have not yet ascended to my Father». Cf. **541.**

248. It is however to be noted that it is not necessarily the continuation of an act already begun that is prohibited (or commanded) by the present form, which may be used also to express the idea of (future) repetition or continuation or the enunciation of a general principle. (Cf. 254).

184   **249.** What has been illustrated above with regard to commands and prohibitions applies also to all the other moods of the present and aorist. Several examples follow:

Acts 15,37f: Barnabas when about to set out with Paul for a second apostolic journey wished συμπαραλαβεῖν τὸν... Μᾶρκον (aorist because the meaning is simply a definite act which he wished). Paul however on account of his experience on the previous journey refused to take (συμπαραλαμβάνειν) him, the present being used because the meaning is not simply that Paul as a matter of fact refused this particular act, but that he regarded it as to be refused on principle, as «the sort of thing» he was not prepared to undertake (not definite act, but manner of acting). (But Moulton thought that it was the idea of duration — having Mark with him for the whole journey — that determined the used of the present!). — In the account of the institution of the sacrament of penance (Jo 20,23) we read « whose sins you shall forgive (ἄν . . . ἀφῆτε) are forgiven, whose sins you shall retain (κρατῆτε) they are retained »; the writer spontaneously uses the aorist for the notion of forgiving, because it is an act which is posited, but the present for that of retaining, because here we have simply continuing in the same state. — Lk 6,47. 49 seems to distinguish two ways of hearing the word of God: ὁ ἀκούων he who hears (as a characteristic or a matter of principle, i. e. present) is he who hears effectively and keeps what he hears, but ὁ ἀκούσας he who hears (as a simple matter of fact, i. e. aorist) is he who hears indeed, but to no effect. — In Lk 18,5 the unjust judge at last decides to give the widow her rights ἵνα μὴ εἰς τέλος ἐρχομένη ὑπωπιάζῃ με. This has been understood to mean that he feared that in the end (εἰς τέλος) she might be stirred up to some act of violence; but this could rather have required the aorist ἐλθοῦσα ὑπωπιάσῃ με; the present verbs give rather the sense « lest she go on to the end coming and slapping me » (εἰς τέλος = till she gets what she wants): what a difference of sense both for the verbs and for εἰς τέλος, owing to the choice of aspect.

185   **250. The inceptive aorist.** The aorist calls for especial attention in verbs which of their nature indicates a state; with these verbs the aorist commonly (but not necessarily) indicate the inception of the state, and this may demand a difference in the translation; e. g., to mention the principal examples occurring in the NT: βασιλεύειν = reign (be king), βασιλεῦσαι may = come to the throne (become king); δουλεύειν = serve (be slave), δουλεῦσαι may = be reduced to servitude (become slave); πλουτεῖν = be rich, πλουτῆσαι may = become rich; πτωχεύειν = be poor, πτωχεῦσαι may = become poor; ἀποδημεῖν = be abroad, ἀποδημῆσαι may = go abroad; κρατεῖν = hold, keep, κρατῆσαι may = take hold of, seize (cf. Heb 4,14 as against 6,18); ζῆν = live, ζῆσαι may = enter into life (1 Thess 5,10) or return to life from death (Mk 5,23); λάμπειν = shine (be shining), λάμψαι may = shine forth (Mt 5,16). Especially noteworthy: πιστεύειν = be a believer, πιστεῦσαι may = embrace the faith (both of course may be rendered « believe » in English), so that according to the reading accepted for Jo 20,31 the gospel may be regarded as addressed to pagans to be converted or to Christians to be confirmed in their faith. (In all cases for the aorist we say « may = », because of course the aorist may be a « global » one as in « ... reigned ten years » as a simple historical statement; cf. 253).

186   251. The application of a similar consideration to the verb ἁμαρτεῖν (aorist: commit sin in the concrete, commit some sin or other), ἁμαρτάνειν (present: be a sinner, as a characteristic « state »), offers a solution to the apparent contradiction between 1 Jo 2,1 and 3,9. In the latter place John seems to suppose that Christians cannot sin, but in 2,1 he admonishes them not to sin. Here however he says γράφω ὑμῖν ἵνα μὴ ἁμάρτητε (aorist: not to commit sin), whereas in 3,9 he says that he who is born of God οὐ δύναται ἁμαρτάνειν (present: be — habitually — a sinner) because he is born of God, i. e. cannot continue the sinful life that was his before his regeneration. (Cf. Rom 6,1 as compared with 6,15).

187   252. The effective aorist. Just as the aorist of verbs indicating states may express the inception of the state, so the aorist of verbs indicating action directed to some end may express the actual attainment of that end. E. g. ἐρωτῆσαι may imply receiving a response to the asking, or παρακαλέσαι (cf. Mk 5,10 παρεκάλει with 5,12 παρεκάλεσαν) may imply successful petition; in Acts 28,14 παρεκλήθημεν ... ἐπιμεῖναι may almost be rendered « we allowed ourselves to be persuaded to stay », so too κωλῦσαι « prevent » (effectively) as against κωλύειν « hinder, impede », Acts 27,43; βαλεῖν may imply hitting the mark. Cf. also Mt 27,20 οἱ ἀρχιερεῖς ἔπεισαν τοὺς ὄχλους with Acts 13,42 ἔπειθον αὐτοὺς προσμένειν τῇ χάριτι τοῦ Θεοῦ; the chief priests effectively persuaded the crowd, whereas the exhortation to fidelity is in the nature of things expressed as a simple exhortation. In Lk 15,16 ἐπεθύμει γεμίσαι τὴν κοιλίαν αὐτοῦ the imperfect expresses a constant (and ever unfulfilled) desire, though indeed the aorist (expressing a desire definitely conceived) would not imply that the desire was fulfilled.

[handwritten: Global—historical fact / no reference to duration or frequency]

188   253. The global aorist. There is perhaps a risk that some may suppose the aorist to express necessarily a « momentary » action because ποιῆσαι = « do » a thing definitively = posit an act, as distinct from ποιεῖν = « be doing » it over a length of time). In fact, of course, the action expressed by the aorist may have occupied a long time, or the reference may be to an act frequently repeated; the aorist will be used so long as the writer wishes simply to record the fact of the act or acts, and not to represent the action as in progress or habitual, i. e. so long as the whole activity expressed by the verb is regarded « globally ». E. g. Jo 2,20 « this temple οἰκοδομήθη for forty-six years » does not mean « for forty-six years the building of this temple was going on » but simply (and hence with the aorist) « the building of this temple took forty-six years » — a historical fact. Paul ἐκάθισεν i. e. « remained » at Corinth a year and six months, Acts 18,11 the aorist simply recording the duration of his stay. In Acts 11,26 ἐγένετο δὲ αὐτοῖς καὶ ἐνιαυτὸν ὅλον συναχθῆναι ἐν τῇ ἐκκλησίᾳ καὶ διδάξαι ὄχλον ἱκανόν: not « habitual activity » but simply the fact. So too Greek (unlike certain other languages in which distinction of aspect is of primary importance, e. g. Russian) can use the aorist where repetition of the act is explicitly reported, so long as the intention is simply to record « globally » the fact, e. g. « five times did I receive (ἔλαβον) from the Jews forty stripes save one... three times was I beaten with rods (ἐραβδίσθην) » 2 Cor 11,24f. In Jo 1,14 καὶ ἐσκήνωσεν ἐν ἡμῖν if the aorist be understood as an « inceptive » one (« took up his abode among us ») the verb may be understood of the dwelling of the Word in the faithful to the end of time; but if it be understood as a « global » one (« dwelt among us ») it refers only to those who as a historical fact were about Christ in his earthly life.

189   254. An aorist of « global » type is often used in categorical prohibitions, e. g. μὴ μεριμνήσητε εἰς τὸν αὔριον Mt 6,34 (i. e. the act is simply not to be posited at all, hence aorist) as against μὴ μεριμνᾶτε 6,25 which enunciates a general principle to be adopted (kind of activity, hence present) (or cf. 246 for the possible sense « stop worrying »).

190   255. In prayers the aorist (often of « global » type) is more commonly used classically, and almost always in ancient liturgies (MOULTON). It is thus not surprising that in the Lord's prayer all the petitions are expressed in the aorist (except the fourth one in its Lucan form, cf. 242), and there is no necessity (however likely such an interpretation may be) to have recourse to an eschatological sense in order to account for the aorists.

191   256. **The gnomic aorist,** i. e. the one used classically in axioms and proverbs, seems not be found in the NT, unless we are to put under this heading, as some have done, several uses of the aorist which present a certain difficulty (but this solution hides the difficulty rather than solves it). Why, e. g. the aorist in « ὡμοιώθη the kingdom of heaven to a man... », Mt 13,24, instead of the usual ὁμοία ἐστίν...? Why has 23,2 the aorist in « the scribes ἐκάθισαν on the seat of Moses » (perfect sense, « have taken their seat »? — in any case the sense is clearly that they now sit...)? — Many aorists are to be found in the parables, sometimes interspersed with presents (e. g. Mt 13,48 etc.) which have nothing in common with the « gnomic » aorist except as perhaps illustrating its origin, inasmuch as they are narrations in historical form, and the gnomic aorist may have arisen from the expression of a fact of past experience as a guide to present or future judgement. It would seem that this is the sense to be attributed to the aorists in the Magnificat Lk 1,51-53, but cf. 259 (*).

192   257. **The proleptic use** of the aorist. There should be no difficulty in accounting for the aorist which after an implicit or explicit condition seem to be used in future sense, as Jo 15,6: « if anyone abide not in Me ἐβλήθη ἔξω ... καὶ ἐξηράνθη » (here the Vulgate renders in the future « mittetur foras et arescet »), or 15,8: « in this ἐδοξάσθη My Father, that you bear much fruit ». These are examples of the proleptic use of the aorist, whereby in vivacious speech what is enunciated as a consequence of the condition is expressed as if it had already come to pass, the condition being regarded as fulfilled (e. g. by the fruit already borne, in the

(*) The question of the « gnomic aorist » is still an open one among scholars, and some suspect that this use of the aorist shows that the aorist expresses the aspect of the action so strongly, that even in the indicative the temporal element may be disregarded (J. HUMBERT, *Syntax* n. 126).

last example). Similarly Gal 5,4 «κατηργήθητε ἀπὸ Χριστοῦ you who seek justification in the law, τῆς χάριτος ἐξεπέσατε »: the relative clause has a conditional sense « if you seek justification in the law » and the aorist as it were dramatically represents the consequence as a historical fact, so as to insist the more on the imminence of the danger run by those who are being warned (so too 1 Cor 7,28; Heb 4,10; Jas 2,4; 1 Pet 3,6b). (Cf. a similar proleptic use of the present and of the perfect in place of the future e. g. Rom 14,23 ὁ δὲ διακρινόμενος ἐὰν φάγῃ κατακέκριται and 1 Jo 5,10b).

258. Some call this usage a « dramatic » aorist, and there seems to be justification for such a term, for verbs indicating sudden emotion such as an access of joy or sorrow, ready adhesion or the like, are often used in the aorist although they refer to present time. Without going further afield for an explanation of such a use, we have modern Greek examples such as νύσταξα (aorist, instead of the present νυσπάζω) to express great fatigue (« je tombe de sommeil »), or κρύωσα (aorist instead of the present κρυώνω) for great cold (« I am frozen »). The aorist (indicative) is even used with future sense, which shows to what an extent it can lose temporal value, (J. Humbert n. 187).

193   259. Hebrew influence is to be suspected in the Magnificat Lk 1,51ff: ἐποίησεν κράτος ... διεσκόρπισεν ὑπερηφάνους ... καθεῖλεν δυνάστας etc., for the Hebrew perfect is used also for the expressions of a universal truth, and is rendered in poetical passages by the LXX in the aorist (DEBR. ed. 8, 333A). Cf. the song of Hannah 1 Sam 2,4f.

194   260. Still in the Magnificat (Lk 1,47) we have the remarkable aorist ἠγαλλίασεν in obvious parallelism with the present μεγαλύνει. This has been explained as a servile version of a Hebrew inverted future (form wayyiktol) which, though it commonly refers to the past, can itself take a present value after a participle with that value (JOÜON, Grammaire §118r). If this explanation be correct, it would point to an underlying written original in Hebrew.

195   261. The aorist participle (as also the remaining moods) does not of itself express any temporal relation, whether absolute (past time) or relative (preceding action etc.). This is all the more to be noted in that

85

in Latin and in many modern languages (e. g. in English for the form
« having -ed ») a relation of time (anteriority) is expressed by the participle, which might seem to correspond to the Greek aorist participle,
and, in general, the participles express various temporal relations. Hence
in translating one is often obliged to render such a relation although it is
not expressed by the Greek form.

Thus e. g. ταῦτα εἰπὼν ἀπῆλθεν is to be rendered « having said this
he went away » on account of the obvious order of the actions and not
simply because the participle is in the aorist; in ταῦτα εἰπὼν ἐψεύσατο,
for example, the case is quite different, the aorist not indicating a preceding action but a concomitant one, or rather, the same action. A quite
clear example of this second type is to be found in Mk 14,39 προσεύξατο
τὸν αὐτὸν λόγον εἰπών, or Lk 15,23 φαγόντες εὐφρανθῶμεν = φάγωμεν
καὶ εὐφρανθῶμεν.

196   262. Since the aorist does not express relative time, which is to be
inferred from the subject matter, it is obvious that the exact interpretation may remain doubtful, e. g. Acts 18,27: when Apollo was to go into
Achaia, προτρεψάμενοι οἱ ἀδελφοὶ ἔγραψαν to the disciples to receive him,
where the sense *may* be that the brothers exhorted Apollo (first) and
(afterwards) wrote, though the more obvious sense is that they wrote
exhorting the disciples to receive him (two verbs referring to the same
action).

263. The participle ἀγαγόντα seems to call for a similar interpretation
in Heb 2,10: ἔπρεπεν γὰρ αὐτῷ (= God) ... πολλοὺς υἱοὺς εἰς δόξαν ἀγαγόντα
τὸν ἀρχηγὸν τῆς σωτηρίας αὐτῶν διὰ παθημάτων τελειῶσαι. The Vulgate renders this as if the participle referred to an antecedent action, so giving the very
obscure « decebat ... eum ... qui multos filios in gloriam adduxerat ...
per passionem consummare ». The participle may however be referred to God
(αὐτῷ; the use of the accusative in the participle is perfectly normal, cf. 394)
and taken as paralleling τελειῶσαι and referring to the same action: it was
fitting that God, so leading many into glory, should ... ». One might perhaps
have expected rather « ... should lead many into glory, consummating ... »,
i. e. with inversion of the rôles of participle and infinitive; but it is not uncom-
mon in good Greek style (and the passage in question is in the epistle to the
Hebrews) that a principal action should be expressed by a participle and a
subordinate one by a main verb. Cf. KÜHNER-GERTH, *Grammatik d. griech.
Sprache* 2,98, where many examples are given. The sense of the passage in question would thus be that it was fitting that God should bring many sons into

glory by consummating through passions the author of their salvation (³).
Cf. also Heb 6,13 and unless I am mistaken 1 Tim 1,12. For a like phenomenon cf. also **376**.

197   264. Grammarians are not agreed as to whether the aorist participle may be understood as referring to a subsequent action (⁴). The NT
passage involved in this controversy is Acts 25,13: 'Αγρίππα . . . καὶ
Βερνίκη κατήντησαν εἰς Καισάρειαν ἀ σ π α σ ά μ ε ν ο ι τὸν Φῆστον
(a variant which is an obvious emendation reads the future participle:
ἀσπασόμενοι). It is generally agreed that the aorist participle cannot
express the meaning of the future one here (i. e. « *in order to* . . . »), and
many either do not admit the reading, or try to understand the aorist
of a simultaneous action, regarding the arrival at Caesarea and the
salutation of Festus as being, as it were, a single action, a « visit of
greeting » (⁵).

198   265. An English reader should find no difficulty in this aorist participle, because it can go directly into English; just as one might say « greeting Festus, they departed » (participle for preceding action) or « greeting
Festus, they said . . . » (concomitant or identical action), so it is quite
normal to say « they went to Caesarea, greeting Festus » (following action),
and there is no *a priori* reason for not using the Greek aorist participle
in the same manner, unusual or inelegant as such a turn of phrase undoubtedly is from a Greek stylistic point of view. A number of analogous cases
are cited from the Acts (⁶), but none of them is apodictic, since it
seems always possible to regard the actions as concomitant or pre-

---

(³) This is the sense given by Helmut KRÄMER in *Wort u. Dienst*, 1952,
pp. 102-107.

(⁴) For a bibliography of this controversy see DEBRUNNER's note to
§ 339,1; 418,1

(⁵) In spite of parallels in the books of Maccabees, in the apocrypha
and in papyri, cf. *Journ. Theol. Stud.* 24 (1923) 183-186 and 403-406, and
against this *ibid.* 25(1924) 286-289.

(⁶) Thus 16,6; 16,23; 17,26; 21,14; 22,24; 23,35; 24,22f (but against this
cf. A. ROBERTSON, *Grammar*, 861-864). I would add Lk 9,22, if εἰπών there
is rightly rendered « adding », « ajoutant » (JOÜON).

ceding (⁷). A passage of some importance in connection with Paul's itinerary is Acts 16,6: Διῆλθον δὲ τὴν Φρυγίαν καὶ Γαλατικὴν χώραν κ ω λ υ θ έ ν τ ε ς ὑπὸ τοῦ ἁγίου πνεύματος λαλῆσαι τὸν λόγον ἐν ᾿Ασίᾳ. ᾿Ελθόντες δὲ κατὰ τὴν Μυσίαν... When were they prevented from preaching in Asia (= Ephesus)? After traversing Phrygia and Galatia (so Ramsay, who understands this of Lystra, Iconium and Antioch)? This would mean that the aorist participle κωλυθέντες referred to an action subsequent to that of the main verb. Usually however it is taken as referring to a preceding one: being prevented by the Spirit from going on to Ephesus from the road-junction at Antioch, they therefore traversed Phrygia-Galatia, which must thus be taken to refer to the northern region.

(⁷) The same may be said of all the passages alleged from other sources, and the chief reason for the almost universal rejection of the use of the aorist participle for a subsequent action is the fact that no example has been found either in the NT or elsewhere in which it is *impossible* to conceive any sense but that of a subsequent action, and on the grounds that such a use cannot be admitted « if all the rules of grammar and all sure understanding of language are not to be given up » (so SCHMIEDEL, and MOULTON and ROBERTSON agree with him). But the following case seems to me to be reasonably certain, inasmuch as (though even here it is not « impossible to conceive » any other sense but that of subsequent action) the Homeric narrative to which the author refers puts it beyond doubt that the sense intended is in fact subsequent action. In Fl. Philostratus, *Vita Apollonii* 1,22 (in CONYBEARE. p. 64) we have: οἱ δὲ δὴ στρουθοί... οἱ παρὰ τῷ ῾Ομήρῳ τί φήσουσιν, οὓς δράκων μὲν... ἐδαίσατο ὀκτὼ ὄντας, ἐννάτην ἐπ᾿ αὐτοῖς τὴν μητέρα ἑλών «... devoured, eight of them, taking in addition to them a ninth, the mother ». No one surely will see here an action regarded as « coincident » with that of the main verb, since the eight are explicitly distinguished (as object of the finite verb « ate ») from the « ninth » taken ἐπ᾿ αὐτοῖς (i. e. subsequently, the participle); and preceding action seems quite out of the question: in any case the succession of events, whatever one may say for the text in question, is quite clear from the Homeric account which that text resumes (11,2,305) in which the mother is said to have flown about bewailing her young while the serpent was devouring them, and to have been herself devoured afterwards: αὐτὰρ ἐπεὶ κατὰ τέκν᾿ ἔφαγεν στρουθοῖο καὶ αὐτήν (317 and 326f). It is however objected that in the Philostratus text the action expressed by the participle becomes prior to its principal verb if the latter be taken as an « understood » repetition of ἐδαίσατο (and the possibility of such an explanation shows how difficult it necessarily is to find any case which cannot possibly be conceived otherwise than as using a participle to express subsequent action).

199   **266.** The case is quite different with Jo 11,2, where after speaking of Lazarus and his sisters, the evangelist describes one of them as the Mary ἡ ἀλείψασα τὸν Κύριον μύρῳ ·καὶ ἐκμάξασα τοὺς πόδας αὐτοῦ ταῖς θριξὶν αὐτῆς. Here it might be argued: either the participles refer to an action preceding that which is being narrated, so that the reference would be to the anointing related in Lk 7, and Mary the sister of Lazarus would be identified as the « sinful woman » of that anointing (= Magdalene ?) (*); or else he is referring to the anointing (certainly by Mary the sister of Lazarus) which he is to relate in 12,3f, and in this case the aorist participle refers to an event subsequent to the time of narration. This argument is however worthless; the participle has the article, and so is not subordinated to any verb, but simply used to describe Mary, and to identify her for the readers of the gospel, among the many Maries, as « the one who anointed... », so that the time with respect to which the anointing is to be considered is the time when the gospel is composed, or read.

267. The same explanation applies likewise to the aorist participle of Mt 10,4, where Judas is described as ὁ καὶ παραδοὺς αὐτόν «the one who betrayed him » — a historical fact from the point of view of writer or reader — and not, of course « who was to betray him ». So too Acts 1,16 Ἰούδας ὁ γενόμενος ὁδηγὸς τοῖς συλλαβοῦσιν τὸν Ἰησοῦν «... to those who took Jesus », the time-reference being « absolute » and not relative to when Judas undertook to guide them. So too in many cases where the participle is not subordinated to another verb. Acts 1,8 « you shall receive the power ἐπελθόντος τοῦ ἁγίου πνεύματος » has an aorist participle referring to future from the « absolute » point of view (« who will come upon you »), and the present participle can likewise be used of the future. The distinction between present and aorist participle is therefore not one of relative time, but only one of aspect.

268. After verbs of perception, or where the sense is of the immediate apprehension of a fact (as distinct from the enunciation or conception of a proposition, which uses the infinitive as in Latin), Greek uses the accusative (or other case according to the syntax) and participle (instead of the infinitive, as in Latin). (In Latin the *present* participle may of course be used directly, i. e. without understanding « esse », but the nuance is different, cf. « video eum venientem » and « video eum venire »: both would have a participle in Greek, as would also « video eum venisse » or « scio eum venisse » etc.) The participle used depends upon

---

(*) On this question cf. U. HOLZMEISTER in *V. D.* 16 (1936), 196f.

the aspect to be expressed, the notion of time (relative or absolute) being only secondary (i. e. being inferred from the aspect and the subject matter); e. g. Mk 8,24 ὡς δένδρα ὁρῶ περιπατοῦντας (present aspect of participle just as of corresponding indicative: I see that they περιπατοῦσιν); Mk 9,1 «shall not taste death till they see τὴν βασιλείαν τοῦ θεοῦ ἐληλυθυῖαν» (i. e. see that it ἐλήλυθεν); Lk 8,46 ἐγὼ ἔγνων δύναμιν ἐξεληλυθυῖαν ἀπ' ἐμοῦ (i. e. knew that it ἐξελήλυθεν); the same with the aorist in the parallel Mk 5,30: «perceiving τὴν ἐξ αὐτοῦ δύναμιν ἐξελθοῦσαν» (i. e. that it ἐξῆλθεν); Acts 9,12: «and he saw a man Ananias εἰσελθόντα καὶ ἐπιθέντα αὐτῷ χεῖρας» (i. e. saw a man A. who εἰσῆλθεν καὶ ἐπέθηκεν).

Since the participle in this usage corresponds to an indicative of direct speech (or relative clause rendering as in the last example) and has the aspect that the indicative would have had, it follows that the aorist participle generally connotes, secondarily, a time relation, inasmuch as it must correspond to an aorist indicative, i. e. to a past tense (but the present participle may correspond to an imperfect as well as to a present, and the perfect one to a pluperfect as well as to a perfect). Cf. the remark above on the participles equivalent to relative clauses (267).

269. The choice of aspects is full of meaning in Lk 10,18: ἐ θ ε ώ ρ ο υ ν τὸν σατανᾶν ὡς ἀστραπὴν ἐκ τοῦ οὐρανοῦ π ε σ ό ν τ α, the reply given by Our Lord to His disciples when on their return from their mission they tell Him they have had power even over demons. In confirmation of this Our Lord says ἐθεώρουν «I saw (constantly or repeatedly = as the disciples were casting out demons; hence the imperfect) Satan's fall (not «Satan falling», because aorist, i. e. not description but fact: «saw that he ἔπεσεν) from heaven». Note that although the fall of Satan was repeatedly seen, the participle need not necessarily for that reason be a present one; the repetition is already expressed by the main verb, and the subordinate one may thus distinguish by the use of present or aorist the aspect proper to the event regarded apart from its repetition (the same applies also to subordinate clauses of time for example). It is thus not necessary to understand this aorist as connoting the prehistorical, definitive fall of Lucifer; but the aorist may be regarded as a «global» one embracing the whole process of the defeat of Satan from the fall of Lucifer throughout the whole history of salvation to the full and final victory in the Last Judgement.

3) The Imperfect

200   270. The imperfect (the past tense corresponding in aspect to the
« present ») exhibits an action not simply as a historical fact (aorist) but
as in progress or repeated or tending towards its end, or as this or that
kind of activity or habit (descriptive).

201   271. Sometimes the mere distinction between aorist and imperfect suffices to throw light on the writer's mental picture and so fill out
with detail an otherwise jejune narrative. Thus the multiplication of
the loaves is related in Mk 6,41 (= Lk 9,16) with two aorists and one imperfect: « He blessed (εὐλόγησεν) and broke (κατέκλασεν) the bread and
went on giving it (ἐδίδου) to His disciples to set before them ». The blessing
and the breaking are simply recorded as facts without reference to duration or repetition, but the handing out of the bread is described by an imperfect as a continuous process, so that we conclude that having (once
for all) blessed and broken the bread, Our Lord multiplied it by continuing to hand it out without exhausting the scanty stock: the multiplication thus took place in the hands of Our Lord Himself.

202   272. Some verbs tend of their nature to be put in the imperfect
when used of past time: 1) verbs of saying, where they introduce direct
speech (especially if it is of some length), because in this case the interest
falls normally not on the fact that this was or was not said (aorist) but on
the exposition of *what* was said (descriptive, imperfect); 2) verbs of asking
or ordering, for a like reason. Thus the Sermon on the Mount is introduced
by ἐδίδασκεν αὐτοὺς λέγων (Mt 5,2), and Paul's speech before Agrippa
by ἀπελογεῖτο (Acts 26,1). In the case of verbs of asking or ordering
there is the additional reason that such acts are of their nature « imperfect »
as calling for completion by an answer or by obedience. For the two classes of verbs just mentioned there is no need to seek far for the explanation of the choice of the imperfect.

The « imperfect » nature of an act of asking or ordering is the more
marked, where the response is lacking (cf. 252.). Thus in the account of
the possessed man and the Gadarene swine, the demon παρεκάλει not to
be cast forth, a vain request, expressed in the imperfect; but the second
request, which was granted, is expressed by an aorist: καὶ παρεκάλεσαν
αὐτόν to be sent into the swine (Mk 5,10.12).

203   273. Not infrequently the imperfect denotes an attempt which was not carried into effect, i. e. the tendency to an end though the action denoted by the verb as such (apart from its aspect) was not in fact performed (whereas in the cases mentioned in the preceding paragraph that action was performed, and what was lacking was the response which it sought). E. g. διεκώλυεν Mk 15,23: John the Baptist wished to dissuade Jesus from being baptized by him, but desisted before Jesus's insistence (hence commonly in English the «present» aspect κωλύειν can be rendered simply «hinder», but the aorist κωλῦσαι by «prevent»); ἐδίδουν Mk 15,23: He did not accept the wine, so that they did not in fact «give» it to Him; ἀπέθνῃσκεν Lk 8,42: the daughter of Jairus «was dying»; Lk 1,59: «ἐκάλουν him . . . Zachary», (but as Zachary insisted that he be called John they did not in fact «call» him Zachary); Lk 5,6: διερρήσ-σετο τὰ δίκτυα (but they did not in fact break).

204   274. The form which, in other moods than the indicative, corresponds in aspect to the imperfect (as well as to the present) of the indicative, is called the «present» (a more satisfactory terminology would have called it the «imperfect», since only aspect is connoted and not present or other time); these forms therefore are used in the same senses as the imperfect, e. g. for unaccomplished tendency (as in the preceding paragraph) «they filled both boats ὥστε βυθίζεσθαι αὐτά» (but they did not sink) Lk 5,7; or ὁ καταλύων τὸν ναὸν καὶ . . . οἰκοδομῶν «who proposed to destroy the temple and rebuild it» Mt 27,40; the mother of the sons of Zebedee came αἰτοῦσα παρ' αὐτῷ but her request was vain, Mt 20,20; Our Lord says to the scribes «you close the kingdom of heaven... you do not go in yourselves and you do not let τοὺς εἰσερχομένους do so» Mt 23,13; or for the sense of description of continuous state: τυφλὸς ὢν (whereas I was: imperfect) ἄρτι βλέπω Jo 9,25. So too the variant reading Jo 3,13 ὁ ὢν ἐν τῷ οὐρανῷ may be rendered not only «who is in heaven» but also «who was in heaven» (cf. 372). So too for repeated action, e. g. ὁ κλέπτων μηκέτι κλεπτέτω «he who used to steal...» Eph 4,28; or Jo 9,8 οἱ θεωροῦντες αὐτὸν τὸ πρότερον «those who were used to seeing him (290) (when he was blind)»; Mt 23,35: «all the blood ἐκχυννόμενον» = «which was (continually) shed»; Acts 26,10 ἀναιρου-μένων αὐτῶν «when they were (to be) killed».

275. An especial use of the imperfect is to describe the action in progress when some other took place: Acts 18,18 « Paul was sailing (ἐξέπλει) to Syria ... and (during the voyage) κατήντησεν εἰς Ἔφεσον ». Cf. also 18,5; 21,5 15; 22,5 etc.

205   **276.** Similarly the infinitive or participle of the « present » aspect is used to describe an action in progress when another took place. In Mk 6,45 Our Lord makes His disciples ἐμβῆναι εἰς τὸ πλοῖον καὶ προάγειν « embark (aorist: simple fact) and go on (present) towards Bethsaida », the present being used for the second infinitive because what is to be expressed is the activity on which they were engaged (when the incident to be narrated took place). Lk 2,41f has καὶ ἀναβαινόντων αὐτῶν ... καὶ τελειωσάντων τὰς ἡμέρας ἐν τῷ ὑποστρέφειν αὐτοὺς ὑπέμεινεν Ἰησοῦς ὁ παῖς ἐν Ἰερουσαλήμ where the infintive ὑποστρέφειν is « present » because it was while they *were returning* that Jesus ὑπέμεινεν (aorist: what happened then); the participle τελειωσάντων is aorist because « they *came* to the end of the days », simple fact expressed, while ἀναβαινόντων though it might of itself conceivably have meant « as they used to go up », in the context clearly means « while they were 'going up' »; and since the event narrated occurred in fact during the return journey, what we have here is an example of the use of the verb ἀναβαίνειν so as to cover (as a technical term) the entire pilgrimage, including the return journey.

4) The Future

277. The future (a secondary formation) is the only « tense » which lies outside the system of distinction of aspect (unless one wishes to regard it as being in fact an additional « aspect » rather than a « tense », cf. e. g. the « future » participle which in fact commonly denoted an « aspectual » rather than a temporal relation — not simple futurity but end in view). It expresses future time, but is also often used to express intention or possibility, so that is has more affinity with the « moods » (or « aspects », as was said above) than with the « tenses ». As regards the Biblical use the following points are to be noted:

206   **278. The present** very often stands **for the future,** apparently owing to the influence of Aramaic, which readily uses the (present) participle especially for the proximate future, e. g. ἔρχομαι Mt 24, 23f; Lk 12,40;

Jo 4,35; 14,13 28; ἐγείρομαι Mt' 27,63; εἰσπορεύομαι Lk 22,10 etc. The fact that this is especially frequent with εἶναι (Mt 10,20; Jo 7,34; 8,31 etc.) and ἔχειν (Mt 6,1; 26,11; Mk 3 39; 14 7; Jo 12,48; 13,8 etc.) is due to the Aramaic rendering of these notions not verbally but by the use of an adverb which is atemporal, but commonly stands for the present ('*it li* in-being for me = I have, cf. *est mihi*; *lait li* not-in-being for me = I have not). Note however that this does not mean that e. g. in Mt 5,46 (6,1) μισθὸν ἔχετε must be taken as standing for a future, because the present is used in such expression in the sense of a reward already laid up with God (cf. μισθὸν οὐκ ἔχετε παρὰ τῷ πατρὶ ὑμῶν 6,1 not παρὰ τοῦ πατρός, and the whole context where the hypocrites are already « paid off », ἀπέχουσιν τὸν μισθὸν αὐτῶν 6,3, whereas those for whom it is laid up will be paid their due: ὁ πατήρ ... ἀποδώσει 6,4, the choice of expression in all cases indicating a metaphor in which the Father is as it were the banker with whom one has an account).

279. The use of the future indicative in the NT has undergone **Semitic influence** in three ways: a) it is sometimes used **modally** like the Semitic form which often connotes only what *may* be, e. g. Mt 7,4 πῶς ἐρεῖς τῷ ἀδελφῷ σου, which Lk 6,42 renders πῶς δύνασαι λέγειν... — Similarly Mt 5,43 καὶ μισήσεις τὸν ἐχθρόν σου where the future may indicate lawfulness (« you may hate ») so that Joüon renders « Tu aimeras ton proche mais tu pourras ne pas aimer ton ennemi ».

280. b) Much more frequently, and in the legal language of the OT almost always, the future is used as a **categorical imperative,** as in the place just cited: ἀγαπήσεις τὸν πλησίον σου, or Mt 5,21 οὐ φονεύσεις, cf. verses 27 and 33, or Mt 21,13 « my house shall be called a house of prayer » where κληθήσεται in accordance with the Hebrew use of the corresponding verb is practically equivalent to ἔσται: « shall be and shall be acknowledged as ». — The same usage is sometimes found outside quotations from the OT, e. g. where the angel says to Mary: « thou shalt call his name Jesus » Lk 1,31, a future which is perhaps to be understood not simply as a prediction (like the preceding ones « thou shalt conceive... and bring forth a son ») but as a command (cf. 1,13). So too Mt 21,2 « if anyone says... ἐρεῖτε (= say!) ». — The future of εἶναι in particular is used in imperative sense « let ... be », e. g. Mk 9,35 « if anyone wish to be first, ἔσται ... the servant of all » (cf. Mt 23,11).

281. It is to be noted however that what we have ascribed in the preceding two paragraphs to a possible Semitic influence has nothing (save perhaps its frequency) which has no counterpart in Greek usage. This is not the case for what follows: c) Occasionally in a « Semitizing » text, a future which it is difficult to account for may be simply neglected and rendered by a present or an imperfect, on the supposition that the future is a servile rendering of a Hebrew imperfect, for this latter is often used with future sense, but is of itself atemporal, expressing only an « aspect » similar to that of the Greek « present » (and imperfect, therefore) whether for present or past or future time. Thus Rev 4,9f καὶ ὅταν δώσουσιν τὰ ζῷα δόξαν... πεσοῦνται οἱ... πρεσβύτεροι... καὶ προσκυνήσουσιν... καὶ βαλοῦσιν where the Vulgate seems to be right in rendering the futures by imperfects; or they might be rendered by the present, if John be taken as describing the habitual order of the heavenly liturgy rather than a particular vision of it; cf. 5,8f; 11,16f; 19,41 (BONACCORSI).

207   282. The future participle in particular drops to a great extent out of use. Luke is almost alone (and in the Acts only) in sometimes using it classically to indicate the purpose of a movement, e. g. ἀνέβην προσκυνήσων 24,11 (cf. 8,27; 22,5; 24,17). Even in other uses the future participle is very rare, e. g. again in Acts 20,22 « I go to Jerusalem, not knowing τὰ συναντήσοντά μοι there ». The future participle is not found in the gospels without a variant reading (cf. Mt 27,49; Lk 22,49; Jo 6,64); in the epistles cf. Rom 8,34; 1 Pet 3,15; 2 Pet 2,13 (variant reading).

208   283. In place of the future participle the present one is used (as in Hebrew and Aramaic), e. g. Mt 26,25 Ἰούδας ὁ παραδιδοὺς αὐτὸν εἶπεν « who was to betray Him »; Mt 25,14 « a certain man ἀποδημῶν » where the context shows the sense to be future. In Jo 17,20 Our Lord says, in the priestly discourse « I ask not for these alone but also περὶ τῶν πιστευόντων », meaning those who « are to believe » and there is thus no force in the argument that since the participle is present the words are those not of Christ but of John. So too Lk 2,34 « a sign to be contradicted » σημεῖον ἀντιλεγόμενον, cf. also Lk 1,35 τὸ γεννώμενον « what is to be born »; Lk 14,31; Acts 21,2f; 26,17.

This must be borne in mind in interpreting the words of institution of the Eucharist Lk 22,19f: τοῦτό ἐστιν τὸ σῶμά μου τὸ ὑπὲρ ὑμῶν διδόμενον (« given for you », which may be understood atemporally) ... τοῦτο τὸ ποτήριον τὸ ὑπὲρ ὑμῶν ἐκχυννόμενον (« shed for you », likewise). A theological argument in favour of the sacrificial character of the Last Supper cannot be based on the mere fact that the participles are present ones (on the grounds that if the reference were to the sacrifice of the cross the future would have been used).

284. The question may be raised, whether the present participle may not at times stand for the future one indicating the end in view, in which case the present participle would itself take on a possible final sense. In Mt 20,20 we have: τότε προσῆλθεν αὐτῷ ἡ μήτηρ... προσκυνοῦσα καὶ αἰτοῦσά τι παρ' αὐτοῦ, where αἰτοῦσα seems to mean the intention of asking; in any case the context puts the request as subsequent only. — So too in Mt 22,16 the pharisees « send to Him disciples λέγοντας » (variant reading). Cf. also Lk 2,45; 14,21; 15,27; 18,23; 19,18; 21,16; 2 Pet 2,9.

5) The Perfect

209   **285.** In essence, though not exactly in use, the Greek perfect tense corresponds to the English one, in that it is not a past tense but a present one, indicating not the past action as such but the present « state of affairs » resulting from the past action. An example of its use contrasted with that of the aorist is provided by Mk 6,14 where Herod, hearing of Our Lord's miracles, says Ἰωάννης... ἐγήγερται ἐκ νεκρῶν, « John is risen from the dead » (present state of affairs, cf. what follows: καὶ διὰ τοῦτο ἐνεργοῦσιν αἱ δυνάμεις ἐν αὐτῷ), whereas in verse 16 he says ὃν ἐγὼ ἀπεκεφάλισα Ἰωάννην, οὗτος ἠγέρθη, with the aorist, expressing the fact of past action (in English the perfect would again be expected; the sense of the aorist may be represented by turning the expression otherwise: « I decapitated John, but he rose again »).

210   **286.** The perfect has often much to offer towards the interpretation of the text. When the Jews say (Jo 9,29): « οἴδαμεν ὅτι Μωϋσεῖ λελάληκεν ὁ Θεός, but we know not whence this man is » the perfect is used instead of the aorist because the sense is of course not that of the simple historical fact « God spoke to Moses » but that of the resultant dignity of Moses as commissioned by God and not, like « this man », without credentials. This sense of the perfect (that Moses is one to whom « God has spoken ») is the essential one for what the Jews are here saying; but it must be noted that the

same perfect has for them a further meaning, namely that what God said to Moses was said once for all and immutably: God « has spoken ». On the other hand, Our Lord Himself, speaking of the same divine declarations, uses the aorist: ἠκούσατε ὅτι ἐρρέθη τοῖς ἀρχαίοις ... because the sense is simply « it was said » as a fact of history, and moreover, not destined to immutability, for He goes on ἐγὼ δὲ λέγω ὑμῖν ... Mt 5,21f.

211 287. In Col 1,16f St Paul establishes Christ's universal primacy on the grounds ὅτι ἐν αὐτῷ ἐκτίσθη τὰ πάντα (aorist: historical fact). Christ is however not only the efficient cause (δι' αὐτοῦ) but also the final cause (εἰς αὐτόν) and as such is even more in the present (and future) than in the past; hence to describe this state of affairs Paul now uses the perfect: πάντα δι'αὐτοῦ καὶ εἰς αὐτὸν ἔκτισται, and adds by way of conclusion: καὶ τὰ πάντα ἐν αὐτῷ συνέστηκεν, a perfect expressing the fact that we and the universe have in Christ our subsistance, our internal cohesion, an intimate relation with one another and with the universe. — What Christ's resurrection was for Paul, namely the beginning, once and for all, of the new αἰών, which is ours, is well illustrated by his use of a perfect along with three aorists in 1 Cor 15,3: « Christ died (ἀπέθανεν) for our sins ... and was buried (ἐτάφη) and is risen (ἐγήγερται — but English has to use past instead of the perfect on account of the following « on the third day ») ... and He appeared (ὤφθη) to Cephas ». — For Jo cf. μεμίσηκεν 15,18. 24.

212 288. It is to be noted that the choice between aorist and perfect is not determined by the objective facts, but by the writer's wish to connote the special nuance of the perfect; if this be not required, the aorist will be used. The use of the perfect in the NT thus shows that the author has in mind the notion of a state of affairs resultant upon the action.

213 289. This has indeed been questioned, because the perfect in later Greek use lost its specific sense and became a **simple narrative tense** like the aorist (*), so that the question arises, whether there are not traces of this

---

(*) This merging of aorist and perfect has resulted for modern Greek in the extinction of the perfect as a distinct simple form, its place having been taken, for the expression of the perfect aspect, by compound forms (normally

evolution in the NT. It is more commonly admitted that there are not, for the examples alleged nearly all allow of other explanations: πέπρακα is used for the aorist because πιπράσκω has no active aorist; ἔσχηκα is used for «I had» Mc 5,15 because the aorist ἔσχον would have given the sense «I took» (¹⁰); γέγονα either has the full sense of the perfect or the evolved one (still not aorist, but present like the perfect) «I am» (¹¹); εἴληφα and εἴρηκα, to be found in Rev only (5,7; 8,5; 7,14; 19,3), are the forms which in contemporary papyri are found as aorists, which suggests that owing to the lack of clearly discernible reduplication they were popularly regarded not as perfects but as aorists.

6) The Pluperfect *Past state of affairs, not present*

214   290. The pluperfect in the NT as in classical use, is simply the past tense corresponding to the (present) perfect, i. e. it indicates a past state of affairs constituted by an action still further in the past; e. g. the parents of the man born blind feared the Jews because these «had agreed (συνετέθειντο) that anyone who acknowledged Jesus as Messiah should be banned from the synagogue» Jo 9,22, and the arrangement still stood. It is to be noted that since Greek does note express relative time as such, the pluperfect is *not* used simply because the action denoted was prior to the past time of the main verb or the narration in general (as Latin or English would use the pluperfect): Greek uses simply the aorist or imperfect according to the aspect required. Thus Mk 6,17 after recounting Herod's notion that Christ was John the Baptist come to life again, inserts the account of the beheading of John beginning simply with an aorist: Herod ἀποστείλας ἐκράτησεν ..., which has to be rendered into English, since it goes back in time, by «*had* sent and arrested...»; in Mk 5,8 the possessed man cries «do not torment me; ἔλεγεν γὰρ αὐτῷ Ἰησοῦς

---

e. g. active ἔχω λύσει and passive ἔχω λυθεῖ, where λύσει and λυθεῖ are forms derived from the aorist stems and regarded as «infinitives» though they are not used as such but only in the formation of the perfect; another formation uses the perfect participle passive: active ἔχω δεμένο, passive εἶμαι δεμένος).

(¹⁰) It may be doubted whether this assertion is correct, cf. Mt 22,28; Mk 2,25; 14,8; Jo 4,17; Gal 4,22; 1 Jo 2,28.

(¹¹) but Mt 25, 6?; 1 Cor 13, 11 ?!

ἔξελθε . . . » where the sense seems to be that Jesus *had* said this. Hence there is no linguistic objection to avoiding the apparent difficulty in « (the parents of Jesus) οὐ συνῆκαν τὸ ῥῆμα ὃ ἐλάλησεν αὐτοῖς » Lk 2,50 by rendering it «. . . had not understood . . . had said . . . » (i. e. before the departure from Jerusalem).

291. Just as the aorist or imperfect, where relative anteriority is involved, may correspond to an English pluperfect, so too the participles (aorist, or present standing for an imperfect) may have to be rendered so as to express the relative time which they themselves do not express. The rendering of an aorist participle by « having -ed » is too usual to need exemplification; for the present participle cf. Mt 14,21; 15,38 οἱ ἐσθίοντες = « those who had eaten »; Lk 23,49 the women αἱ συνακολουθοῦσαι (« who had followed ») Him from Galilee stood by the cross.

X. THE MOODS

215   295. As ideas of what constitutes a « mood » are often somewhat vague, some explanation may not be out of place here. In any verbal enunciation we may distinguish between the action expressed and the manner in which it is envisaged. The verbal « voices » and « tenses » regard the action itself (the voices relating it to its subject, the tenses fixing it in time — or, as aspects, exhibiting it simply or as in progress etc.).

The « moods » or manners of envisaging the action regard the degree of actuality which is attributed to it, or rather, its relation to actuality: an action may be represented simply as realized (the indicative) or as an eventuality (subjunctive) or possibility (optative) or as to be realized by another (imperative).

We say that the action is « represented », not that it is « asserted » or « affirmed », because often there is no assertion or affirmation, e. g. in questions, exhortations etc.

296. The « moods » thus express various mental attitudes to the reality of the act in question (¹). It is of great importance not to lose sight of this subjective character possessed by the moods no less than by the aspects. What matters is how the act is conceived by the speaker, not its objective nature. E. g. Jo 13,8 ἐὰν μὴ νίψω σε οὐκ ἔχεις μέρος μετ' ἐμοῦ one might have expected the future (as the Vulgate translates) since we have a condition regarding the future; but the speaker conceives and expresses the matter as already actual, with the present indicative, which adds to the urgency of the warning.

(¹) « Die Modusformen beziehen sich lediglich auf die geistige Auffassung des Redenden », KÜHNER-GERTH II, 1, p. 202. Hence ancient grammarians called them διαθέσεις ψυχῆς, and cf. the non-grammatical sense of the word « mood » in English. The infinitive and the participle are in this sense not « moods » since they do not express of themselves such an attitude: the infinitive is rather a verbal substantive (naming the action) and the participle a verbal adjective (associating it with a subject), and in use they may correspond to, and so share the characteristics of, the various « moods » (when they take the place of finite verbs).

297. The subjunctive, it was said, represents an action as an «eventuality », i. e. as in some way lacking actuality: a more apt term than that sometimes used, « probability ». Hence in main clauses it is used in exhortations (« let us . . . ») and in prohibitions with the aorist (μή and aorist subjunctive, e. g. μὴ μεριμνήσητε, and not — as with prohibitions with the « present » aspect — the imperative) and in deliberations (τί ποιήσωμεν;) where NB that the mood corresponds, as is logical, to that of the corresponding affirmative — or negative — reply; so τί ποιήσομεν; regards simply a future fact, ποιήσομεν . . . , whereas τί ποιήσωμεν is answered by ποιήσωμεν . . . « let us do (this) » similarly in rhetorical questions referring to the future as Lk 11,5 τίς ὑμῶν ἕξει φίλον καὶ εἴπῃ αὐτῷ or Lk 23,31 « if this be done in the green wood, in the dry τί γένηται ».

298. In subordinate clauses the general rule for Greek is that the same mood is used in indirect speech as would have been in the direct speech (as also the same «tense »), in both principal and subordinate clauses (the exceptions to this rule are the substitution of infinitive or participle for other moods, and the possible use of the optative in place of indicative or [ἄν +] subjunctive in historic narration, cf. 346).

1) The Moods in Conditional Clauses

299. A conditional proposition of itself asserts merely the connection between what is enunciated by its two clauses, the subordinate one which proposes a condition (and so is called protasis, from προτείνω) and the main one which declares the outcome (apodosis) connected with it.

300. Originally the two clauses, however close their association, were syntactically independent (as. e. g. « do this and thou shalt live » = « if thou do this thou shalt live »), and despite the subordination of the protasis this independence remains inasmuch as each of the two clauses has its own mood according to its own sense; it is only because the mood required depends in the nature of things from the same situation for each clause, that certain correspondences between the moods are usual.

301. Conditions may be particular or general ones, according as they regard a particular event in the concrete (e. g. « if he did that, he was wrong », « if he is coming he will be here soon ») or a kind of event in general (e. g. « if he were to do that, he would be wrong », « if [ever] » he comes, tell him . . . »). It is to be noted that the use of the one form or the other depends largely on the intention of the speaker; thus what is in fact a particular case may be referred to in a general expression, e. g. « if (ever) anyone thinks that he is wrong » may in the circumstances be a less direct way of saying « if (some definite person) thinks that (here and now) he is wrong »; just as with the form of a particular condition the word « anyone » may cover in fact a particular person, as 1 Cor 3,12. 14. 15. 17, where Paul seems to be speaking in general since he says « if *anyone's* work . . . » etc., but the form is that of a concrete condition (εἰ and the indicative, not ἐάν and the subjunctive), which suggests that Paul is in fact thinking of a particular case or cases.

302. Of the six classes of conditionals distinguished by certain grammarians, **five classes** occur in the NT, namely A) the simple or « real » condition (the concrete case), B) the « unreal » one, C) the « eventual » or « probable » one, D) the « possible » one, and E) the « universal » one.

224 **303.** A) In **simple conditions**, for particular cases whether in the past or in the present (or in the future, but here only if the future event is to be presented in very concrete fashion, otherwise the « eventual » form is used), the condition and its consequence are simply stated without reference to whether the condition is in fact fulfilled or not: εἰ with the indicative (normally; theoretically with any form which without the εἰ would make a principal statement) in the protasis; in the apodosis the form required by the meaning to be expressed, which is expressed as it would have been expressed independently of the condition (e. g. indicative: « if he did that, he was wrong »; imperative: « if he did that, punish him »; subjunctive: « if he did that, let us punish him »; optative: « if he did that, may God punish him; infinitive or participle where these replace any of the other moods). In the NT e. g. Jo 15,20 εἰ ἐμὲ ἐδίωξαν καὶ ὑμᾶς διώξουσιν; Gal 5,18 εἰ δὲ πνεύματι ἄγεσθε, οὐκ ἐστὲ ὑπὸ νόμου; cf. Mt 4,3; Lk 16,11; 22,42; Acts 5,39; Rom 4,2; 8,10; Gal 2,17; Rev 20,15.

304. Very often (not to say always, for the NT) this form is used in cases where the fulfilment or non-fulfilment of the condition is in fact known or supposed; but this circumstance is to be gathered from the context; the grammatical form is indifferent to it, and means simply what it says, namely « if..., then... ».

305. It is nevertheless obvious that in this form of condition the fulfilment of the condition (including that of a negative one) is in a certain sense « supposed » i. e. taken as a basis of argument, in the sense that « If A, then B » may be paraphrased « let us suppose that A is true; it then follows that B is true »; hence the name « real » condition which is also given to the « simple » condition. The supposition in question, i. e. the treatment of the matter as a concrete case, is naturally often called for by the introduction, in what precedes, of such a case, so that εἰ may often be rendered « if therefore » or « if indeed ».

218   306. Thus the «reality» of the condition does not mean that the speaker regards the condition as fulfilled, indeed the opposite may be the case, but only that the condition in question is treated not as a generality but as a case which for one reason or another is a concrete one. Thus in Mt 12,26f καὶ εἰ ὁ σατανᾶς τὸν σατανᾶν ἐκβάλλει... καὶ εἰ ἐγὼ ἐν Βεελζεβοὺλ ἐκβάλλω τὰ δαιμόνια... we have a « real » condition (and the εἰ may be rendered « if in reality » or the like) but the fulfilment of the condition is obviously not admitted as real by the speaker; since however it had been asserted by His adversaries, it is a case which has been raised in the concrete and therefore a « real » condition (*). This is even better illustrated in the parallel text Mk 3, 24-26: here the question of Satan casting out Satan has been introduced, and the impossibility of this shown by three conditional propositions:

ἐὰν βασιλεία ἐφ᾽ ἑαυτὴν μερισθῇ, οὐ δύναται σταθῆναι
καὶ ἐὰν οἰκία ἐφ᾽ ἑαυτὴν μερισθῇ, οὐ δυνήσεται... στῆναι
καὶ εἰ σατανᾶς ἀνέστη ἐφ᾽ ἑαυτὸν... οὐ δύναται στῆναι.

Here the « real » condition of the third proposition (« real » as in Mt because it is the case proposed and being refuted) is offset by two generalities adduced to prove it: « if (ever, in general, hence not « real » condition) any kingdom... and if ever any house... and (in the particular

---

(*) Cf. e. g. ROBERTSON, Grammar, p. 1008: « This is a good example (cf. also Gal 5,11).... since the assumption is untrue in fact, though assumed to be true by Jesus for the sake of argument ».

case under discussion, hence «real» condition) if (therefore!) Satan...» (*).
Cf also Lk 16,30f; 23,37; 1 Cor 15,15; Gal 1,8f.

219   307. Let us now take an example in which the reason for the choice
between «real» conditions and generalities is not so obvious from the context as in the case discussed above. In Acts 5,38-39 Gamaliel urges his
colleagues to leave the apostles alone because if their work is of men it
will come to nothing, whereas if it is of God it cannot be brought to nothing.
In the Greek text, however the two conditions of this dilemma are differ-
ently expressed:

ἐὰν ᾖ ἐξ ἀνθρώπων... καταλυθήσεται
εἰ δὲ ἐκ θεοῦ ἐστιν, οὐ δυνήσεσθε καταλῦσαι

The latter condition, the «real» one, may well be rendered «but if in
fact...», but this does not necessarily imply that Gamaliel thought
that this was the fact. He might indeed have been led to use the «real»
form of condition because in his opinion it was «real» in the sense that
the condition was fulfilled; but he may equally have expressed the condition as a «real» one for the same reason as in the case discussed in the
last paragraph, namely because this was the contention of the apostles,
and so the concrete supposition to be discussed; but even apart from this
there is yet another psychological explanation of the use of a «real» condition for the second member despite the generality of the other member
(in fact, both members might have been expected to be expressed as «real»
conditions, since they represent immediate suppositions under discussion;
but since the former member is expressed as a generality the expression
of the latter one as a «real» condition calls for explanation): in a sense,
the condition «if it be of God» is a more actual and pressing one (and
hence calls for expression as a «real» condition); if the work happens to
be of men, it does not matter very much what is done about it; but if
in fact it is of God it matters very much!

220   308. It is an astonishing fact that even scholars sometimes overlook
what has just been said and seem to forget that, εἰ even in a «real» condition still means «if» and not «because» or the like.

(*) There is therefore no need to take the third member as «unreal»
(as e. g. RADERMACHER, ed. 2, p. 176), though both sense and form would
here allow it to be taken as such.

Thus on the example just cited (Acts 5,38) we read in Radermacher (⁴) « the distinction in the speech of the Pharisee Gamaliel is a very significant one, and indeed one which seems to show (« die wohl lehrt ») that this discourse . . . has received from the author of the Acts a form unconsciously influenced by that author's own opinion » (i. e. that of Luke). He then remarks to ἐὰν (ἡ ἐξ ἀνθρώπων) « as the foes of Christianity think . . . », and to εἰ δὲ ἐκ θεοῦ ἐστιν « this then (in the speaker's view) is the fact ». « Gamaliel himself would more properly have formulated these two conditions vice versa. But here the speaker is the author of the Acts, who is convinced of the truth of his doctrine » (⁵). — From what has been said above it is obvious that this conclusion, so categorically expressed, is unfounded, since such an explanation is only one among several which would suffice to account for the text (cf. those given at the end of the preceding paragraph).

221   **309.** In the account of the Transfiguration Mt 17,4 we read: « Lord, it is good for us to be here; if it is thy wish (εἰ θέλεις), let us make three tabernacles . . . »; here the « real » condition is in any case normal, as the reference is to the particular present circumstance; but one may also suspect that the impetuous Peter in fact anticipates as it were the fulfilment of the condition and regards it to some extent as a « real » i. e. « realized » one (cf. the main verb ποιήσωμεν « let us make » of the reading rendered above; Merk's text has however ποιήσω, which might be future), and means in effect « unless you forbid us ».

On the other hand the leper says, Mt 8,2 « Lord, if it be thy wish (ἐὰν θέλῃς) thou canst cleanse me ». The choice of an « eventual » or « general » condition instead of a « real » one does not imply the least doubt even as to the Lord's good will (it is of course obvious that there is no doubt as to the Lord's power); for it is to be accounted for simply by the speaker's modesty and restraint; instead of saying « if you wish (here and now) you can cleanse me (= please do so, here and now) », he says « if ever you wish, you can (at any time) cleanse me (= I trust you will have mercy on me in your own good time) ».

222   **310.** In Lk 17,6 we have: εἰ ἔχετε (« real » condition) πίστιν . . ἐλέγετε ἄν . . . (« unreal » apodosis). The « unreal » apodosis might seem to call for an « unreal » protasis, but on reflection it is seen that this is not

---

(⁴) *Neutestamentliche Grammatik*, ed. 2, 1925, p. 176.

(⁵) The same interpretation is to be found in F. JACKSON and K. LAKE, *The Beginnings of Christianity*, II, p. 29f (following RADERMACHER): « Here the author betrays himself as composer of the speech as he unconsciously has stepped into the place of the person speaking ».

the case. The protasis is « real » because it regards a present concrete question (and does *not* suppose that the condition is unfulfilled, or at least, the form does not express this supposition), for Our Lord is replying to the apostles' request « increase our faith », which supposes that they have faith, and in his reply Our Lord takes up this proposed (and thus « real ») condition: « if you have indeed faith (as you suppose) ... ». As for the apodosis, it expresses what follows on that supposition, but the « unreal » form is called for by the subject matter: « you would say to this tree: be uprooted and carried into the sea, and it would obey you », which is a paratactic way of saying « *if* you said ... it would obey you », an « unreal » supposition independently of the realization or non-realization of the condition (i. e. as is obvious, the fact of having faith does not necessarily imply that they *would* use it to transport the tree! — but only that that would be possible). Our Lord's thought and expression is thus more complex than appears in the Vulgate and other versions, and the example illustrates the independence of syntax in the apodosis (cf. 300, 303).

223 311. There are other cases too in which a condition which might have been expected to take the « unreal » form of expression takes instead the « real » one, e. g. Mk 9,42 and its parallel Lk 17,2 of the man who should scandalize « one of these little ones »: καλόν ἐστιν αὐτῷ μᾶλλον εἰ περίκειται μύλος ὀνικὸς περὶ τὸν τράχηλον αὐτοῦ καὶ βέβληται εἰς τὴν θάλασσαν. There is no need here to speak as some do of grammatical incongruity and prefer for that reason the variant reading of D and W which have the « unreal » forms περιέκειτο and ἐβλήθη (*). It seems to me rather that there is a great depth of meaning in this remarkable and almost violent use of the « real » type of expression instead of the « unreal », one, as if Our Lord wished to represent as vividly as possible (with the perfect!) « that man is well off thrown into the sea ... ». Somewhat similarly Gal 5,11: ἐγὼ δέ, ἀδελφοί, εἰ ἔτι περιτομὴν κηρύσσω, τί ἔτι διώκομαι; Here the condition is certainly objectively unrealized, and one might have expected the « unreal » form, and a straightforward apodosis οὐκέτι ἐδιωκόμην ἄν. The unlooked-for deviation from the normal mode of expression calls attention to the great vivacity and emotion of the passage:

(*) Debrunner 371,3 « Übergriff in das Gebiet des Irrealis ». Zorell (εἰ 1,1, c) « εἰ cum praes. aliquoties ponitur pro condicione irreali ».

the subject is placed in the emphatic initial position: « As for me, brethren . . . », the condition is expressed not as « unreal » but as « suppose I still preach circumcision », and for the apodosis a rhetorical question is substituted. Cf. also 2 Cor 11,4; Jo 8,39.

312. We may thus say, in brief: the « real » type of condition puts the condition simply as such, in the concrete, and so at least « supposes » the condition as realized (as an element of argument), and indeed frequently the realization of the condition is believed or even asserted in the context by the speaker or another.

229   313. B) « Unreal » condition: the protasis represents the condition as not in fact realized, using (even if the time referred to is not past but present or even future) a historic « tense » of the indicative (aorist, imperfect, or pluperfect, according to the aspect desired and quite independently of the time referred to), while the apodosis likewise uses a historic « tense » of the indicative (not, of course, necessarily the same tense as the protasis, since the aspect desired need not be the same) with the particle ἄν (it may thus be noted that the only formal distinction between an « unreal » condition and a « real » one referring to past time is the ἄν in the apodosis).

314. As was said in the preceding paragraph, the choice of « tense » whether in protasis or in apodosis depends entirely on the aspect and not on the time referred to; and it is all the more necessary to note this, in that some defective grammars teach that « the aorist is used of past time and the imperfect of present time ». In the nature of things the aorist normally refers to past time (there is no « present aorist » in the indicative) and to refer to present time it is normal that the imperfect be used (being of the same aspect as the present indicative); but what of the case in which past time is referred to, but in the « present » aspect, i. e. where the simple statement in the indicative would use the imperfect? Clearly, the « unreal » condition will likewise use the imperfect. — For examples in the NT of imperfect for present time and aorist for past time cf. Jo 18,36: « if my kingdom were (ἦν) of this world, my servants would strive (ἄν . . . ἠγωνίζοντο) . . . » and Mt 11,21: « if in Tyre the miracles had come to pass (ἐγένοντο) . . . , they would have done penance (ἄν . . . μετενόησαν) ».

315. The following paragraphs however give examples in which the false rule just referred to does not hold, since the imperfect is used with reference to past time (316) or the aorist for other than past time (317).

316. Imperfect for « unreal » past: Mt 23,30: εἰ ἤ μ ε θ α ἐν ταῖς ἡμέραις τῶν πατέρων ἡμῶν, οὐκ ἄν ἤ μ ε θ α αὐτῶν κοινωνοί — but of course some may say: the reference is not to past but to present time; we are not transferred to the time of our fathers, but that time to us: « if were we (now!) in the time of our fathers... » — As for the explanation that the imperfect is used because εἶναι has no aorist, it is obvious that if the writer had wanted an aorist would have used γενέσθαι, as is usual in Greek including the NT); cf. also Jo 11,21. 32. — But Heb 8,7 has: « for if the former (convenant) had been irreproachable (ἦν ἄμεμπτος) place would not have been sought (οὐκ ἄν... ἐζητεῖτο) for a second one »; and — an especially clear example — Heb 11,15 says that the patriarchs regarded themselves as in exile on earth, meaning that they sought a fatherland, but this was not the one they had left, because « if they had been thinking of (ἐμνημόνευον) the one they had left, they would have had (εἶχον ἄν) time to return to it »: the reason for the « present » aspect is obvious from the meaning of the verbs: permanent state and not definitive act.

317. Aorist of present time (rarer for the reason mentioned above, the normal inapplicability of the aorist aspect to real present time but here the « present » is the atemporal one): Lk 12,39 = Mt 24,43: « if the master of the house knew (ᾔδει which is a pluperfect form) at what hour the thief was to come, he would of course watch (ἐγρηγόρησεν ἄν, aorist) and not let (οὐκ ἄν εἴασεν) his house be burglarized ». This perhaps suggests a « gnomic » use of the aorist (256) or the frequent use of the aorist in parables, but the aptness of the aorist aspect is obvious (definite act, and the definitive prevention of the burglary; one might indeed say that the imperfect [= « present » aspect = watching habitually and warding off burglary in general] would have been apter if the master of the house did not know when the thief was to come but of course it could have been used here in the sense of « would be watching »). — In Mt 24,22 the reference is to the (eschatological) future, and the aorist is used: εἰ μὴ ἐκολοβώθησαν αἱ ἡμέραι ἐκεῖναι οὐκ ἄν ἐσώθη πᾶσα σάρξ (but here some refer to the prophetic use of the past to represent vividly the future!). — In Jo 14,28: εἰ ἠγαπᾶτέ με, ἐχάρητε ἄν... the imperfect is used in the protasis and the aorist in the apodosis; surely we are not to attempt to understand the sense as being « if you loved me now you would have rejoiced in the past... »; it seems clear enough that the reference is to a present situation but without the present expression of the joy as « you would be glad ». (If one wishes to render the aspect in English one may say: « If you loved me, your reaction would be one of joy »). Cf. Acts 18,14; Jo 15,22; 19,11.

318. Whatever may be said in favour of the various reasons adduced to account for these uses as departing from the « rule » that associates the choice of tense with the time referred to, it will be plain to anyone who is accustomed (as those who formulated the « rule » were not) to « aspectual » verbal usage, that the real reason for the choice of « tense » is the choice of aspect (in any case it is obvious that the « tenses » used, though indicative, do not have their normal temporal values) (').

230   **319.** The particle ἄν in the apodosis was ordinarily omitted in classical usage with verbs meaning obligation, fitness, necessity etc., e. g. καλὸν ἦν, ἔδει, ἔχρην. In Hellenistic usage this omission is extended to other verbs, e. g. Gal 4,15: εἰ δυνατόν, τοὺς ὀφθαλμοὺς ὑμῶν ... ἐδώκατέ μοι (without ἄν).

225   **320. C) Eventual** (« probable ») **conditions** of the future: a future eventuality (commonly enough « probable » to a greater or less degree, but the term « probable » is misleading as applied to this class of condition, as it may quite properly be used of an eventuality regarded as highly unlikely to arise) is expressed by ἐάν with the subjunctive in the protasis, the apodosis being free to use any form permitted by the circumstances of the expression; e. g. Mt 21,3 Our Lord sends two disciples to bring him the ass and foal for His entry into Jerusalem, adding « and if anyone says (ἐάν ... εἴπῃ) anything to you, you shall say (ἐρεῖτε) ... ». Irony (as well as the wish to conceal one's opinion) allows the use of this form for an impossible condition, treated simply as an eventuality, as when God says Ps 49,12 (LXX; Hebrew 50,12) ἐὰν πεινάσω, οὐ μή σοι εἴπω, ἐμὴ γάρ ἐστιν ἡ οἰκουμένη ... — This type of condition is not really distinct from the type E, as may be seen by posing the question to which type one is to assign e. g. Jo 14,15 ἐὰν ἀγαπᾶτέ με, τὰς ἐντολὰς τηρήσετε or (all the more as the subject is indefinite) verse 23 of the same chapter: ἐάν τις ἀγαπᾷ με, τὸν λόγον μου τηρήσει ... (cf. 327).

321. The subjunctive of this type of condition is sometimes found without explicit conditional form (i. e. without ἐάν, even the ἄν which

---

(') We read in fact in E. SCHWYZER - A. DEBRUNNER, *Griechische Grammatik,* p. 348f; 686: « Für die Wahl des Tempus ist der Aspekt massgebend », i. e. even in « unreal » conditions the « tense » is chosen according to the aspect desired. Cf. J. HUMBERT, *Syntaxe grecque,* § 285.

should accompany the mood being thus absent) e. g. Lk 11,5 - 7: τίς ἕξει
φίλον καὶ ε ἴ π η αὐτῷ... κἀκεῖνος ἔσωθεν ἀποκριθεὶς ε ἴ π η... (or is this
to be assigned to type E?); cf. in the LXX Eccl. 9,14 an entire passage
with four subjunctives.

226　　　**322.** The use of this type of condition, instead of the « real » type,
is normal whenever the reference is to the future (where the use of the
« real » type would insist explicitly on the concrete conception of the future event), so that its use instead of εἰ + future indicative does not imply
anything as to the speaker's opinion of the likeliness of the condition (does
not, e. g. imply that he doubts its fulfilment, except of course in so far as
any expression in conditional form means « if .. » and not « when... »).
E. g. on 1 Cor 16,10 ἐ ὰ ν δὲ ἔλθῃ Τιμόθεος ALLO admits that the use of
ἐάν certainly implies a doubt, and shows by a long psychological consideration that this doubt is not incompatible with the certainty which Paul
expresses in 4,17 (ἔπεμψα ὑμῖν Τιμόθεον), so that J. WEISS was not justified in rejecting the unity of the epistle on account of this « contradiction ».
As we have said, the argument in favour of Paul's doubt may be accepted
in so far as it is founded on the use of a conditional instead of a temporal
clause (ἐάν instead of ὅταν) (*) but the fact that condition is expressed by
ἐάν with the subjunctive in particular, as distinct from εἰ with the indicative, is completely irrelevant, so long as the form is not an « unreal » one.

228　　　**323.** D) A « possible » condition, of itself atemporal, but in the nature of things referring commonly, for practical purposes, to the future,
is expressed by a protasis with the optative (but the protasis is often
not expressed) and an apodosis with ἄν and the optative, the choice of
« tense » being in both clauses determined by the aspect desired. There
is no complete example of this in the NT, but an apodosis without express protasis is found 1 Cor 14,10; 15,37; 1 Pet 3,14; 3,17. Note that
the choice of this form (like that of a general condition ἐάν + subjunctive referring in fact to a particular case) depends on the speaker's intention; thus in 1 Pet 3,14 we have ἀλλ' εἰ καὶ π ά σ χ ο ι τ ε διὰ δικαιοσύνην,
μακάριοι and again verse 17 « it is better to suffer for doing good, εἰ θέ-

---

(*) « perhaps » because « gelegentlich kommt die Bedeutung des ἐάν sehr
nahe an die von ὅταν heran (Is 24,23; Amos 7,2; 1 Jo 2,28; Jo 12,32; 14,3;
1 Cor 16,10; 2 Cor 5,1; 13,2; Col 4,10; Heb 3,7) » W. BAUER, Griech. - Deutsches
Wörterbuch, under ἐάν 1 d.

λοι τὸ θέλημα τοῦ θεοῦ, than for doing evil ». In both cases the condition is expressed as a theoretical possibility (type D) rather than as an envisaged eventuality (type C, E), although St Peter well knows that in fact such sufferings are eminently probable in the Christian life, and indeed perhaps already a reality for his readers. His tact, however, leads him, when speaking of sufferings to those who are seeking to avoid them, to put the matter on the theoretical plane.

324. This point is not without its importance for exegesis: it is well known that a difficulty has been seen in the fact that in the first part of St Peter's first epistle (1.3-4,11) the trials of the Christians are spoken of in an almost hypothetical manner (1,6; 3,17) whereas later (4,12ff) concrete trials are presupposed. For Preisker this offers grounds for the view that 1 Peter is a baptismal liturgy set down in writing, the first part being for catecumens, the second part for the entire Christian community.

227

325. E) A general (universal) condition in the (atemporal) present, referring to any case of the kind expressed, uses ἐάν with the subjunctive in the protasis, and any form of general expression (commonly though not necessarily the present indicative) in the apodosis, e. g. Jo 11,9: ἐάν τις περιπατῇ ἐν τῇ ἡμέρᾳ οὐ προσκόπτει or 2 Tim 2,5: ἐὰν δὲ καὶ ἀθλῇ τις, οὐ στεφανοῦται, ἐὰν μὴ νομίμως ἀθλήσῃ. Cf. also Mk 3,24; Jo 7,51; 12,24; 1 Cor 7,39f.

326. A condition which is objectively a general one may be (more vividly) expressed as a concrete « real » condition, i. e. with εἰ and the indicative (cf. **301** above), e. g. Lk 14,26: εἴ τις ἔρχεται πρός με καὶ οὐ μισεῖ... τὴν ψυχὴν ἑαυτοῦ, οὐ δύναται εἶναί μου μαθητής.

327. The distinction between types C and E, though certain grammarians make it, is not a linguistic or grammatical one, but a purely extrinsic one based on the subject-matter (and on an analysis according to the speech-habits of some other language than Greek): cf. above, end of **320** and e. g. Jo 8,31: ἐὰν ὑμεῖς μείνητε ἐν τῷ λόγῳ τῷ ἐμῷ, ἀληθῶς μαθηταί μού ἐστε or 1 Jo 1,9 ἐὰν ὁμολογῶμεν τὰς ἁμαρτίας ἡμῶν, πιστός ἐστιν καὶ δίκαιος ἵνα ἀφῇ ἡμῖν... where likewise it is superfluous to ask oneself to which class the example is to be assigned. Cf. also Mk 1,40; Jo 19,12.

328. A universal condition in the past (« if A happened B would happen », the meaning being « whenever A happened, B used to happen ») was classically expressed by a protasis with εἰ and the optative, and an apodosis with the imperfect indicative (normally, because of the meaning; but other forms are possible). The dropping out of use of the « historic-sequence » optative has left the NT with no examples of this form (for the form which could take its place cf. 358).

329. The **relative independence** between protasis and apodosis (and so the subjective nature of the moods) is clear from cases where protasis and apodosis belong to what are, in the classification of certain grammarians (who associate too rigidly the types of protasis and of apodosis), different « types », e. g.

a) Acts 8,31 πῶς γὰρ ἂν δυναίμην (apodosis of type D used, as always in the NT, absolutely, i. e. without the formally corresponding protasis), ἐὰν μή τις ὁδηγήσῃ με (type C of protasis; as we said above, 320, the apodosis may use any form according to what is to be expressed; here that form happens to be the one above).

b) Mt 8,31 εἰ ἐκβάλλεις ἡμᾶς, ἀπόστειλον ἡμᾶς... (a « real » condition; apodosis syntactically free, and here the imperative is called for but some grammars make it seem that the imperative, since it refers to the future, should be regarded as an apodosis for type C); and cf. Mt 5,29 30; 18,8 9; Lk 14,26; 1 Cor 9,11; 2 Tim 2,12.

c) Lk 17,6 εἰ ἔχετε..., ἐλέγετε ἄν (a « real » protasis, the a-podosis, syntactically free, being in the form of an « unreal » one used absolutely, its formally corresponding one being suppressed, or rather, used as a paratactically expressed protasis itself, cf. above, 310).

330. What has been said above concerning conditional clauses applies equally to classical and to Hellenistic Greek. The **anomalies** of Hellenistic usage in this matter can be reduced to a certain confusion between the particles ἄν (ἐάν) and εἰ.

331. Thus we have ἐάν with the future, e. g. Lk 19,40 ἐάν οὗτοι σιωπήσουσιν, οἱ λίθοι κράξουσιν (cf. Rev 2,22) and even with the present indicative: ἐὰν οἴδαμεν, ὅτι ἀκούει ἡμῶν... 1 Jo 5,15 (cf. 1 Thess 3,8). In the former example Our Lord is replying to the Pharisees who have asked Him to bid his disciples be silent; other example is preceded by: « this is the confidence which we have . . . that (the Son of God) hears us »; hence in the latter case εἰ and not ἐάν was to be expected; in the former case ἐάν with the subjunctive would have been quite normal, but εἰ with the future indicative is probably intended, since the condition, though a future one, is a very concrete one (cf. 333).

332. On the other hand εἰ instead of ἐάν is found with the subjunctive, an anomaly very rare in classical usage but frequent in Hellenistic Greek and in the LXX in particular. Where it occurs in the NT it is almost always possible to point to a special reason for it. Thus Lk 9,13 the disciples reply « we have only five loaves, εἰ μήτι . . . ἡμεῖς ἀγοράσωμεν . . . βρώματα » where the subjunctive would be called for as « deliberative ». — In I Cor 14,5 ἐκτὸς εἰ μὴ διερμηνεύῃ the form εἰ μή is perhaps used as being a common formula, ἐάν μή being little used. The same seems to hold for the use, instead of ἐάντε, of εἴτε . . . εἴτε with the subjunctive in IThess 5,10 εἴτε γρηγορῶμεν εἴτε καθεύδωμεν.

333. Εἰ with the future (instead of ἐάν with the subjunctive) is of course perfectly correct and classical, so long as the condition is to be represented as a concrete one; in the NT it is found about twenty times, e. g. 2 Tim 2,12 εἰ ἀρνησόμεθα, κἀκεῖνος ἀρνήσεται ἡμᾶς.

334. It may be noted that in these anomalies the mood used is the one that might have been expected; the confusion is between the conjunctions εἰ and ἐάν (337).

2) In Relative Clauses

232   335. The importance of what has been said of conditional clauses, and in particular of the « real » type of condition and the « eventual » or « universal » one, is all the greater in that the same principles apply also to (indeterminate) relative clauses, under which heading are included, in addition to those introduced by relative pronouns (ὅς, ὅστις, ὅσος, οἷος etc.), those introduced by adverbs of time (ὅτε, ὡς, ἕως οὗ, ἄχρι οὗ etc.) or place (οὗ, ὅθεν etc.) or comparison (ὡς, καθώς, ὥσπερ etc.). An affinity between indeterminate relative clauses and conditional clauses is easily seen (cf. « he who says this is wrong », « if anyone says this, he is

wrong», «whenever» «wherever» «if ever» etc.) and in the use of the moods
(and, for the subjunctive, of ἄν along with the relative or conjunction) all the
usages are theoretically distinguishable for relatives that were distinguished
for conditionals. In practice the important distinction is that between
the use of the indicative as in «real» conditions, and the use of ἄν with
the subjunctive in «eventual» or «general» ones, the distinction between
εἰ (with indicative) and ἄν (with subjunctive) corresponding to that
between ὅς (τις) and ὅς (τις) ἄν (the two are found together in 2 Cor 8,12),
between ὅτε and ὅταν, ἕως and ἕως ἄν, ὅπου and ὅπου ἄν etc., i. e. ἄν
(in Hellenistic usage often abusively ἐάν) with the subjunctive indicates
an eventuality or generality, and the indicative (without ἄν) a concrete
«reality»:

    as εἴ τις θέλει, λέγει   so too ὅστις θέλει λέγει   («real»)
    as ἐάν τις θελήσῃ, ἐρεῖ   so too ὅστις ἂν θελήσῃ ἐρεῖ   («eventual»)
    as ἐάν τις θέλῃ, λέγει   so too ὅστις ἂν θέλῃ λέγει   («general»).

233   336. Just as the regular constructions are analogous, so too we find
analogous Hellenistic anomalies (cf. 330-334):

        1) ἄν with the future indicative:

    as with ἐάν e. g. Lk 19,40 ἐὰν σιωπήσουσιν . . . κράξουσιν
    so with ὅς ἄν e. g. Mk 8,35 ὃς ἂν ἀπολέσει . . . σώσει
    or with ὅταν e. g. Rev 4,9 ὅταν δώσουσιν . . . πεσοῦνται

        2) ἄν with present or past indicative:

    as with ἐάν   e. g. 1 Jo 5,15 ἐὰν οἴδαμεν . . . οἴδαμεν
    so with ὅταν   e. g. Mk 11,19 ὅταν ὀψὲ ἐγένετο, ἐξεπορεύοντο
    or with ὅσοι ἄν e. g. Mk 6,56 ὅσοι ἂν ἥψαντο . . . ἐσῴζοντο (cf. 358).

        3) subjunctive without ἄν:

    as with εἰ   e. g. 1 Cor 14,5 ἐκτὸς εἰ μὴ διερμηνεύῃ
    so with ὅστις e. g. Jas 2,10 ὅστις . . . τηρήσῃ
    or with ἕως e. g. Lk 13,35 (οὐ μὴ ἴδητέ με) ἕως εἴπητε (*)

234   337. It is clear from all these examples that moods have kept their
original nuances, but that the grammatical association established for

_____

(*) With ἕως and the subjunctive the particle ἄν is often omitted, and
with ἕως οὗ, μέχρις οὗ etc. almost always.

classical usage between the subjunctive and the particle ἄν does not hold so strictly, so that εἰ and ἐάν or ὅτε and ὅταν etc. are confused. This tendency has led in modern Greek to the extinction of the weaker forms εἰ and ὅτε in favour of ἐάν and ὅταν, used with indicative or subjunctive alike (the distinction between « real » and « eventual or general » still being expressed by the choice of mood).

235
338. To return to problems of exegesis, some have asked what we may conclude as to the thought or expectation attributed to the Blessed Virgin, in what she said to the servants at Cana, by the Greek form of what she said: ὅ τι ἄν λέγῃ ὑμῖν, ποιήσατε Jo 2,5. The answer is, that the only point worth noting in the form of expression is the present (not aorist) λέγῃ, which focusses attention on what is to be said rather than on the fact of its being said, and that is natural enough; for the rest, all that can be gathered is what can be gathered from the meaning of what she said, namely « do what He tells you, whatever it is ». The question seems to have been prompted by the idea of a distinction between a « probable » and a « general » condition and the notion that the speaker in the former case regards the fulfilment of the condition as « probable ». Since the distinction between these conditions seems to consist uniquely in the fact that the « general » condition is said to have its apodosis in the present indicative (how is one to say « do what He tells you » with a present indicative?), the principle would seem to be « when a condition is enunciated by ἐάν with the subjunctive, the speaker regards its fulfilment as probable unless he uses the present indicative in the apodosis » — and this is a principle which no linguist can be expected to take seriously.

339. Almost all of what has been said above (**296-338**) with concessions to a traditional manner in which grammarians have presented conditional and other clauses may be considerably simplified, as J. P. SMITH suggests, as follows:

1) Greek usage distinguishes between the determinate or concrete and the indeterminate or abstract (for actions, « eventual »), in the use or omission of the article with substantives, in the forms of certain pronouns and adverbs of conjunction, e. g. ὅς the one who », ὅστις « one who » etc. (cf. **215**), and with verbs (so that approximately one may render the indicative as « posit the act . . . » and ἄν with the subjunctive as « posit an act . . .»); thus one may distinguish e. g.

ὅς with the indicative (both subject and act determinate): « the one who does this action (or « . . . did », « . . . will do » etc).

ὅς ἄν with the subjunctive (subject determinate, act indeterminate)

The Moods

« *the* one who does *such an* act »
ὅστις with the indicative (subject indeterminate, act determinate)
« *such a* one as does *this* act » (or « . . . did » etc.)
ὅστις ἄν with the subjunctive (both subject and act indeterminate)
« *such* a one as does *such* an act ».

Note that mere futurity is sufficient to give « indetermination » to the act and so to be rendered by ἄν with the subjunctive, even if the speaker is in fact thinking of a definite foreseen act, for so long as the act remains future it is not really « concrete » but only a mental object; the use of the indicative future would thus insist on the determinate foreseen nature of the act. As for past acts, they are of their nature determined by their realization, but may be represented in « general » form, classically by the use of the optative in the subordinate clause, Hellenistically by the insertion of ἄν along with the indicative (358).

2) The « conditional tense » of English and various other languages corresponds more or less exactly to the Greek principal verb with ἄν and the optative (abstracting from the realization or non-realization of condition and consequence) or ἄν and historic indicative (for non-realization). As in English and other languages, this form is readily used absolutely i. e. without express protasis, cf. « who would have thought it? » etc. Sometimes the protasis is easily supplied, e. g. « he would never do that » (sc. « even if such and such an occasion arose » or the like); sometimes however this form is used in Greek as in certain other languages (not usually in English, however, which prefers « might » to « would » in such cases) in modest statement or in wondering question or the like (« now, what would that mean? ») — and in this use, which is not thoroughly literary, the ἄν is (in popular use) omitted, the optative alone remaining, as in Lk 1,29, Our Lady was wondering what sort of salutation that « might be », εἴη without ἄν (an « oblique optative » would be out of place here!). Note that this « conditional tense » is an autonomous form with a meaning of its own which may be set alongside the indicative for instance as a form of main-clause expression.

Where the protasis formally corresponding to a « conditional tense » is to be expressed, it uses the same mood and « tenses » (but without ἄν) as the corresponding apodosis (but of course the choice of « tense » depends on the aspect desired for the protasis, which need not be the same as that desired for the apodosis).

3) Further distinctions of « probable » or « possible » or the like tend to hinder rather than assist the student, who has but to observe the distinctions already exposed (« conditional tense », and the distinction between the « concrete » indicative and the « eventual » ἄν + subjunctive) and judge the sense according to the meaning which results; the psychological nuances will be supplied automatically by the usages of his own language (examples: 322, what does ἐὰν δὲ ἔλθῃ Τιμόθεος imply as to Paul's expectation? — answer: exactly what « if Timothy comes » does in English; 338, what does ὅ τι ἂν λέγῃ ὑμῖν, ποιήσατε imply as to Our Lady's expectations? — answer: exactly what « whatever He tells you, do it » does in English).

3) In Final Clauses

236   340. Ἵνα in « final » sense, classically used with the subjunctive (or the « oblique » optative) is in Hellenistic and NT usage found also **with the future indicative** (though there is nearly always a variant reading with the subjunctive), e. g. Lk 14,10 « take the lowest place so that ... the one who invited you may say (ἵνα ... ἐρεῖ) » or 1 Cor 13,3 « even if I give my body to be burnt (ἵνα καυθήσομαι) » (¹⁰).

237   341· This is not astonishing considering the affinity between the future and the (aorist) subjunctive both in origin (the future seems to be a variant on that subjunctive) and in sense (both as it were regarding an expectation and not a realized fact). Hence also after ἐάν (and other forms with ἄν) the future is found instead of the subjunctive (cf. **333, 336**). This affinity accounts for the use with final ἵνα of the future indicative, and of the future only; the present indicative with final ἵνα is to be regarded even in Hellenistic or NT Greek as a « corrupt » use. In 1 Cor 4,6 ἵνα μὴ ... φυσιοῦσθε and Gal 4,17 ἵνα αὐτοὺς ζηλοῦτε the verbal forms are to be regarded not as syntactical aberrations (indicative instead of subjunctive) but as morphological ones (subjunctive identical in form with indicative on the analogy of verb in -άω).

238   342. A special case is that of a future indicative following upon a subjunctive with ἵνα, e. g. Jo 15,8 ἐν τούτῳ ἐδοξάσθη ὁ πατήρ μου ἵνα καρπὸν φέρητε καὶ γενήσεσθε ἐμοὶ μαθηταί, cf. Jo 12,40 (LXX). Some here take the last clause, on account of its future, as independent (« that you bear fruit; and [so] you will be my disciples », a main statement added to what precedes) (¹¹), but there is no need to interpret in this manner, since the future may be parallel with the subjunctive, as is especially to be seen from the occurence in parallel of the same two forms but in the opposite order, e. g. Rev 22,14 ἵνα ἔσται ... καὶ εἰσέλθωσιν.

(¹⁰) The same usage is found classically with ὅπως (often), and μή (rarely), but never with ἵνα.

(¹¹) This would indeed be in accordance with the general Semitic preference for coordination rather than subordination, so that from indirect speech they pass as soon as possible to direct, and in relative clauses the dependence on the relative is readily abandoned, cf. e. g. 2 Pet 2,3 οἷς τὸ κρίμα ἔκπαλαι οὐκ ἀργεῖ, καὶ ἡ ἀπώλεια αὐτῶν (for καὶ ὧν ἡ ἀπώλεια) οὐ νυστάζει, or 1 Cor 8,6 (the same usage is also found in classical Greek); cf. **515ff**.

239   343. In **relative clauses** (of determinate type; for indeterminate ones see above 335ff) a final sense sometimes leads to the use of the subjunctive (without ἄν) or the future (both usages are also found classically) e. g. Acts 21,16 ἄγοντες (ἡμᾶς) παρ' ᾧ ξενισθῶμεν Μνάσονι = παρὰ Μνάσονα ἵνα παρ' αὐτῷ ξενισθῶμεν, or Lk 7,4 of the centurion ἄξιός ἐστιν ᾧ παρέξῃ τοῦτο (future for subjunctive, which itself stands for the classical infinitive with ἄξιος). — Cf. also Mt 21,41; Mk 14,14; Lk 11,6; 22,11; Acts 6,3. Such a subjunctive may however sometimes be a «deliberative» one (cf. 243).

240   344. **Fear or anxiety** is expressed by the conjunctions μή, μήπως, μήποτε, generally with the subjunctive (or, as in other like uses, with the future indicative, e. g. Mk 14,2; Heb 3,12; Col 2,8); but here the independence of Greek syntax (as contrasted with Latin, where the corresponding *ne* must have the subjunctive) is illustrated by the fact that, in classical as in NT Greek, if what follows the conjunction is not an eventuality (subjunctive) but in the past (or real, i. e. not atemporal present), and so in the concrete already realized or unrealized, the indicative is used. An example of both moods in the same passage is to be found in 1 Thess 3,5 μή πως ἐπείρασεν ὑμᾶς ὁ πειράζων καὶ εἰς κενὸν γένηται ὁ κόπος ἡμῶν, «lest the tempter has tempted you (fact, i. e. either he has or he has not, indicative) and our labour be (apprehension, not determinate fact, whether temptation has occurred or not) in vain»; so too Gal 2,2 μή πως εἰς κενὸν τρέχω ἢ ἔδραμον, the first verb is doubtless to be understood not as an indicative (real present = I am now in fact running) but as subjunctive (atemporal of present aspect = I at any time be running) while the second is past and so indicative. Cf. also Gal 4,15.

345. In 2 Tim 2,25 we have what may seem a strange expression of preoccupation: the apostle exhorts Timothy to clemency and moderation in dealing with the adversaries of the faith μήποτε δῴη αὐτοῖς ὁ θεὸς μετάνοιαν. The sense seems to be «lest they be persons to whom God proposes to grant repentance», i. e. the eventuality is not one to be avoided if possible, but one to be borne in mind with precaution (and this is, in the last analysis, all that is expressed by μή etc., as distinct from ἵνα μή).

4) In Indirect Speech

241   **346.** English and various other languages, when reporting speech in a narration in past time, put likewise into the past what would in the direct speech be present, and change correspondingly other tenses of direct speech (e. g. « I *was* here before, I *am* here now and I *will* be here again » becomes « [he said that] he *had been* there before, he *was* there then, and he *would* be there again »). Greek, as has been said with regard to the perfect and with regard to the participles, never expresses the notion of relative time by a verbal form; and in indirect speech in particular, retains the same tense as would be used in direct speech ([11]) (the classical possibility of using the « oblique optative » instead of the indicative or [ἄν +] subjunctive of direct speech in historic sequence still left the « tense » = aspect unchanged). The « oblique optative » is rare in Hellenistic usage, and in the NT is to be found in Luke only, where he represents elegant speech of e.g. Festus who tells Agrippa that it is not the way of the Romans to condemn a man πρὶν ἢ ὁ κατηγορούμενος κατὰ πρόσωπον ἔχοι τοὺς κατηγόρους τόπον τε ἀπολογίας λάβοι... (Acts 25,16). The other possible examples are all in questions where the optative may be a potential one without ἄν (e. g. Lk 1,29, cf. above 339). Where ἄν is found, the use must be potential, since the oblique optative is never accompanied by ἄν. (So e. g. Lk 1,62 where they asked Zachary τί ἄν θέλοι καλεῖσθαι αὐτόν («what he would like him to be called»; so nine times in Lk, six times in Acts).

242   **347.** As examples of the **retention of the tense** of direct speech we may cite Lk 18,9: « He said to certain ones πεποιθότας ὅτι εἰσίν δίκαιοι (= convinced that they *were* ...)»; and Acts 6,1: the Greeks raised against the Hebrews a complaint ὅτι παρεθεωροῦντο ... αἱ χῆραι

([11]) E. g. Mk 6,55 ὅπου ἤκουον ὅτι ἐστίν « where they heard that He *was* ». Hence in Acts 16,3 « for, they knew that his father *had been* (ὑπῆρχεν) a gentile », one may conclude that his father was dead (« ... that his father *was...* » would have had ὑπάρχει), were it not that certain (rare) exceptions are found such as Jo 2,25 « He knew what was (ἦν) in man », where direct speech would have the present; cf. also Jo 6,6; 8,27; 11,51; 12,16; Acts 17,13 etc.

αὐτῶν. This latter example is the more important in that the unwary may translate it e. g. « that their widows were being passed over », without reflecting that if the meaning were that the Greeks said « our widows are being passed over », the Greek would have had the present and not the imperfect tense. Hence either the sense is « that their widows had been passed over », where the « had been » corresponds to a « were being » and not simply « were » of direct speech, or the ὅτι must be taken as causal and the translation must be « because their widows were being passed over », or finally, one must suppose that Luke was led by a confusion of thought into using the imperfect appropriate to ὅτι « because » although he intended ὅτι « that ». Cf. also 2 Thess 2,4 of the antichrist in the temple ἀποδεικνύοντα ἑαυτὸν ὅτι ἐ σ τ ί ν θεός (present because the action is e-quivalent to « I am God »).

243   348. Not only the tenses, but also the moods of direct speech are retained when it passes into indirect (with the exception, here, of the « oblique optative » and the obvious exception of the passage of finite verbs into infinitive or participle), a point to be noted by those weak in Greek but used to Latin usage, in that a subjunctive of Greek indirect speech cannot result, as a Latin one could, from the passage from direct speech, but must correspond to a direct use of the subjunctive (thus 2 Cor 3,5 οὐχ ὅτι... ἱκανοί ἐσμεν though Latin renders « simus »). Thus in Mk 9,6 Peter proposes to build three tabernacles, οὐ γὰρ ᾔδει τί ἀπο-κριθῇ (cf Mk 14,40). The Latin « quid diceret » might mean « not know-ing what he said » but the Greek can not have this meaning, since this supposes the direct question τί ἀποκρίνομαι « what answer am I giving? » which in indirect speech would have become τί ἀποκρίνεται (or, to keep the aorist of the text, the meaning « did not know what he [had] said » would have had τί ἀπεκρίθη corresponding to Peter's question τί ἀπεκρίθην); the subjunctive supposes for Peter the question in the subjunctive τί ἀποκριθῶ (deliberative) and the meaning is thus « not knowing what answer to give »; on the contrary the parallel Lk 9,33 μὴ εἰδὼς ὃ λέγει means « not knowing what he was saying ». — Simi-larly Mt 6,25: « be not solicitous τί φάγητε ἢ τί πίητε ... » are delibera-tive subjunctives; the question is not the factual one « what (in fact) shall we eat ... ? » but « what are we to eat? » Cf. also Mt 8,20; Mk 8,1f; Lk 12,17.

349. There are however cases in which a subjunctive in indirect speech is to be accounted for not simply by a subjunctive in the corresponding direct speech, but by the presence of a nuance corresponding to that of the (Hellenistic) ἵνα with the subjunctive e. g. Lk 12,36 « waiting πότε (their master) ἀναλύσῃ from the wedding » i. e. they were waiting « for him *to return* » (not simply to know the answer to the theoretical question when he would return), just as e. g. Mk 6,36 ἵνα ... ἀγοράσωσιν ἑαυτοῖς τί φάγωσιν, though a « deliberative subjunctive » may be invoked, means in effect « buy themselves something *to eat* », and cf. the future corresponding to a subjunctive with the relative in Lk 7,4 discussed above 343. Cf. also Php 3,12. Hence DEBRUNNER 368 speaks of « the extension of the subjunctive (in indirect speech) beyond its limits in the classical language ».

5) In Consecutive Clauses

244   350. The consecutive conjunction has two constructions: with the indicative if the speaker wishes to indicate the actual realization of the consequence; with the infinitive otherwise (i. . e. so long as the speaker has no special need to indicate the actual event). It would seem that the latter (« non-committal ») construction gained ground in the course of time, in the sense that in classical usage a less important reason sufficed for the use of the indicative than in later times; however that may be, the indicative is used in the NT twice only, as against over fifty uses with the infinitive, a circumstance which attracts especial attention to the cases with the indicative. Thus where Jo 3,16 we read that « God so loved the world ὥστε τὸν υἱὸν αὐτοῦ τὸν μονογενῆ ἔδωκεν, we have the right to suppose that by using the indicative the writer wishes to insist on the actual fact of the incarnation. Similarly we may suppose that indignation moved St Paul to use the stronger indicative when he wrote that Peter's ὑπόκρισις was shared by the other Jews ὥστε καὶ Βαρνάβας συναπήχθη αὐτῶν τῇ

(¹²) I. e. twice only where ὥστε introduces a subordinate clause with the indicative, leaving out of account the frequent use of ὥστε with an indicative (or imperative etc.) introducing a main clause and meaning « so », « therefore », as e. g. in the conclusion to the parable about the sheep to be rescued on the Sabbath, Mt 12,12: ὥστε ἔξεστιν τοῖς σάββασιν καλῶς ποιεῖν.

ὑποκρίσει (Gal 2,13). It must however be noted that these two examples would not justify such insistence upon them were it not that they
are in such contrast to the usual practice of using the infinitive with ὥστε.

6) Consecutive and Final Clauses

245   351. The distinction between consecutive and final clauses lies in
the fact that a consecutive clause declares the end which in the nature
of things is reached by something, whereas a final clause declares the end
which someone intends to reach. There is thus a considerable affinity
between the two types of clause, and it is not astonishing that there should
be a tendency to confuse the two kinds of clause (cf. in English « so as
to » used frequently in final sense though primarily consecutive). In Biblical use a confusion of the two notions is perhaps helped by the Hebrew
idea that God is the principal and universal cause of all that happens.

246   352. Thus constructions used classically in final sense only are now
used in consecutive sense, e. g. the infinitive with τοῦ, as Rom 7,3 « but
if her husband is dead she is freed, τοῦ μὴ εἶναι αὐτὴν an adulteress
if she be with another husband » (also Rom 8,12; Lk 24, 16; Heb 11,5).
So too εἰς τό (which though it does not of itself indicate more than direction, without distinguishing between final and consecutive, yet commonly
has final sense) as Rom 1,20: the gentiles could have known God from
creatures, εἰς τὸ εἶναι αὐτοὺς ἀναπολογήτους for not having done so
(cf. 4,11; Heb 11,3). The very conjunctions ἵνα and ὥστε can be interchanged at times, so that ὥστε may have an obviously final sense or ἵνα
an obviously consecutive one. Thus Lk 4,29, the people of Nazareth led
Christ to the crest of the hill ὥστε κατακρημνίσαι αὐτόν (cf. Lk 9,52; 20,20;
Mt 10,1; 27,1 and perhaps Mt 24,24 according to the interpretation of
Mk 13,22), while Jo 9,2 asks who had sinned, the man born blind or his
parents, ἵνα τυφλὸς γεννηθῇ (and cf. Lk 9,45; 1 Thess 5,4; 1 Cor 5,2;
9,24; 2 Cor 1,17; Jo 6,7; 11,37?; Gal 5,17; 1 Jo 1,9; Rev 9,20; 13,13. 15;
22,14). Thus it is finally only from the context that the distinction between
final and consecutive sense can be gathered in Hellenistic usage.

247   353. The question has a certain exegetical importance e. g. in Rom
11,11 μὴ ἔπταισαν ἵνα πέσωσιν, where ἵνα can indeed be taken in a final

sense, but also in a consecutive one, as the Vulgate does in fact take it. —
In Lk 9,45 the disciples do not understand Our Lord's reference to His
passion because it was veiled from them ἵνα μὴ αἴσθωνται αὐτό, which might
give grounds for interpreting their misunderstanding as divinely ordain-
ed, whereas the Vulgate is right in rendering in a consecutive sense (« ut
non » instead of « ne »). The double sense of ἵνα was well known to ancient
grammarians, and thus e. g. Chrysostom on Rom 5,20 νόμος δὲ παρεισ-
ῆλθεν ἵνα πλεονάσῃ τὸ παράπτωμα remarks τὸ δὲ ἵνα ἐνταῦθα οὐκ αἰτιο-
λογίας πάλιν ἀλλ' ἐκβάσεώς ἐστιν ([14]).

7) The Optative

248   354. In Hellenistic and Biblical Greek the optative is much rarer
than in classical Greek.

249   355. a) The optative **expressing a wish** is still found in the NT in
38 examples, 29 of which are in Paul (the formula μὴ γένοιτο alone fifteen
times). Elsewhere the imperative takes its place, or a circumlocution
with βούλομαι, θέλω or ὄφελον, or (once) a future for a desire possible
of attainment but not seriously entertained (Gal 5,12) ([15]).

250   356. b) The **potential optative** for modest assertion has (unlike
its counterpart in questions) disappeared from popular speech, and is
to be found in Luke alone, who uses it with obvious aiming at literary
effect, e. g. where Paul is made to say to Agrippa εὐξαίμην ἄν Acts 26,29,
or to Felix εἴ τι ἔχοιεν πρὸς ἐμέ Acts 24,19. In place of this optative
we often find the future, e. g. πῶς κρινεῖ ὁ θεὸς τὸν κόσμον Rom 3,6;
ἐρεῖ τις 1 Cor 15,35; or the imperfect, as Acts 25,22 ἐβουλόμην for βου-
λοίμην ἄν; Rom 9,3 ηὐχόμην; Gal 4,20 ἤθελον. For the potential optative in conditions see 323.

_____

([14]) Migne, PG 60,878; cf. also 59,307.

([15]) A wish which is regarded as no longer capable of fulfilment is Hellenistically rendered by ὄφελον treated as a particle (classical Greek would
have the verbal form ὤφελον with the infinitive) with the « unreal » (i. e.
historic tense) indicative, e. g. ὄφελον ἀνείχεσθέ μου 2 Cor 11,1; ὄφελον ἐβα-
σιλεύσατε 1 Cor 4,8.

251   **357.** c) For the oblique optative see 346.

252   **358.** d) The optative used classically for iteration («generality)» in historic sequence is no longer in use, its place being taken in the NT by the use of ἄν (giving generality as with the subjunctive) with the historic tenses of the indicative (so as to put it into the desired past time), e. g. Mk 6,56b ὅσοι ἄν ἥψαντο ἐσῴζοντο. So too Mk 3,11; 6,56a; 11,19; 15,6 in Codex Bezae; Acts 2,45; 4,35; 1 Cor 12,2.

XI. THE PARTICIPLE

The use of the participle in the NT (¹) is not free from Semitic influence; under this heading we have:

253   360. The so-called periphrastic construction (²), consisting in the use, instead of a simple verbal form, of a participle with the verb εἶναι (³), a usage favoured in Hellenistic Greek by the general tendency to greater expressiveness. E. g. ἑστὼς ἐπὶ τοῦ βήματος Καίσαρός εἰμι (Acts 25,10) is a much stronger and more picturesque expression than ἕστηκα ἐπὶ τοῦ βήματος Καίσαρος. Even in a less dramatic and rhetorical context, however, we occasionally perceive the especial force of a circumlocution of this kind. E. g. when we read of the child Jesus ἦν ὑποτασσόμενος αὐτοῖς (Lk 2,51) this expression with the present participle certainly brings out more effectively His continued and daily submission than either the simple imperfect ὑπετάσσετο or the use of an adjective as ἦν ὑπήκοος.

254   361. In the NT circumlocution is so frequent for the imperfect in particular that it can scarcely be explained otherwise than as due to Aramaic influence. The use of the periphrastic construction has in the NT a distribution which gives more than a half of the total number of occur-

---

(¹) G. RUDBERG, Zu den Partizipien im NT. (Coniect. neot. 12, Lund 1948, pp. 1-38) deals with only the asyndetic use of the participle.

(²) Gudmund BJORK, Ἦν διδάσκων, Die periphrastichen Konstruktionen im Griechischen, Uppsala 1940. The author rejects Aramaic influence in Luke (p. 67ff) and ascribes the frequency of the construction to the disposition of Luke, « der sich im konkreten Situationsbild und im malerisch geprägten Einzelausdruck in gleicher Weise gefällt ». I take this quotation from E. HÄNCHEN, Die Apostelgeschichte, on Acts 1,10.

(³) It occurs once even with ὑπάρχειν (frequent Hellenistically for εἶναι), Lk 23,12 ὑπῆρχον γὰρ (sc. Herod and Pilate) ἐν ἔχθρᾳ ὄντες: « they had been (214) hostile to each other». Another remarkable case is to be found in the same chapter, 23,19: ἦν (sc. Barabbas)... βληθεὶς ἐν τῇ φυλακῇ.

rences to the writings of Luke alone. When the comparison is restricted
to the periphrasis of the imperfect alone, Luke still is far ahead other writers: his gospel has about 30 examples and the Acts about 24, of which
17 are found in the earlier or Palestinian section of the book, and only
7 in the rest of it (chapters 13-28) (MOULTON). This seems to suggest that
this Aramaizing use is to be attributed rather to Luke's sources than
to his own ways of expressing himself, but against this we have HOWARD's
observation (p. 451) that though this construction is very frequent in
the sections proper to Luke, he avoids it where he finds it in Mark, while
on the other hand using it even in passages parallelled by Mark, where
Mark does not use it.

255   362. The only case in which this construction raises a serious question
for exegesis is Jo 1,9: ἦν τὸ φῶς τὸ ἀληθινὸν ὃ φωτίζει πάντα ἄνθρωπον,
ἐρχόμενον εἰς τὸν κόσμον. Here the question arises, whether ἐρχόμενον refers to τὸ φῶς, as it is referred by the punctuation adopted above (Merk,
Nestle), or to ἄνθρωπον, as the Vulgate, for example, renders it: in other
words, is ἦν ... ἐρχόμενον a periphrastic construction or not? The periphrastic construction is to be found in John nine times (*), save that it
has been noted that the verb εἶναι almost always retains a more or less
independent force, as e. g. 1,28 ὅπου ἦν ὁ Ἰωάννης βαπτίζων which seems
to mean not simply « where John was baptizing », but « where John
was, (and was) baptizing ». As for the distance between the ἦν and the
ἐρχόμενον (eight intervening words), we may perhaps compare John's
own 2,6: ἦσαν δὲ ἐκεῖ λίθιναι ὑδρίαι ἓξ κατὰ τὸν καθαρισμὸν τῶν Ἰουδαίων
κείμεναι . . . , though here too ἦσαν may keep its verbal force. (This independence of εἶναι in John is of course irrelevant to the interpretation
of the passsage in question, ἦν . . . ἐρχόμενον, since there too the ἦν
obviously can in any interpretation have independent force, indeed if
ἐρχόμενον be referred to ἄνθρωπον, is completely independent). Cf. also
Lk 23,19 ὅστις ἦν διὰ στάσιν τινα γενομένην ἐν τῇ πόλει καὶ φόνον βληθεὶς
ἐν τῇ φυλακῇ and Acts 19,14: ἦσαν δέ τινος Σκευᾶ Ἰουδαίου ἀρχιερέως
ἑπτὰ υἱοὶ τοῦτο ποιοῦντες.

two things at the same time

256   363. « Graphic » participles are those which express a concomitant
or preceding action which is implicit in the verb to which they are added,

----

(*) 1,9. 28; 3,23 (= 10,40); 2,6; 11,1; 13,23; 18,25. 30 .

certain idioms however adding such participles as a matter of course. The participle very often expresses corporal movement or position. Thus, in Semitic idiom, one who does something in another place does it ἀπελθών (Mk 14,12); one who goes away, does so, ἀναστάς or ἐγερθείς or πορευθείς (Hebrew *wayyaqom wayyabo'*), one who asks a question, does so προσελθών or προσερχόμενος; he who teaches in solemn manner does so ἀνοίξας τὸ στόμα αὐτοῦ (*); he who touches does so ἐκτείνας τὴν χεῖρα αὐτοῦ; one who teaches or writes or casts accounts or judges is said to do so καθίσας; he who gives, gives λαβών; he who sees, sees ἀναβλέψας (Lk 21,1); perhaps also he who does something by another's agency does so ἀποστείλας (*); finally the apostles are bidden to go and speak σταθέντες in the temple (Acts 5,20).

364. It must be noted in general that « graphic participles » are « Semitisms » inasmuch as they render a Semitic mannerism of speech by expressing what in ordinary Greek would not be expressed at all; but the manner of expression is not Semitic, i. e. the use of the participle is quite Greek and foreign to Semitic usage, which in these expressions has a coordinate finite verb.

257   **365.** It is clear that such participles are mere speech-mannerisms, whose sense is not as a rule to be insisted upon. Hence for example it is entirely without justification that preachers sometimes see the Pharisee's pride as expressed in the participle σταθείς... προσεύχετο Lk 18,11, as if it meant that he took up a specially prominent position so as to be seen. In fact, the publican also prays ἐστώς (μακρόθεν, it is true): indeed the Jews (like a great part of the Christian church) normally prayed standing. — Hence too ἐστώς occasionally means nothing more than mere presence in a place, e. g. Jo 3,29; 6,22; 18,18 25; Acts 1,11; 5,25.

258   **366.** Similarly the very common example of this pleonastic participle, ἀποκριθείς εἶπεν became to such an extent an empty formula that it is even sometimes used where there is nothing preceding to which an « answer » can be referred (*), just as is also the underlying Hebrew for-

(*) Mt 5,2; (13,35); Acts 8,35; 10,34; (18,14).
(*) Mt 2,16 ἀποστείλας ἀνεῖλεν « had (him) killed »; Mk 6,17; Acts 7,14; Rev 1,1.
(*) Cf. Mk 9,5; 11,14; 12,35; Mt 11,25; 12,38; 17,4; 28,5 (HOWARD, p. 453).

127

mula *wayya'an wayyo'mer*, to which there corresponds in Aramaic the asyndetic *'anah we'amar*.

259   367. In the use of this formula attention has been called to a difference between John and the synoptics. The latter use the Hebraizing formula (of the LXX), rendered however more Greek in expression by the subordination of the verb «answer» in the form of a participle (ἀποκριθείς), whereas John, as he never uses the participle and generally uses an asyndetic formula, seems to be closely following the Aramaic usage. Moreover, other redundant participles so frequently found in the synoptics, such as ἐλθών, ἀπελθών, ἀφείς, ἀναστάς etc. are lacking in John, who coordinates in Semitic fashion, e. g. 7,37 εἱστήκει καὶ ἔκραξεν, cf. 9,8 καθήμενος καὶ προσαιτῶν, 11,29 ἐγείρεται καὶ ἔρχεται, 12,44 ἔκραξεν καὶ εἶπεν, 13,26 «and having dipped bread, λαμβάνει (though He must have already «taken» it to dip it) καὶ δίδωσιν Ἰούδᾳ.

260   368. After verbs of saying, asking, answering, and also of deliberating (Lk 5,21; 12,17), thinking, writing (Lk 1,63) the object-clause is commonly introduced in Hebrew by the infinitive *le'mor*, equivalent in sense to «saying» and rendered λέγων by the LXX. Hence the great frequency of the same usage in the NT also (cf. 391).

The stereotyped nature of this participle is especially evident when it is added to the same verb λέγειν, as εἶπεν... λέγων Lk 7,39; (12,26; 15,3); 20,2.

261   369. In quotations from the LXX we find also participles used to render the **Hebrew absolute infinitive** used to emphasise a finite verb, e. g. ἰδὼν εἶδεν (Acts 7,34 = Ex 3,7); εὐλογῶν εὐλογήσω σε καὶ πληθύνων πληθυνῶ σε (Heb 6,14 = Gen 22,17); or Mt 13,14 = Is 6,9 where the two ways of rendering the Hebrew absolute infinitive are found together, i. e. the «internal» dative and the participle: ἀκοῇ ἀκούσετε... καὶ βλέποντες βλέψετε.

262   370. It is however to be noted that in all these usages there is scarcely anything that cannot be formally parallelled in ancient Greek from Homer onwards; but this does not prevent us from seeing in them, and especially in their frequency, a Semitic tinge in the writers or, at least, in their sources.

only aspect!

263   371. Note that the present participle does not express time but only the aspect; thus e. g. John the Baptist even after his death is called ὁ βαπτίζων (= «he who used to baptize» i. e. past tense, but imperfect, so present participle as contrasted with e. g. «he who baptized Jesus» which would be aorist and so ὁ βαπτίσας τὸν'Ιησοῦν), and the Gadarene energumen after his cure is called not only ὁ δαιμονισθείς and ὁ ἐσχηκὼς τὸν λεγιῶνα but also simply ὁ δαιμονιζόμενος (Mk 5,15. 18). Here as also for John the Baptist the expression is a sort of quasi-proper name for the man (so ὁ βαπτίζων = ὁ βαπτιστής). Cf. Heb 7,9 Levi ὁ λαμβάνων δεκάτας, Php 3,6 Paul διώκων τὴν ἐκκλησίαν.

264   372. So too in Paul sometimes a present participle should not on the mere grounds of its present form be understood necessarily as referring to «real» present time, or indeed to present time at all. E. g. 1 Thess 1,10 Jesus is called ὁ ῥυόμενος ἡμᾶς ἐκ τῆς ὀργῆς τῆς ἐρχομένης («He who saves», atemporal present) but the Vulgate renders with a past tense «qui eripuit nos», though a rendering with the future «qui eripiet nos» would be equally justifiable (cf. 282f), or a present «qui semper eripit nos ». So too 1 Thess 2,12 (5,24) God is called ὁ καλῶν ὑμᾶς εἰς τὴν ἑαυτοῦ βασιλείαν, and the Vulgate has «qui vocavit vos», a defensible translation, in that God's definitive call makes Him the one who «calls» (atemporal present, hence the participle), but insistence on the form of the participle is justified also, in that it expresses God's quality as the one who always calls, just as his (timeless) quality of «giver» is expressed by ὁ διδοὺς (Vulgate: qui dedit τὸ πνεῦμα αὐτοῦ τὸ ἅγιον (1 Thess 4,8); it is correct in these cases to see the atemporal present of «characterization (generality)» cf. also ὁ ὢν εἰς τὸν κόλπον τοῦ πατρός Jo 1,18; ὁ ὢν ἐν τῷ οὐρανῷ 3,13 (variant reading); the Lamb of God ὁ αἴρων the sins of the world, 1,29. In Semitizing texts there is the additional point that the Hebrew participle is quite atemporal and may refer to past, present or future.

265   373. Peter and Paul seem to use the participle with imperative sense, e. g. Rom 12, 9-19, where a series of exhortations is expressed by seventeen participles without a finite verb: ἀποστυγοῦντες τὸ πονηρόν, κολλώμενοι τῷ ἀγαθῷ . . . , the first ten participles containing also two simple adjectives: εἰς ἀλλήλους φιλόστοργοι . . . . τῇ σπουδῇ μὴ ὀκνηροί. This series of participles is then taken up by three imperatives, verse 14:

εὐλογεῖτε τοὺς διώκοντας ὑμᾶς ... and two infinitives: χαίρειν μετὰ χαιρόντων ... after which there follow seven more participles along with two imperatives. Cf. also 1 Pet 2,12. 18; 3,1. 7. 9. 15f. The adjectives and participles would require us to «understand» ἐστέ (a form which remarkably enough is never found in the NT) so that the participles would be periphrastic constructions. It may further be remarked that as the participle is not a «mood» but an adjective, it may according to the context take on various modalities, including that of the imperative, in exhortations. (On a probable connection of this kind of expression with Semetic idiom cf. JOUON, Grammaire de l'Hébreu biblique § 121 e note 2).

374. A similar usage is that whereby Paul after a finite verb goes on with coordinate participles, as he does with remarkable frequency in 2 Cor, e. g. 5,12 οὐ πάλιν ἑαυτοὺς συνιστάνομεν ὑμῖν, ἀλλὰ ἀφορμὴν διδόντες (for δίδομεν) ὑμῖν καυχήματος ὑπὲρ ἡμῶν, and similarly 6,3; 7,5; 8,19; 9,11. 13; 10,4. 15 (twice); 11,6.

375. A similar but opposite usage is that of continuing after a participle with καί and a finite verb, especially in Rev, e. g. 2,2 ... τοὺς λέγοντας ἑαυτοὺς ἀποστόλους καὶ οὐκ εἰσίν, as also 2,9. 20; 3,7. 9 etc.; similarly Jo 5,44; 2 Jo 2 διὰ τὴν ἀλήθειαν τὴν μένουσαν ἐν ἡμῖν καὶ μεθ' ἡμῶν ἔσται. Cf also Mt 13,22; Lk 5,18; 8,12. 14; Jo 1,32; 1 Cor 7,37; 2 Cor 6,9; Col 1,26. (BONACCORSI).

376. Occasionally puzzlement, and sometimes perhaps also exegetical difficulty, is caused by the expression in a participle of what is the principal notion, while the finite verb expresses what is but a circumstance, e. g. Mk 2,23 the disciples started ὁδὸν ποιεῖν τίλλοντες τοὺς στάχυας, where if ὁδὸν ποιεῖν meant simply «walk» one would have expected «started τίλλειν τοὺς στάχυας ὁδὸν ποιοῦντες »: KLOSTERMANN suspects that an underlying parataxis (ὁδὸν ποιεῖν καὶ τίλλειν) has been awkwardly rendered (« ungeschickte Wiedergabe einer aram. Parataxe ») (but cf. note to 228 above); so too Lk 13,28; Rom 4,19: « μὴ ἀσθενήσας in faith regarded his body as dead », on which W. BAUER (Wörterbuch) remarks « wie oft, der Hauptbegriff durch das Partizip ausgedrückt ». For a similar phenomenon in ancient Greek cf. 263.

377. Here and in many other cases there would seem to be an underlying Aramaic circumstantial clause which although subordinate is expressed paratactically, waw + pronoun + verb, cf. Mk 1,19: He saw James . . .
and John . . . « and they preparing their nets » as an Irishman might have
said (καὶ αὐτοὺς . . . καταρτίζοντας). Note how Mk does not render
literally the Aramaic circumstantial clause (which would have given καὶ
αὐτοὶ καταρτίζοντες) but as a concession to Greek syntax makes the participle depend on the principal verb εἶδεν, putting the αὐτούς in the accusative. Similarly Lk 13,28. Cf. M. BLACK, An Aramaic Approach . . . ,
1954, p. 63f.

XII. THE INFINITIVE

The Hellenistic use of the infinitive, as compared with the classical one, shows considerable modification: in certain usages the infinitive is more frequently employed than in classical Greek, and in others less frequently.

266   380. a) The infinitive is **less frequent**, and very much so, in the uses for which its place is taken by the conjunctions ἵνα (406 ff) and ὅτι. This latter conjunction is used oftener than in classical Greek after verbs of saying (instead of the infinitive; as also with verbs of perception, instead of the participle, but indirect speech with the participle has survived better than indirect speech with the infinitive), and is also normal (in contrast with good classical usage) with verbs of opinion.

b) On the other hand the infinitive is **more frequently** used:

267   381. α) in that it takes the place, after verbs of motion, for the indication of the end in view, of the classical future participle (cf. 282f), e. g. Mt 20,28: οὐκ ἦλθεν διακονηθῆναι ἀλλὰ διακονῆσαι.

268   382. β) in that the use of the **infinitive with the article** is widely extended in Hellenistic Greek, a tendency which in the NT seems at least in part reinforced by the frequent use of the infinitive with prepositions in Semitic idiom.

269   383. Especially frequent is the infinitive with τοῦ, not so much in dependence upon a substantive (e. g. ὁ χρόνος τοῦ τεκεῖν αὐτήν Lk 1,57) as independently, with final or consecutive sense (cf. 352) e. g. (final) «Herod sought the child τοῦ ἀπολέσαι αὐτό» Mt 2,13; (consecutive) «nor did you repent afterwards so as to believe him (τοῦ πιστεῦσαι αὐτῷ)» Mt 21,32; cf. Acts 7,19; 20,20; Rom 7,3.

270   384. The same consecutive infinitive with τοῦ is found with substantives of which it is more or less independent, e. g. «God has given them... ὀφθαλμοὺς τοῦ μὴ βλέπειν καὶ ὦτα τοῦ μὴ ἀκούειν» = eyes such as do not see..., Rom 11,8 = LXX; or «seeing that he had πίστιν τοῦ σωθῆναι» = such faith that he could be saved, Acts 14,9 (Paul however is

accustomed to express this kind of consecutive sense with prepositions, εἰς τό and πρὸς τό).

271   385. When **several such infinitives** (final or consecutive) follow one another, Luke likes to add τοῦ before the second (or third) infinitive, while leaving the first without article, thus twice in the « Benedictus », Lk 1,77: « thou shalt go before the face of the Lord ἑτοιμάσαι ὁδοὺς αὐτοῦ, τοῦ δοῦναι γνῶσιν ... » and again: « the Orient from on high visited us ἐπιφᾶναι τοῖς ἐν σκότει ... τοῦ κατευθῦναι τοὺς πόδας ἡμῶν » 1,78f. Perhaps also the τοῦ δοῦναι ἡμῖν of 1,73b is to be understood as a third member coordinate with the preceding infinitives ποιῆσαι ἔλεος ... καὶ μνησθῆναι, notwithstanding the interpretation of the Vulgate, which makes it depend upon « the oath which he swore », rendering « daturum se nobis ».

272   386. Luke's predilection for τοῦ with the infinitive (twenty times in the gospel, seventeen times in the Acts) leads him (and also sometimes James) to use τοῦ pleonastically with e. g. an object-infinitive as Lk 4,10 = LXX « he hath given his angels command concerning thee τοῦ διαφυλάξαι σε » or 5,7 καὶ κατένευσαν τοῖς μετόχοις ... τοῦ συλλαβέσθαι αὐτοῖς, (cf. also 17,1; Acts 3,12; 15,20; 21,12 etc.), or the subject-infinitive, e. g. with ἐγένετο Acts 10,25: ὡς δὲ ἐγένετο τοῦ εἰσελθεῖν τὸν Πέτρον. Note however that this usage supposes some « futurity » in the verbal notion, e. g. as the context shows, this last expression means « when Peter was about to go in ». Where there was a notion of refraining or restraining or the like, even classical usage admitted τοῦ with the infinitive (genitive of separation), e. g. Lk 4,32; 24,16; Acts 10,47; Rom 15,22; 2 Cor 1,8.

273   387. Among the various uses of the infinitive with prepositions, special mention is due to **the temporal use with ἐν τῷ**. Such a use is of itself quite Greek, but its regular use in the temporal sense may be attributed to Hebrew influence; and since such a use is not Aramaic, its frequence, especially in Luke, is to be attributed to the influence of the LXX (about thirty times in the gospel, but rare in Acts: 2,1; 8,6; 9,3; 11,15; 19,1).

274   388. This is further confirmed by the fact that this use is found especially often (about twenty times) along with another LXX usage char-

acteristic of Luke, namely the introductory formula καὶ ἐγένετο with a finite verb (the LXX construction) e. g. Lk 2,6 ἐγένετο δὲ ἐν τῷ εἶναι αὐτοὺς ἐκεῖ ἐπλήσθησαν αἱ ἡμέραι.

275   389. Moreover, just as in Luke's gospel the more Hebrew form of this construction (ἐγένετο with καί and a finite verb) is very frequent, while in the Acts we find the Greek construction (ἐγένετο with the infinitive), so too the accompanying temporal expression is usually in the Gospel the Hebrew one ἐν τῷ with the infinitive, which occurs only once in the Acts, at any rate in conjunction with ἐγένετο (19,1). This almost certainly indicates deliberate imitation of the LXX in the gospel. For other signs of this imitation see 199, and on this Lukan tendency in general cf. H. F. D. SPARKS, *The Semitisms of St Luke's Gospel*, in *J. Th. St.* 44 1943), 129-138, and *The Semitisms of the Acts*, in *NTS* 1 (1950), 16-28.

276   390. Where ἐν τῷ with the infinitive is used temporally, the present infinitive naturally indicates, in general, contemporary action, and the aorist preceding action; not that the forms indicate of themselves any relation of time, but because the aspect which they indicate normally corresponds

---

(¹) In the Lukan formula ἐγένετο three constructions are to be distinguished:

1) ἐγένετο with a finite verb not preceded by καί (the construction used by the LXX which often omits the καί necessary to Hebrew idiom), e. g. Lk 2,6 ἐγένετο... ἐπλήσθησαν.

2) ἐγένετο with καί and a finite verb (the « Hebrew » construction) e. g. Lk 9,51 ἐγένετο ἐν τῷ συμπληροῦσθαι τὰς ἡμέρας... καὶ αὐτὸς... ἐστήρισεν...

3) ἐγένετο with the infinitive (the « Greek » construction), e. g. Acts 16,16 ἐγένετο δὲ πορευομένων ἡμῶν... παιδίσκην τινὰ ὑπαντῆσαι ἡμῖν.

The distribution of these constructions in the Gospel and Acts is very significant; the author uses this favourite construction of his in his Gospel 22 times after the manner of the LXX, 11 times after the Hebrew manner, and only 5 times after the Greek manner, whereas in the Acts he uses it 15 times in the Greek manner and never in either of the other two manners. — Note that in Mt, with the exception of 9,10 (the « Hebrew » construction), we have this formula five times, in the LXX construction, but always in a similar place, namely concluding the five great discourses that make up the plan of the Gospel: 7,28; 11,1; 13,53; 19,1; 26,1: καὶ ἐγένετο ὅτε ἐτέλεσεν Ἰησοῦς τοὺς λόγους τούτους (and a finite verb follows). On this formula there is an article by JOHANNESSOHN, *Das biblische καὶ ἐγένετο u. seine Geschichte*, in *Z. f. vergl. Sprachwissensch....* (1926), 161-212. And see Klaus BEYER, *Semit. Syntax im NT I*, (1962) p. 41-60.

to those relationships (cf. the imperfect or aorist indicative for past time in a corresponding temporal clause) e. g. Lk 9,29 ἐν τῷ προσεύχεσθαι αὐτόν «when he was praying» (present aspect, so imperfect indicative) but ἐγένετο ἐν τῷ ἐλθεῖν αὐτὸν εἰς οἶκον «when he (had) entered a house» (aorist): the present represents the action in progress, the aorist represents it simply as posited. Cf. in Luke the aorist infinitives 2,27; 3,21; 9,34. 36; 11,37; 14,1; 19,15; 24,30; Acts 11,15; and the present infinitives 5,1. 12; 8,5. 42; 9,18. 29. 33. 51; 10,35. 38; 11,1. 27; 17,11. 14; 24,4. 15. 51; Acts 8,6; 19,1 (PLUMMER, on Lk 3,21). Note in 3,21 and 9,34 that the use of the aorist does not exclude contemporaneousness of action: ἐν τῷ βαπτισθῆναι ἅπαντα τὸν λαόν means simply «when the whole people was baptized» *not* in the sense «... had been baptized», nor in the sense «was being baptized», but simply «on the occasion of the baptism».

277   391. Πρὸς τό with the infinitive usually has final sense, but the preposition itself merely indicates direction without specifying whether the direction is intended or not, and it is reasonable to doubt whether the sense is final in Mt 5,28 ὁ βλέπων γυναῖκα πρὸς τὸ ἐπιθυμῆσαι αὐτήν. Indeed the sense need not even be consecutive; in the passage in question one would expect the sense «with concupiscence» simply, and this may in fact be the sense intended, if the πρὸς τό can be understood as a servile rendering of a Semitic (Hebrew or Aramaic) le ⊦ infinitive which, though of itself it means «to(wards) ... » and so has final or consecutive sense, may also be used without any such connotation and simply with the sense «... - ing». The classical example is the very frequent Hebrew le'mor used to introduce direct speech; of itself it means «to say» but it is used simply in the sense «saying»; whence in the NT the very frequent λέγων or λέγοντες (cf. 368).

278   392. It is therefore well, in dealing with Semitizing texts, to bear in mind the possibility of rendering an infinitive (with or without τοῦ, εἰς, πρός) by «... - ing». Hence e. g. JOÜON (*) in the «Benedictus» rightly renders the infinitives ποιῆσαι ἔλεος and μνησθῆναι by participles, «faciens misericordiam ... recordatus», Lk 1,72. So too in the Magnificat, Lk 1,54, «recordatus» for μνησθῆναι, cf. also Mt 21,32 (cf. 383); Acts 7,19 (?); 15,10: «why do you tempt God ἐπιθεῖναι ζυγόν = setting a yoke...» (cf. Ps 77,18); Gal 3,10; Php 3,10 (?).

(*) *Verbum Salutis V, L'Évangile de Notre-Seigneur Jésus-Christ,*

279   393. The case of the subject of the infinitive as such (and hence that of participles or other adjectives or nouns in agreement with it) is the accusative. If however it be identical with the subject of the verb on which it depends, and be not expressed by a reflexive (in the accusative), what agrees with it is put into the nominative, e. g. Rom 1,22 φάσκοντες εἶναι σοφοί (but with expressed subject of the infinitive e. g. Acts 5,36 Θευδᾶς λέγων εἶναι τινα ἑαυτόν). So too Rom 9,3 ηὐχόμην ἀνάθεμα εἶναι αὐτὸς ἐγώ. This rule is to be noted so as not to refer wrongly to the main verb a nominative which belongs to the infinitive. E. g. Lk 1,9f has (Ζαχαρίας) ἔλαχε τοῦ θυμιᾶσαι εἰσελθὼν εἰς τὸν ναόν, where εἰσελθών goes with θυμιᾶσαι and not with ἔλαχε.

394. If the subject of the infinitive (not otherwise expressed) is identical with an element of the main clause in the genitive or dative words agreeing with it may be put into the genitive or dative as the case may be, or into the accusative (and so a distinction of sense is possible: accusative if the reference is to the subject of the infinitive as such, genitive, or dative if the reference is immediately to the element of the main clause: contrast Acts 15,22 ἔδοξε τοῖς ἀποστόλοις... ἐκλεξαμένους... πέμψαι with Lk 1,3 ἔδοξε κἀμοὶ παρηκολουθηκότι... γράψαι). Cf. Acts 26,20 ἀπήγγελλον τοῖς ἔθνεσιν μετανοεῖν... ἄξια... ἔργα πράσσοντας and 15,22; or Mt 18,8 « it is better for thee (σοι) to enter life... χωλὸν than to be thrown into the everlasting fire ἔχοντα two hands »; cf. Lk 5,7; Mk 6,9 (where the infinitive is lacking); Rom 1,29.

395. Not only the subject but also the object of the infinitive may be left unexpressed as such, if it stand in the same relation to the principal verb also. On this fact FRIDRICHSEN founds an excellent interpretation of king Agrippa's obscure expression, Acts 26,28: ἐν ὀλίγῳ με πείθεις χριστιανὸν ποιῆσαι, the subject of ποιῆσαι being understood as that of the main verb, and the object likewise (i. e. you would persuade me that you have made me a christian). In confirmation he points to a remarkable parallel in Xenophon Mem. 1,2,49 where Socrates' accuser says that he taught the young to despise their parents πείθων μὲν τοὺς συνόντας αὐτῷ σοφωτέρους ποιεῖν τῶν πατέρων i. e. persuading those who frequented him that he rendered them wiser than their parents (both subject and object of the infinitive being omitted as identical with those of the main verb) (Coniectanea neot. III [1938]).

XIII. CONJUNCTIONS

1) The Use of εἰ.

In addition to its use in conditional clauses whether «real» (303ff) or «unreal» (313ff) or «potential» (323), the particle is also used in Biblical Greek:

280   400. a) as a Hebraism in emphatic negation in the form of an oath. The conditional form is explained by the ellipse of an imprecatory formula: «(May God do thus and thus to me) if...», e. g. ἀμὴν λέγω ὑμῖν εἰ δοθήσεται... = (a sign) shall certainly not be given (to this generation), Mk 8,12; cf. Gen 14,23; 1 Sam 3,14. That this formula was intelligible Greek is suggested by 3 Kings 1,52, where the Greek text has εἰ πεσεῖται for «shall not fall» though the Hebrew is not so expressed. — Thus εἰ introduces a negative oath («certainly not...»), to which the affirmative (not found in the NT) would thus be εἰ μή... (Hebrew 'im lo'), e. g. 3 Kings 21,23... ἐὰν δὲ πολεμήσωμεν αὐτοὺς κατ' εὐθύ, εἰ μὴ κραταιώσομεν ὑπὲρ αὐτούς «... surely we shall be stronger than they».

281   401. b) as an interrogative particle in direct questions, e. g. Lk 13,23 κύριε, εἰ ὀλίγοι οἱ σῳζόμενοι; cf. Mt 12,10; Lk 22,49; Acts 1,6 etc., perhaps owing to Hebrew influence, since 'im (= εἰ) introduces also direct questions (usually, it is true, disjunctive ones), cf. Gen 17,17 where as frequently the interrogative particles ha and 'im are used parallelly. Hence the great frequency of this use of εἰ in direct questions in the LXX. In Greek this usage was perhaps favoured by the regular use of εἰ:

282   402. c) as interrogative particle in indirect questions (¹), whether α) in true questions, e. g. Lk 23,6 ἐπηρώτησεν εἰ ὁ ἄνθρωπος Γαλιλαῖός ἐστιν,

---

(¹) The distinction between this εἰ (introducing noun-clauses of indirect question) and the εἰ introducing (adverbial) clauses of condition may be paralleled by that dealt with below (416 on) between ὅτι introducing noun-clauses (indirect statement) and ὅτι introducing adverb-clauses (causal).

283   403. β) in virtual questions expressing an uncertain expectation associated with an effort to attain something, e. g. Php 3,12 διώκω δὲ εἰ καὶ καταλάβω, so that it would seem that a verb must be « understood » such as « to try (if I can...)»; or Rom 1,10 δεόμενος εἴ πως εὐοδωθήσομαι. Cf. Mk 11,13; Acts 8,22; 17,27; 20,16; 27,12; Rom 11,14 etc. — In the NT the εἰ is followed by the subjunctive or the future (only once a classical optative, Acts 17,27, and never, as is usual in classical Greek, ἐάν with the subjunctive) (¹).

284   404. γ) in much the same sense as ὅτι after verbs expressing emotion (astonishment, admiration, indignation) e. g. Mk 15,44 ἐθαύμασεν εἰ ἤδη τέθνηκεν; Acts 26,8 τί ἄπιστον κρίνεται παρ' ὑμῶν εἰ ὁ Θεὸς νεκροὺς ἐγείρει;

285   405. Despite the variety of uses for εἰ, it is difficult to know what to make of Lk 12,49 καὶ τί θέλω εἰ ἤδη ἀνήφθη. A common version (the Vulgate's interpretation) understands « I am come to set fire to the earth, and what do I desire but that it be already enkindled »; but this certanly does not correspond to the Greek text, which seems rather (of itself, but not according to the context) to mean « and what (more) do I desire if it be already kindled ». Some have tried to render the expression as an exclamation: « would that it were already enkindled » (²), but against this it is objected that a desire incapable of fulfilment is never expressed in Biblical Greek by εἰ (? see below), nor can one appeal to Lk 19,42 where Our Lord says to Jerusalem εἰ ἔγνως..., because this is simply an « unreal » condition whose apodosis is suppressed (as in the regular English « if only...! »). Most adopt a sense close to that of the Vulgate and understand « how I wish it were already enkindled », justifying this by the statement that εἰ can introduce the object of the verb θέλω, a statement founded on one Biblical example, Sir 23,14 θελήσεις εἰ μὴ ἐγενήθης, and on Herodotus 6,52; 9,44 (B. WEISS). The εἰ of this text would thus belong to 404 above, θέλω being understood in the sense « be glad », a sense which perhaps should be noticed in lexica. A solution based on an underlying Semitic idiom alone has been suggested by H. SEPER in Verb.

_____

(¹) As classical Greek uses for such clauses ἐάν and not εἰ alone, others treat them as conditional (DEBR. 375).

(²) Seeing in τί θέλω εἰ the equivalent of a rabbinical formula meaning « would that »

Dom. 36 (1958), 147-153. On the basis of Jos 7,7b and the probable Hebrew original of the Greek text of Sir 23,14 and on Is 9,14, he suspects
that εἰ here stands for Hebrew *lu* (or the Aramaic equivalent) « would
that », and renders the expression as a double exclamation: « how I desire it! Would that it were already enkindled! ».

2) The Use of ἵνα.

286   **406. a) Ἵνα in place of the infinitive.** The following seems to
have been the way in which ἵνα lost its final sense: in classical usage ἵνα
with the subjunctive introduced only strictly final clauses, i. e. not
object or subject clauses but adverbial ones indicating the end in view,
« in order that . . . ». Later it began to be more and more used for the
infinitive expressing the object (which in a certain sense is an « end in
view ») with verbs of asking, commanding or the like (« ask him *to do* this »
etc. , now expressed in the form which is properly that of a final clause
« ask him in order that he may do this »).

287   **407.** In Hellenistic usage ἵνα becomes frequent in place of such an
infinitive, e. g. ἠρώτησεν αὐτὸν ἵνα ἀπέλθῃ instead of ἠρώτησεν αὐτὸν
ἀπελθεῖν. From this beginning the use of ἵνα was extended to other types
of infinitive, and in the end (in modern Greek) the infinitive hås disappeared and is expressed by (ἵ)να with the subjunctive. In the NT there
are many traces of the earlier stages of this extension of ἵνα.

288   **408.** Thus ἵνα is used not only for the object-infinitive with verbs
of asking, exhorting, commanding (where ὅπως also is used: Lk 7,3; 10,2;
11,37), but also for the subject-infinitive as e. g. συμφέρει ὑμῖν ἵνα ἐγὼ
ἀπέλθω Jo 16,7 instead of ἀπελθεῖν με for the subject of συμφέρει; cf.
1 Cor 9,18: τίς οὖν μού ἐστιν ὁ μισθός; ἵνα εὐαγγελιζόμενος ἀδάπανον
θήσω τὸ εὐαγγέλιον.

289   **409.** On ἵνα for the consecutive infinitive see above 350ff.

290   **410.** Finally ἵνα takes the place of the **epexegetic infinitive** e. g.
« this is eternal life, ἵνα γινώσκωσι . . . » Jo 17,3, especially in John, where
it is commonly used (as in the example just cited) to « explain » (whence
the term « epexegetic ») the content of a preceding demonstrative; so

411-413 Conjunctions

also e. g. 15,8 ἐν τούτῳ ἐδοξάσθη ὁ πατήρ μου ἵνα καρπὸν πολὺν φέρητε; 15,12 αὕτη ἐστὶν ἡ ἐντολὴ ἡ ἐμή, ἵνα ἀγαπᾶτε ἀλλήλους. These examples admit more or less a final sense, but there is no trace of such a sense in e. g. Jo 15,13: μείζονα ταύτης ἀγάπην οὐδεὶς ἔχει, ἵνα τις τὴν ψυχὴν αὐτοῦ θῇ ὑπὲρ τῶν φίλων αὐτοῦ, or in an extreme case such as Lk 1,43: καὶ πόθεν μοι τοῦτο, ἵνα ἔλθῃ ἡ μήτηρ τοῦ κυρίου μου πρὸς ἐμέ, on which DEBRUNNER (394) remarks that the ἵνα is used « not quite correctly », since the clause expresses what has actually taken place: for the infinitive expressing a statement of fact seems to be the only one for which ἵνα can not be used. Cf. also Mk 11,28; Mt 8,8; Lk 7,6; Jo 1,27; 2,25; 16,2. 32. In these examples, what is « explained » by the infinitive is always a noun or pronoun. Verbs can also be similarly « explained » (i. e. the content or motive or manner of the action), e. g. Jo 8,56: « Abraham rejoiced ἵνα ἴδῃ τὴν ἡμέραν τὴν ἐμήν » or Php 2,2; Jo 5,7; 9,22; Gal 2,9.

411. Ἵνα seems also to be found in place of (τοῦ with) an infinitive in dependence upon a substantive, e. g. Jo 12,23 ἐλήλυθεν ἡ ὥρα ἵνα δοξασθῇ ὁ υἱὸς τοῦ ἀνθρώπου, cf. 428; 18,39 ἔστιν συνήθεια ὑμῖν ἵνα ἕνα ἀπολύσω; cf. 1 Cor 9,18.

291   412. b) Causal ἵνα. The extent to which ἵνα has evolved from its original final sense is clear from the fact that in later Greek it was certainly used also in causal sense, and that not merely in a few isolated cases, but so as to be explicitly listed for this use by grammarians, e. g. Apollonius Dyscolus (2nd cent. A. D.): « this particle has two uses, the one causal (αἰτιολογικὴν) and the other final (ἀποτελεστικήν) ». He cites as an example: ἵνα ἀναγνῶ, ἐτιμήθην, ἵνα λοιδορήσω, ἐπεπλήχθην (⁴). Indubitable examples of this use are in fact found in patristic literature.

292   413. It is disputed, however, whether the causal use of ἵνα is to be admitted for the NT. The question arises principally in connection with the well known difficulty of Mk 4,12: « To those that are without all is in parables, ἵνα they look indeed but see not ». Here the blindness of « those that are without » seems to be given as the end in view, the reason for which parables are used instead of plain speech, and this goes ill with what follows in the same chapter,

(⁴) Ed. SCHNEIDER, 510,16 (p. 243), cf. also 511,30. I take the quotation from PERNOT, Études sur la langue des Évangiles (1927), p. 19f, where the reader may find further information concerning this problem.

verse 33: « and in such parables He spoke to them according as they were able
to hear ». There is no difficulty in the parallel text Mt 13,13: « I speak to them
in parables because (ὅτι) they look without seeing and listen without hearing »,
where the incomprehension of the people is not the end to which the use of
parables is directed, but a fact on account of which parables are used. The
question thus arises whether Mark's ἵνα may not mean the same thing as
Matthew's ὅτι. PERNOT (loc.' cit.) tried to show that it could, citing in addition to later grammarians and patristic examples some texts from the NT
itself, namely Jo 8,56 « Abraham ... rejoiced ἵνα ἴδῃ my day », where
however ἵνα is generally taken as standing for the infinitive (⁶). A parallel text
is cited from a papyrus (BGU IV 1081 line 3, of the 2nd or 3rd century A, D.)
ἐχάρην ἵνα σε ἀσπάζομαι, and cf. Pap. Giss. 17 line 5, of the 2nd cent.: ἠγω-
νίασα ... ἵνα ἀκούσω = « on hearing »).

293   414. From Rev are cited 22,14 and 14,13, but these texts also can be
otherwise explained (⁶). Rev 22,14 has « blessed they who wash their garments
in the blood of the Lamb ἵνα their power be in the tree of life and they enter
the city by the gate »; obviously this ἵνα can be understood not only causally
(« because ... ») but also finally (« so that ... »). Rev 14,13 likewise has « blessed (the dead that die in the Lord) ... ἵνα (they rest from their labours) »,
but here ἵνα may be used absolutely with the sense « let them rest ...! » (⁷)
cf. 415.

294   415. c) Ἵνα in **independent wish** or exhortation: That ἵνα can in
the NT be used absolutely with the sense of an imperative or the like
is shown by examples such as Eph 5,33: « let each one love his wife (ἀγα-
πάτω), and let the wife fear her husband (ἵνα φοβῆται) »; cf. 2 Cor 8,7. This

---

(⁶) Cf. DEBR. 392,1 a, seeing as the only possible sense « he longed with
desire, rejoiced that he was to ... ».

(⁶) ALLO, Apocalypse (1933), p. CLVIII: Aux deux passages 6,11 (read:
22,14) et 14,13 ... ἵνα peut équivalo'r à ὅτι (BOUSSET, SWETE)

(⁷) Although causal ἵνα in the NT is generally rejected, it is noteworthy
that in a modern commentary (Göttingen 1937) LOHMEYER renders the ἵνα
of Mk 4,12 by « quia, weil », remarking « ἵνα bedeutet in der Koine ... auch,
wenngleich seltener, 'weil' », though he cites authors of contrary opinion.
On this whole question see also WINDISCH, Die Verstockungsidee in Mk 4,12
und das causale ἵνα der späteren Koine, in ZNTW 1927, and Biblica 17(1936),
512ff, where U. HOLZMEISTER reviews (in a negative sense) the findings of
Fr. LA CAVA in favour of causal ἵνα in Ut videntes non videant (Marietti 1933);
and Ne quando convertantur (1935). This author sees causal ἵνα also in Rom 5,20,
6,1; 1 Cor 7,34; 3 Jo 8; 2 Cor 4,7; to which must be added 2 Cor 12,9 in La
Scuola Cattolica (1937). Cf. also Una lettera di Sant'Isidoro Pelusiota in Divus
Thomas (Piacenza 1936), pp. 529-533.

being so, in Mk 5,23 also ἵνα is not necessarily to be regarded as introducing indirect speech (mixed with direct, as the verb is second person instead of third) after the preceding « begged », but may simply be used absolutely, in a quotation of direct speech: Jairus « begged Him ... ἵνα ἐλθὼν ἐπιθῇς τὰς χεῖρας αὐτῇ » (= «... 'come and lay hands upon her' » in this latter interpretation). These three examples are generally admitted; but the same usage is found Mk 2,10 (?); 5,12; 10,51; 12,15.19; 1 Cor 16,15f; 2 Cor 13,17; Tit 3,13. Moreover, some render as imperatives the ἵνα clauses Jo 13,34; 1 Cor 5,2; 14,1; Col. 2,4; Rev 14,13 (ᵃ). Finally, Our Lord's words to those who arrested Him (Mk 14,49): ἀλλ' ἵνα πληρωθῶσιν αἱ γραφαί are not necessarily to be understood as·an ellipsis (as often in Mattew's own style, e. g. 26,56 and parallels), i. e. « (this happens) that the Scriptures may be fulfilled », but may express Our Lord's acceptance of the Father's will: « let the Scriptures be fulfilled! » — In modern Greek νά (= ἵνα) with the subjunctive is sometimes found for the imperative.

3) Ὅτι in Noun-Clauses and Causal Clauses.

416. The conjunction ὅτι has two uses. One of these is causal, introducing adverb-clauses, « because ... »; the other introduces noun-clauses, « that ... », whether as object of the verb (of saying, perceiving, and — Hellenistically — thinking, etc.) e. g. οἴδαμεν ὅτι ἀληθής εἶ (Mk 12,14) or as subject e. g. Gal 3,11: ὅτι δὲ ἐν νόμῳ οὐδεὶς δικαιοῦται ... δῆλον (ᵇ). The use of the same word ὅτι in two senses so different from each other may at times lead to ambiguity, e. g. where Simon the Pharisee, seeing the sinful woman kissing Jesus's feet, thought « if this man were a prophet, he would surely know who and what manner of woman this is, ὅτι she is a sinner ». Lk 7,39. This clause with ὅτι may equally well be understood as a noun-clause dependent upon « would know », i. e., « (namely) that she is a sinner », or as an adverbial clause « Because she is a sinner ». So too Lk 1,45; 2,11.

(ᵃ) A. R. GEORGE, *The Imperatival Use of ἵνα in the NT*, in *J. Th. St.* 45(1944), 56-60, and A. P. SALOM under the same title in *Aust. Bi. R.* 6(1958), 123-141.

(ᵇ) This ὅτι when introducing direct speech is equivalent to our colon (:); it is very common in Mark and John, perhaps owing to the influence of Aramaic, which uses *di* (Hebrew *ki*) in the same way; e. g. Jo 10,36.

295

296 417. Some have sought to diminish, by an appeal to the ambiguity of ὅτι, the difficulty caused by Mt 2,23: « and He came and dwelt in the city ... of Nazareth, that might be fulfilled which was said by the prophets, ὅτι Ναζωραῖος κληθήσεται; for although the Messiah is called by Isaiah (11,1) *neser* flower (from the root of Jesse) », it is nowhere written that he « would be called » *neser*. Hence it is convenient to be able to translate not « *that* he would be called a Nazarene », but « (the prophecy is fulfilled) *because* he will be called a Nazarene ». Κληθήσεται moreover may be understood as a servile version of a Semitic « future » which can equally well be rendered as a present. The quotation from « the prophets » would thus be reduced to the single word *neser*. So ZAHN, HARNACK, HOLZMEISTER.

418. Ὅτι is found in the two senses in the same text in Gal 3,11: ὅτι δὲ ἐν νόμῳ οὐδεὶς δικαιοῦται ... δῆλον ὅτι ὁ δίκαιος ἐκ πίστεως ζήσεται, but one may wonder which is to be taken in which sense (i. e., which declares what is « clear », and which gives the reason why it is clear). It would seem that the first ὅτι is « that » and the second « because », inasmuch as it offers a reason, i. e. an argument, in the form of a Scriptural text, which as such has no need of justification. Hence the sense would seem to be « it is clear *that* nobody is justified by the law *because* (as the Scripture teaches us) the just man lives by faith ».

419. This ambiguity is troubling to the exegete in Gal 4,6: ὅτι δέ ἐστε υἱοί, ἐξαπέστειλεν ὁ θεὸς τὸ πνεῦμα τοῦ υἱοῦ αὐτοῦ εἰς τὰς καρδίας ὑμῶν ... Is the adoption as sons of God the reason why God sends the Spirit (causal ὅτι), or is the sending of the Spirit crying « Abba, Father » an argument showing that we are sons of God (ὅτι « that, frequently used by orators in this manner, i. e. introducing a proposition whose demonstration follows)? This latter interpretation seems to be the better one, but the problem cannot be solved on purely linguistic grounds.

297 420. Even within the causal sense of ὅτι there is a distinction which has a certain importance. In general ὅτι, like « because » in English, gives a reason why the fact is as it is stated to be, or why something happens, as e. g. Jo 5,16 ἐδίωκον ... Ἰησοῦν, ὅτι ταῦτα ἐποίει ἐν σαββάτῳ; but sometimes it is used to give the reason for which what precedes is known to be so, or is said, or the reason why a question is asked, e. g. Mt 8,27 (= Mk 4,41), after the calming of the storm they « wondered, saying: who is this, ὅτι the winds and the sea obey him? » Here ὅτι gives the reason fo the asking of such a question, not for a statement of fact. So too frequently in the Scriptures, e. g. Heb 2,6 (= Ps 8, 5f) « What is man, ὅτι thou bearest him in mind, or the son of man ὅτι thou visitest him? » cf. Lk 4,36; 11,18; 13,2; Jo 2,18; 7,35; 14,22; Gen 20,9; Judges 14,3; 1 Sam 20,1; 3 Kings 18,9 (¹⁰).

298   421. The reason whereby a thing is known to be so is indicated by a simple « because » in many colloquial expressions, such as for example « He is dead, because he lived in the middle ages »; in Greek it would be better, in such cases, to use not ὅτι but γάρ.

299   422. This use of ὅτι has acquired a considerable importance in connection with the text which from patristic times onwards has been used — as it still is — to show that « perfect charity » has the power· of forgiving sins (¹¹). In Lk 7,47 Our Lord says of the sinful woman « many sins are forgiven her, ὅτι she has loved much », a text which, taken outside its context, might seem clear enough. The context, however, renders the interpretation just referred to almost impossible; for Our Lord goes on at once do add, « but he to whom less is forgiven, loves less », with evident reference to the parable whereby He had shown Simon that the greater mercy calls forth the greater love of gratitude. Our Lord applies this parable to the love so exuberantly manifested by the sinful woman, so that the logical sequence is: as the love which results is the greater, according as the debt which is cancelled is greater, so this woman's love is so great because so many sins have been forgiven her; in other words, the sense demanded by the context (and confirmed by Our Lord's own words in verse 47b) is « she loves because she is forgiven », and not « she

---

(¹⁰) Some admit for all these examples a « consecutive » ὅτι, e. g. W. BAUER, *Griechisch-deutsches Worterbuch* (ed. 5, 1958) under ὅτι, 1 d (col. 980), F. - M. ABEL, *Grammaire* ..., § 79 (p. 353): « ὅτι, Hebr 2,6; Mt 8,27 ... présente un des sens de *ki* hébreu, sens consécutif, qui n'est pas contraire au génie grec ». But since nearly all the biblical examples are of the same type (ὅτι after a question) and admit readily enough a causal sense, I do not see the need to lay down a further, consecutive, sense for ὅτι. The one exception would be 1 Tim 6,7 οὐδὲν γὰρ εἰσηνέγκαμεν εἰς τὸν κόσμον, ὅτι οὐδὲ ἐξενεγκεῖν τι δυνάμεθα, but the text is here uncertain, for some witnesses have δῆλον ὅτι which is also implied by the Vulgate's « ... haud dubium quod ... ».

(¹¹) For this and what follows, cf. D. BUZY in *Verbum Salutis* VI, *Les Paraboles*, p. 253ff on the parable of the two debtors and its application to the sinful woman.

is forgiven because she loves ». And this is in fact the sense of the Greek expression, so long as the ὅτι is understood in the special causal sense which gives the reason not why the fact *is* so, but whereby it is *known* to be so: « Many sins have been forgiven her, because she loves much » with « because » in the same sense as for example: « he has come into money, because he is spending freely ». Thus the text is ambiguous of itself, owing to the ambiguity of ὅτι, and the sense must be gathered from the context; here Our Lord's own addition « but he to whom less is forgiven loves less » admits of only one interpretation of the causal relationship: the love is caused by the forgiveness and not vice versa. The parallelism and the opposition expressed by the « but » (δέ) demands the same causal relationship in the preceding expression, i. e. the sense of ὅτι « because » which has just been proposed.

This interpretation, the only one satisfying logic (because it is an application of the parable) and grammar (because of the parallel member just mentioned), obviously supposes the sinful woman to have been aware that she was forgiven even before Our Lord said so; and in this one may perhaps see a difficulty (¹⁹). Cf. also 427.

4) The Ambiguity of the Aramaic Particle *di* (¹⁹).

300   423. The ambiguity of the Aramaic particle *di* could not but give rise to variant renderings of the underlying oral or written Aramaic tradition; for this particle can have no fewer than seven values: relative pronoun, genitive case, the conjunction ὅτι (in both of the two senses just explained), or ἵνα or ὅτε or ὥστε.

301   424. a) **Causal ὅτι instead of the relative pronoun.** Where Mt 13,16 has « blessed are the eyes because (ὅτι) they see », Lk 10,23 has « blessed are the eyes which see (οἱ βλέποντες) ». Where Mt 6,5 has causal ὅτι, the Vulgate supposes a text with the relative: « cum oratis non eritis sicut hypocritae qui (but the Greek has ὅτι) amant... ». Similarly Mk 4,41 « who is this, that (ὅτι) the wind and the sea obey him » might well have been « who is this, whom the wind and the sea obey », a form of text

---

(¹⁹) For this difficulty see Buzy, *loc. cit.*, p. 258f, where it is also shown that the view exposed above is not lacking in patristic backing (p. 261f).

(¹¹) On this point f. M. Black, *An Aramaic Approach*, pp. 52-62.

which is in fact supposed by some Old Latin (ff² i q « cui »); cf. Mt 5,45. For Jo 8,45 ἐγὼ δὲ ὅτι τὴν ἀλήθειαν λέγω, οὐ πιστεύετέ μοι (which in Greek would mean « you do not believe *that* I am telling the truth ») the Vulgate has « ego si . . . », but two manuscripts have « qui » instead of « si ». In Jo 9,16f also the Vulgate has a relative for the Greek ὅτι: « tu quid dicis de illo qui aperuit oculos tuos? » Finally Jo 5,39 « search the Scriptures because (ὅτι, Vulgate « quia ») ye think ye have in them eternal life » is in the Old Latin a (b) e ff² rendered « . . . Scripturas in quibus putatis habere... », a reading confirmed by the Egerton Papyrus (before 150) and for other reasons known to be as anciently attested as the reading of our Greek NT manuscipts (¹⁴).

302   **425. b) Ἵνα instead of the relative pronoun** seems to have some probability for Jo 5,7 « I have nobody to (ἵνα for ὅς?) put me in the pool ». Similarly perhaps 1,8; 6,30. 50; 9,36; 14,16 (BURNEY). Ἵνα for the relative seems to account for the difference, and at the same time show the original agreement between Mk 4,22 and Mt 10,26: for Mk has οὐ γάρ ἐστίν τι κρυπτὸν ἐὰν μὴ ἵνα φανερωθῇ, rendered by the Vulgate « non enim est aliquid absconditum quod non reveletur », which corresponds exactly to Mt ... ὃ οὐκ ἀποκαλυφθήσεται and to Lk 8,17 ὃ οὐ φανερόν γενήσεται. Mark's ἵνα may stand for the ambiguous *di* which in Mt and Lk is rendered in a more obvious manner by the relative pronoun.

303   **426. The same ambiguity** perhaps provides an explanation of how Mk 4,12 came to have the difficult ἵνα which seems to make Jesus say that He taught in parables *in order that* (ἵνα) « seeing they see not, lest they be converted and their sins be forgiven ». One may suppose that the Aramaic source, with its ambiguous *di*, was rather to be rendered, with a relative, « οἵτινες (= inasmuch as they) see not . . . », which would give the same sense as Mt 13,13 « because they see not . . . (ὅτι) », and would also correspond to the Targum of the Isaiah quotation which begins « Go and say to this people which hears and understands not . . . », for here Mk, along with the Targum, against the Hebrew and the LXX, has « (lest they be converted) and their sins be forgiven ». We have therefore three different renderings all corresponding to Aramaic *di*: Mk ἵνα, Mt ὅτι, LXX (as compared with the Targum) ὅς. This point is certainly not lacking in importance for those who seek to know what Jesus really

---

(¹⁴) M. E. BOISMARD in *Revue Biblique*, 1948, pp. 3-34.

said, or rather, in what sense He meant what He is known to have said. The difficulty still remains, however, that Mark certainly seems to have understood the Aramaic *di* in a final sense Cf. 413.

304   427. c) **eannsnl ὅτι instead of ὅτι introducing direct speech.** As we have already seen (422), in Lk 7,47 the parable of the two debtors to whom their debt was remitted ought, from the whole tenor of the passage, to end as follows: «wherefore I say to thee, he who has been forgiven many sins loves much, while he who is forgiven less loves less ». In fact, however, we have only the second member of the parallelism to be expected, while instead of the first member we have «many sins are forgiven her, ὅτι she has loved much». The loss of the parallelism may be attributed to the ambiguity of the particle *di*; for the parallelism is restored if we suppose *di* to have been used twice in the Aramaic original, and to have been (on both occasions) misunderstood in rendering into Greek: « I say to thee *di* many sins are forgiven her *di* she loves much ». In the Greek version the first *di* was taken as introducing the direct speech which follows, and so was not rendered into Greek at all, while the second *di* was rendered ὅτι , presumably understood as causal. If however the first *di* be taken as a relative, and the second as introducing the direct speech enunciating the predicate (whose subject is enunciated by the relative clause), we have: « I say to thee, (he) who is forgiven many sins (. . .) loves much »: here (. . .) represents the second *di* which in English usage is to be left untranslated. I mention this hypothesis on account of its interest, without thereby attributing to it a high degree of   probability.

305   428. d) **Ἵνα or ὅτι instead of ὅτε.** The temporal use of the particle *di* is but a variety of its use as a relative, the latter having temporal force with a temporal antecedent. Burney cites six examples from Jo e. g. 16,2 « the time is coming Ἵνα (instead of ὅτε or ᾗ) anyone that kills you will think... ». The same formula ἔρχεται ὥρα Ἵνα is found also in 12,23; 13,1; 16,32. It is to be noted moreover that the same Johannine ἔρχεται ὥρα is elsewhere followed by ὅτε: 4,21 23; 5,25; 16,25; and once by ἐν ᾗ: 5,28; so that it seems clear that ὥρα Ἵνα and ὥρα ὅτε are alternatives equivalent to each other, so that there is no need to suspect any final nuance in the Ἵνα.

306   429. There remain two cases in which not Ἵνα but ὅτι seems to stand for ὅτε: Jo 9,8: « the neighbours who had seen him before, ὅτι (instead of ὅτε?) he was a beggar », and Jo 12,41: « thus said Isaiah ὅτι (codex Bezae: ὅτε, Vulgate: « quando ») he saw His glory ». Finally some include here also Jo 8,56: « your father Abraham exulted Ἵνα ἴδῃ (for ὅτε εἶδεν?) My day ».

XIV. THE NEGATIVES

440. a) The distinction (at times a subtle one) of classical usage between the negatives οὐ (« objective » or « factual ») and μή (« subjective » or « conceptual ») is so simplified in Hellenistic Greek that it may be said that in practice for the NT οὐ is used with the indicative (¹) and μή with the other moods, including the infinitive and the participle (²).

441. Hence ambiguities may arise in the NT which would not arise in classical usage, e. g. Gal 6,9 « let us not be remiss in doing good, for when the time comes we shall reap μὴ ἐκλυόμενοι »: in classical usage the sense would be ἐὰν (or ὅσοι ἂν) μὴ ἐκλυώμεθα, but in the NT the sense may be that of οὐκ ἐκλυόμενοι, i. e. simply « tirelessly ». Similarly Rom 8,4: ἐν ἡμῖν τοῖς μὴ κατὰ σάρκα περιπατοῦσιν (classically « inasmuch as we do not walk . . . ») might in NT usage mean simply « who (as a matter of fact) do not walk . . . ».

442. Can μή mean « except »? The question has a certain importance in connection with the « divorce clauses »; for it is obviously likely that the two expressions (Mt 5,32 and 19,9) have the same meaning, i. e. that μὴ ἐπὶ πορνείᾳ means the same thing as the previous παρεκτὸς λόγου πορνείας. The meaning would of course be the same if μή could mean «except», but this is with good reason denied by many scholars. In this passage however, μή not only may but should mean « except », not that μή = « ex-

---

(¹) So even in « real » conditions and once even in a « unreal » one, Mt 26,24 = Mk 14,21. Μή with the indicative: Tit 1,11 ἃ μὴ δεῖ and Jo 3,18 in a causal clause, a usage singular in the NT but not rare Hellenistically (Debr. 428,5).

(²) Οὐ instead of μή is natural where οὐ belongs to a particular word, with which it often merges to give a single notion, e. g. Php 1,16 οὐχ ἁγνῶς = « insincerely »; 1 Cor 7,9 εἰ οὐκ ἐγκρατεύονται « if they are incontinent »; 2 Thess 3,10 εἴ τις οὐ θέλει ἐργάζεσθαι « if anyone is unwilling to work ». So too with participles e. g. Col 2,19 οὐ κρατῶν τὴν κεφαλήν, the sense being « relinquishing, rejecting ». Cf. Mt 22,11; Lk 6,42; Jo 10,12; Acts 7,5; 1 Pet 1,8.

cept » is of itself admissible, but because μή is here dependent upon the introductory ὅσοι ἄν which is equivalent to ἐάν τις (« whoever = if anyone dismiss his wife μὴ ἐπὶ πορνείᾳ... ») and thus we have (ἐὰν) μή = « unless », i. e. « except ». Both expressions, therefore, lay down the same true exception; as for the interpretation of the exception cf. Verb. Dom. 38 (1960), 193-212.

308   443. b) Οὐ in the legal language of the OT is used with the future indicative to express prohibition: οὐ φονεύσεις. In the NT (apart from quotations from the OT) the same usage is found, but very rarely, in the mouth of Christ, e. g. Mt 6,5 οὐκ ἔσεσθε ὡς οἱ ὑποκριταί, 20,26 οὐχ οὕτως ἔσται ἐν ὑμῖν. Cf. 280.

309   444. c) Οὐ μή with the aorist subjunctive (probably because the sense is οὐ φόβος ἐστὶν μή) or with the future indicative (*) is used classically as an emphatic negative for the future. In the NT the use of this construction has become more frequent, while the emphasis seems to have decreased, as is to be seen especially where it is used in relative clauses, e. g. Mk 13,2 οὐ μὴ ἀφεθῇ ὧδε λίθος ἐπὶ λίθον ὃς οὐ μὴ καταλυθῇ or in questions, e. g. Rev 15,4 τίς οὐ μὴ φοβηθῇ, or in expressions of anxiety like Mt 25,9 μήποτε οὐ μὴ ἀρκέσῃ...

Outside the book of Revelation, where it occurs sixteen times, this construction is almost limited to quotations from the LXX and the words of Jesus (57 out of 61 occurrences in the gospels), so that Semitic influence might have been suspected, were it not that it has no Semitic equivalent, so that the LXX renders the simple Hebrew lo' indiscriminately by οὐ or by οὐ μή.

Nor can the frequency of the construction in the NT be explained from popular Greek usage, for in the papyri οὐ μή is rare, and is always very emphatic. Hence Moulton (p. 192) suggests that its use is due to the feeling of the writers that it is peculiarly suited, as being especially decisive, to sacred utterances.

In the majority of the NT uses, therefore, οὐ μή may be said to express « prophetic » emphasis. In the other uses it expresses, as in Greek in general, an « emotional » emphasis, and it is to be noted that it is never used by the Evangelists (or by Luke in Acts) in their own narrative

---

(*) Mt 26,35; Mk 13,31; 14,31; Jo 10,5; Gal 4,30.

but only in quoting the spoken word (Mt 16,22; 26,35 = Mk 4,31; Jo 13,8; 20,25, and perhaps Lk 1,15; Jo 11,56). So too there is the usual emphasis in the four places where Paul has οὐ μή, and the same applies to the epistles in general (whose style is naturally closer to the vivid one of speech).

310   445. d) In **disjunctive** propositions, it is a Semitic peculiarity to express one member negatively so as to lay more stress on the other, saying « not A but B » where the sense is « not so much A as B » or « B rather than A ». A well-known example is Hos 6,6, where the author himself indicates the sense of the idiom by the parallel second member: « I desire mercy and *not* sacrifice; and the knowledge of God *more than* holocausts ». In the NT cf. 1 Cor 1,17 οὐ γὰρ ἀπέστειλέν με Χριστὸς βαπτίζειν ἀλλὰ εὐαγγελίζεσθαι, Mt 10,20 οὐ γὰρ ὑμεῖς ἐστε οἱ λαλοῦντες ἀλλὰ τὸ πνεῦμα; Jo 12,44 ὁ πιστεύων εἰς ἐμὲ οὐ πιστεύει εἰς ἐμὲ ἀλλὰ εἰς τὸν πέμψαντά με, cf. also Mk 9,37; Lk 10,20; Jo 7,16. This idiom reflects the same mentality as that which uses « hate » to say « love less » (cf. Lk 14,26 with Mt 10,37).

One may thus judge how weak are the arguments against the antiquity of the Mosaic legislation with respect to worship founded on Jer 7,22f: « I did not speak with your fathers and did not command them in the day in which I led them forth from the land of Egypt with regard to holocausts and victims, but this is the command which I gave them: hear my voice... and walk in every way that I have bidden you... » which is but another way of saying: obedience is better than sacrifice (*). Note however that the contrary may occur, i. e. the sense of μᾶλλον... ἤ may really be « not... but », as « and men loved darkness rather than light » Jo 3,19. So too 12,43; Acts 4,19; 5,29; 27,11; 1 Tim 1,14; 2 Tim 3,4; Heb 11,25.

311   446. e) Instead of οὐδείς we find the Semitic οὐ... πᾶς (= the Hebrew lo'... kol), e. g. Mt 24,22 οὐκ ἂν ἐσώθη πᾶσα σάρξ; Acts 10,14 οὐδέποτε ἔφαγον πᾶν κοινόν. Similarly, but this is not so exclusively Semitic, we have πᾶς... οὐ, e. g. πᾶς λόγος σαπρός... μὴ ἐκπορευέσθω

(*) This Semitic idiom and its importance for exegesis has been dealt with, with many examples, by Heinz KRUSE, *Dialektische Negation als semitisches Idiom*, in *Vetus Testamentum* 4(1954), 385-400.

Eph 4,49, and εἴς ... οὐ, e. g. Mt 10,29 καὶ ἓν ἐξ αὐτῶν οὐ πεσεῖται ἐπὶ τὴν γῆν, which occurs also in Greek in the sense « not even one ».

447. Since οὐ may introduce a question (expecting the answer « yes » like the negative-interrogative in English, Latin *nonne*, as against μή ... = Latin *num*, i. e. expecting the answer « no »), some have suggested as a solution to the difficulty of Jo 2,4 the version: « what is that to me and to thee? Is not my hour already come? » and M. – E. Boismard regards this as not merely a possibility but a probability on the grounds that in every other case in the NT (but unfortunately there are only two such cases) where οὔπω follows a question, it is itself also interrogative: Mk 4,41: « why are you afraid? Have you still no faith? » and especially Mk 8,17 (= Mt 16,9) where, just as Mary remarks the lack of wine at Cana, the disciples are troubled because they have no bread with them, and Jesus says to them: « Why do you make account of your lack of bread? Do you still not know or understand? » (*Du baptême à Cana*, 1956, p. 156).

XV. THE PARTICLES

1) The Particle καί.

312 **450.** To a certain extent any popular speech tends to eschew the subordination of ideas and the accurate and explicit expression of their logical connection. This is especially the case in Semitic speech, which further (if not « therefore ») lacks that variety of particles and conjunctions with which languages, especially in literary usage, and above all Greek, can and do express nuances of logical connection.

451. This Semitic habit of paratactic thought and expression sometimes accounts for texts which, to those accustomed to more accurate subordination, must seem obscure, or at least strange. Thus e. g. we read in 1 Cor 12,3 « none that speaks in the Spirit of God says ' Jesus is anathema', and none can say 'Jesus is Lord' but in the Holy Spirit ». At first sight this seems perfectly clear and straightforward: with the Spirit none can reject Christ, and without the Spirit none can accept Him. Some have however seen in the first of the two statements a reference to pseudo-charismatics who « in the Spirit » said « Jesus is anathema », and there has been much discussion as to who they might be; and thanks to the attention thus drawn to the passage, it has been noticed that the seemingly obvious sense is not so good as the one which is obtained by understanding a subordination of comparison: not simply « none can say in the Spirit 'Jesus is anthema' and none can say without the Spirit 'Jesus is Lord' », but « *just as* none can say ... » (which is obvious), « *so* none can say , ... » (which is what Paul wishes to show).

This type of construction (the coordination of two assertions, of which one is merely a comparison for the demonstration of the other) is not foreign to the OT, indeed is very frequent in Prov, e. g. « the heaven above and the earth below and the heart of the king (are) inscrutable » 25,3; so too 25,3. 23. 25. 27; 26, 7. 9. 14 etc.

452. Also in other cases (i. e. without underlying comparison) the apparent paradox of one of two members can be solved by its subordination,

e. g. Rom 6,17 «thanks be to God that you were slaves to sin but have been obedient ...» i. e. «that *although* you were ... yet you have been...». Similarly perhaps Mt 11,25 (= Lk 10,21) «I confess to Thee, Father, ... because Thou hast hidden these things from the wise ... and revealed them to little ones», i. e. «because *though* ...». Hence also Jo 1, (16) 17 «... we have received ... grace for grace, for the Law was given by Moses, grace and truth have been wrought by Jesus Christ» may, according to the exegete's opinions, be understood as «for *whereas* the Law...», so that the conjunction «for» introduces properly only «grace and truth...»; the same seems to apply to the conjunction μήποτε in Lk 14,8f; καθώς in 1 Jo 3,12; for γάρ see below, 472ff.

453. It may likewise happen that a question extend properly to the second only of two clauses, but seem on account of the coordination to extend to both, e. g. Mt 18,21 «how often shall my brother offend me and I forgive him? » So in the OT Isa 50,2 «why did I come and there was no man, why did I call and there was none to hear? », i. e. «why *when* I came, was there no man...?» For this and similar Semitic idioms see JOÜON, *Grammaire* ... 161 k.

We may now come to the various uses of coordinating καί which in the NT offer more or less clear indications of the Semitic character of the writer's thought, or of his sources. Under this heading we have:

313   454. a) the monotonous frequency, unknown to Greek literature, of καί used at the beginning of each narration and of each sentence of the narration. This usage, which is not an Aramaic but rather a Hebrew one, is especially conspicuous in Mark.

314   455. b) the « neutral » use of simple καί for:

α) «and yet », e. g. Mt 6,26 οὐ σπείρουσιν ... καὶ ὁ πατὴρ τρέφει αὐτά. Cf. Mt 3,14; 10,29; and especially John 1,10; 3,11; 5,43; 6,70; 7,28 30; 8,20; 9,30; 10,25; 16,32.

β) « but », e. g. Mk 12,12 «they sought to take Him καὶ they feared the multitude»; Jo 14,30; Acts 10,28b; 1 Cor 16,12b.

γ) «so that» final or consecutive, e. g. Mt 5,15 «they light a candle and set it ... on a candlestick καὶ it lights all » (Vulgate: « ut luceat»); Lk 5,1; 24,26. — Mk 8,25 «and he began to see, and was cured καὶ saw everything clearly » (Vulgate: « ita ut clare videret »); Lk 11,44; Rom 11,35.

δ) «when», e. g. Mk 15,25 «it was the third hour καί they crucified Him»; Lk 19,43.

ε) relative pronoun, e. g. Lk 6,6 «and there was a man there καί
his (= «whose») right hand was paralysed»; 1,49; 19,2; 24,18. — Under
this heading we may put also the passages where a relative clause is continued (as also in normal Greek usage) with καί... αὐτοῦ etc. instead
of another relative, e. g. 2 Pet 2,3 «whose judgement is without end and
their perdition sleeps not»; Rev 17,2.

ζ) «that is», e. g. Acts 5,21 «they assembled τὸ συνέδριον καί
πᾶσαν τὴν γερουσίαν» (unless πᾶσα ἡ γερουσία is a different body from
the sanhedrin?); Gal 6,16 «peace upon them (= the new creation) καί
(=« that is»?) upon God's Israel». Perhaps too Jo 4,10 can be rendered
« if thou knewest the gift of God, that is (καί) who it is that says to thee...».

316   456. c) καί with a finite verb, instead of the Greek construction
with infinitive alone, after introductory ἐγένετο. This καί, rendering
the conjunction which is obligatory in Hebrew, is often omitted by the
LXX and so also by Luke (22 times without καί, eleven times with καί).
Cf. 389.

318   457. d) καί corresponding to the Hebrew « apodotic *waw* » to introduce the main clause after a subordinate one, e. g. after a temporal clause:
καὶ ὅτε ἐπλήσθησαν ἡμέραι ὀκτώ... καὶ ἐκλήθη Lk 2,21; or a conditional
one: ἐάν τις ἀνοίξῃ τὴν θύραν καί (variant reading) εἰσελεύσομαι Rev 3,20;
after ὡς Lk 7,12; Acts 1,10. Perhaps also after ἐν τῷ with infinitive Lk
2,27f (cf. Ezek 47,3).

458. The existence of this usage sometimes renders it uncertain in Hebrew
whether a *wayyiqtol* or *weqatal* is a continuation of the subordinate clause
or is the verb of the main clause. A celebrated example is to be found in the
« law of Moses » which, according to the scribes (Mt 19,7; Mk 10,3f) not only
permitted but prescribed divorce, Deut 24,1-4. This passage, rendered in accordance with the scribes' interpretation (which is also, for that matter, the
Vulgate's) gives: (if a man take a wife ... and she find not favour in his eyes...
he shall write a bill of divorce ... and *shall send* her away from his house ...»,
a law prescribing the bill of divorce and the dismissal of the wife. In fact however the law does not directly touch divorce; for it presupposes the existing
custom of divorce, and is concerned merely with setting limits to its use, by
laying down that after divorce « the first husband, who dismissed her, shall
not have the right to take her back to wife ...» and this only is the real main
clause; for the ten coordinate clauses which precede all belong to the condi-

tional element, and their sense is clear if, instead of taking the *waw* as apodotic, we take it as simply conjunctive « and », so as to render: «... *and write*... *and send*... » etc. Hence not even the bill of divorce (declaring the wife free to contract a new marriage) is here prescribed; it is merely taken into account as an existing institution. The saying of the scribes in Mt 19,7 is an arbitrary interpretation of a legal text which owing to the ambiguity of the particle *waw* admitted such an interpretation. (Cf. B. N. WAMBACQ in *Verb. Dom.* 33[1955], 331-335).

319   **459.** The situation is different where καί introduces a question, e. g. 2 Cor 2,2 εἰ καὶ ἐγὼ λυπῶ ὑμᾶς, καὶ τίς ὁ εὐφραίνων με; for the second καί connotes a previously expressed circumstance (« then... ») and is to be found without a preceding clause, e. g. Mk 10,26 καὶ τίς δύναται σωθῆναι (so too Mk 4.13; 9,12; 10,26; Lk 1,43; 10,29; 20,44; Jo 9,36; 14,22). Php 1,22 also seems to have a similar direct question, so that perhaps one should punctuate εἰ δὲ τοῦτό μοι καρπὸς ἔργου, καὶ τί αἱρήσομαι; οὐ γνωρίζω. Like καί τί in such questions we find also τί καί, e. g. 1 Cor 15,29 « if the dead do not rise, τί καὶ βαπτίζονται ὑπὲρ αὐτῶν », Lk 13,7; Jo 8,25; Rom 3,7; 8,24.

320   **460.** e) καί coordinating two ideas one of which depends upon the other as being a further determination of it: περὶ ἐλπίδος καὶ ἀναστάσεως... ἐγὼ κρίνομαι (= « the hope of resurrection ») Acts 23,6; and perhaps twice in Acts 14,17: ὑετοὺς διδοὺς καὶ καιροὺς καρποφόρους (« weather fruitful by reason of rain ») ἐμπιπλῶν τροφῆς καὶ εὐφροσύνης (« gladness given by food »). So too Mk 6,26 διὰ τοὺς ὅρκους καὶ τοὺς ἀνακειμένους (« the oath in presence of the guests »), or with two verbs Lk 6,48 ἔσκαψεν καὶ ἐβάθυνεν (« deepened by digging »); cf. Mk 5,19 ὅσα... σοι πεποίηκεν καὶ ἐλέησέν σε (« what mercies He has shown thee »); 11,24 ὅσα προσεύχεσθε καὶ αἰτεῖσθε (« whatever you ask in prayer »). This is the figure called « hendiadys ».

321   **461.** f) perhaps to be included under this heading: καί after a final clause to introduce a further effect, e. g. Jo 15,8 ἵνα καρπὸν φέρητε καὶ γενήσεσθε ἐμοὶ μαθηταί, unless indeed the καὶ γενήσεσθε itself also depends upon ἵνα (cf. 342).

322   **462.** καί readily means « also », and thus is sometimes to be found is stereotyped manner after διό, διὰ τοῦτο, e. g. διὰ τοῦτο καὶ ἡ σοφία τοῦ θεοῦ εἶπεν Lk 11,49. The expression διὰ τοῦτο καί seems to be so stereotyped as to separate the καί from the idea to which it belongs and seem to apply it to something to which it does not belong, e. g. διὰ τοῦτο καὶ ἡμεῖς εὐχαριστοῦμεν 1 Thess 2,13, or διὰ τοῦτο κἀγώ... ἔπεμψα 3,5, where the καί does not belong to the pronouns, but to the verbs (or rather, to the whole clause).

323   463. A very frequent usage which would seem to belong to this class is that where καί immediately follows the relative pronoun ([1]) without there seeming to be any special reason for its insertion ([2]). This occurs especially where the relative clause is not a subordinate one but an independent one.

In two places it is of some importance for exegesis to know whether such a καί was to be rendered « also » or simply to be omitted in translation:

464. 2 Cor 3,5f: « not that we are sufficient to think anything of ourselves, as of ourselves, but our sufficiency is from God, ὅς καί has made us apt ministers of the new covenant . . . ». If the καί is a stereotyped and colourless one, the text refers only to the capacity to carry out efficaciously the apostolate; but if the καί is to be understood as meaningful, the text refers to this « too », i. e. the apostle's need of divine aid is merely a particular case of the universal need of grace, without which we can do nothing. It is in this sense that the Council of Orange cited the passage (DENZINGER 180) as a proof of the necessity of grace for every act profitable to salvation.

465. In Php 2,5 τοῦτο φρονεῖτε ἐν ὑμῖν ὃ καί ἐν Χριστῷ Ἰησοῦ, if καί is to be rendered « also » we have a comparison between the sentiments of the faithful and those of Christ; but if the καί is otiose, the sense may be simply « entertain among yourselves the sentiments which are ἐν Χριστῷ Ἰησοῦ » the latter expression being the well-known Pauline formula, and the meaning being: the sentiments fitting in a member of Christ's mystical body.

2) The Particle τε.

324   466. The particle τε occurs eight times in St Luke's gospel, and 158 times in his Acts. This huge disproportion is noteworthy; for since the particle in question is an insignificant one which the author, had he wished,

---

([1]) As I have never found a list of these texts, I here add a more or less complete one: Mt 10,4; Mk 3,19; Lk 6,13f; 7,49; 10,30. 39; Jo 8,25 (?); Acts 1,3. 11; 7,45; 10,39; 11,30; 12,4; 13,22; 17,34; 22,5; 24,6 (twice); 16,10. 26. 29; 26,10. 12 (l. v.); 27,23; 28,10; Rom 4,22; 5,2; 8,34; 9,24; 1 Cor 1,8; 2,13; 4,5; 11,23; 15,1-3 (four times); 15,29f; 2 Cor 1,22; 3,6; 5,2 (variant); Gal 2,10; Col 1,29; 2,11f; 3,15; 4,3; Eph 1,11. 13 (twice); 2,22 Php 2,5; 3,10. 12. 20; 4,9; 1 Thess 2,13; 5,24; 2 Thess 1,5. 11; Heb 1,2; 6,7; 7,2. 4; 1 Pet 2,8; 3,19. 21.

([2]) CADBURY has written briefly on this in *J. B. L.* 42(1923), 157.

might again and again have used instead of καί, the enormous difference of frequency between the same author's two works cannot be explained as due to the subject matter as such, but must be the result of deliberate choice of style (admittedly founded on the subject matter) on the part of the writer. The use of τε is thus a further argument to add to what has already been said with regard to the different constructions used in the gospel and in the Acts with the Lukan καὶ ἐγένετο... (389; cf. also 199). It is also to be noted that of the 158 occurences in Acts, 112 are in in the second part (chapter 13 on).

The correlative use τε... τε (as distinct from the usual τε ... καί) is found once only in the NT, and that in the mouth of Paul before A-grippa, Acts 26,16, i. e. in highly rhetorical style.

3) The Particle δέ.

325 **467.** The particle δέ nearly always implies some sort of contrast, but is sometimes also used with « progressive » or « explanatory » force, meaning « and moreover », « and at that » (where the contrast is still there, namely with an existing or possible false estimate). This value of δέ is usually obvious from the context, e. g. « obedient μέχρι θανάτου, θανά-του δὲ σταυροῦ » Php 2,8 (cf. also Acts 24,19; Rom 3,22; 9,30; 1 Cor 2,6; 10,29; Gal 2,2; Php 1,23; 1 Tim 1,14). Sometimes, however, it may — at least as a hypothesis — be appealed to where it is not obvious, in order to solve difficulties. Thus for example in the obscure passage Gal 2,3–6 one may perhaps lessen the obscurity and find a satisfactory logi-cal sequence by supposing only one principal statement (that Titus was not forced to be circumcised) followed by two δέ–clauses which merely explain or reinforce it (the negative of the principal statement retaining its force throughout) so that St Paul's justification is that Titus was not obliged to be circumcised, neither *indeed* (δέ) on account of the false brethren nor *indeed* by those who seemed to be something (*).

4) Confusion between εἰ μή and ἀλλά.

468. The expression εἰ μή « if not », « unless », but in the sense « a-part from », « except », is not seldom found where ἀλλά was rather to be

---

(*) Cf. M. BRUNEC in *Verb. Dom.* 25(1947), 280-288.

expected, e. g. Mt 12,4: David ate the shewbread « which it was not lawful for him to eat ... but (εἰ μή) only for the priests ».

469. Even in classical usage εἰ μή is to be found for ἀλλά, and conversely ἀλλά for εἰ μή (DEBR. 448,8), but the frequency with which the two seem to be interchanged in the NT is perhaps to be accounted for in particular by the fact that in Aramaic one and the same particle 'ella (= 'en « if » + la « not ») is used indifferently in both senses. The two Greek renderings are found in parallel use in Mk 4,22: « for there is nothing hidden ἐὰν μή to be revealed, nor anything concealed, ἀλλά to be brought to light ».

470. 'Αλλά « but (only) » was to be expected rather than εἰ μή in Mk 6,5; Lk 4,25-27 (twice); Rom 14,14; Gal 1,7; 2,16; 1 Cor 7,17; Rev 21,27. Moreover, in Gal 1,19 « (apart from Peter) I saw no other apostle εἰ μή James the brother of the Lord », the strict sense of εἰ μή implies that Paul regards James as an apostle; but this conclusion cannot be drawn with certainty, because εἰ μή may be used instead of ἀλλά.

For the converse use of ἀλλά instead of εἰ μή cf. Mk 4,22b; 9,8: « they saw nobody ἀλλά Jesus alone ».

471. Interchange between εἰ μή and ἀλλά does not however solve all the difficulties in this connection, and recourse is perhaps to be had to the general observation made by ZAHN on Jo 3,13: there are many cases in which εἰ μή introduces an exception to a rule which has not in fact been expressed with sufficient logical rigour, e. g. Jo 5,19 « the Son can do nothing *of Himself*, save (ἐὰν μή) what He see the Father doing » (can He then do that *of Himself?*). Unless one bore in mind this loose habit of expression and the frequency with which it occurs along with εἰ μή, one would have to conclude from Jo 3,13 that the speaker was not Jesus but the evangelist, and that he was speaking of the glorified Jesus teaching the church through His Spirit; for the text has: « none has mounted to heaven (so as to be able to teach us of heavenly things) εἰ μή He who came down from heaven, the Son of Man »; to account for the εἰ μή we must understand « none (of those on earth) *has been in heaven* — because none has mounted to heaven — save ... ».

5) Γάρ.

472. Γάρ has almost always causal and explanatory force, but note: a) the argument may be based on an *opposition*, e. g. Php 3,20 destruction is the end of the worldly, ἡμῶν γὰρ τὸ πολίτευμα ἐν οὐρανοῖς ὑπάρχει. Similarly Gal 3,10; 5,5.

473. b) Sometimes γάρ seems to have the sense of δέ, as is perhaps suggested by the frequency of variant readings, in which it seems likely that δέ is a «correction» for a γάρ whose causal sense is not apparent. Hence W. BAUER (*Wörterbuch*) notes in the last place under γάρ that it can be used also «anknüpfend und fortführend», and so with much the same sense as δέ. If this be so there is no point in seeking a causal sense in the following texts: especially in Paul: Rom 1,18; 2,25 («of course»); 4,3. 9; 5,7; 12,3; 14,5; 1 Cor 10,1; 2 Cor 1,12; 10,12; 11,5; Gal 1,11; 5,13; 1 Tim 2,5; but a similar usage is to be found in Luke: 1,15; 12,58 (cf. Mt 5,25); 14,28; Acts 2,34; 4,34a; 8,39; 13,27; 15,28; 16,37; 23,11.

474. c) In other places the difficulty of understanding γάρ is to be solved by keeping its causal force but noting that sometimes the real reason is expressed in the second place only, preceded by something not alleged as a reason but merely conceded parenthetically as well known (clas· sically μὲν γάρ... δέ) cf. Acts 13,36f, where the prophecy «thou shalt not give thy Holy One to see corruption» is justified: «Δαυὶδ μὲν γάρ... saw corruption, ὃν δέ God has raised from the dead did not see corruption».

475. The μέν however is often omitted, and the reader must judge from the subject matter to what the γάρ refers, e. g. Mt 18,7 οὐαὶ τῷ κόσμῳ ἀπὸ τῶν σκανδάλων· ἀνάγκη γὰρ ἐλθεῖν τὰ σκάνδαλα, πλὴν οὐαὶ τῷ ἀνθρώπῳ, δι' οὗ τὸ σκάνδαλον ἔρχεται. The reason for the οὐαὶ τῷ κόσμῳ is not the inevitability of scandals, but what follows: οὐαὶ τῷ ἀνθρώπῳ... So too Mt 22,14 «for many are called but few are chosen» means «for (though many are called) few...». Cf. also Mt 24,6.

476. In the examples cited above the sense is clear from the subject matter; but a like interpretation may serve to remove exegetical difficulties in other cases also, where the sense is not so clear. Thus in Jo 20,17

159

one may perhaps take what immediately follows the γάρ as being paren-
thetical, as in the preceding examples, and render « Do not keep hold
of me, for (I am not yet ascended to My Father) go rather to My brethren and tell them . . . » (γάρ with an imperative offering no difficulty
in Greek), i. e. « let go of me because you must go . . . ».

477. It is to a like use of γάρ that P. LÈON-DUFOUR has recourse
in justification of a new interpretation of the difficult passage Mt 1,18-22,
rendering the angel's words: « Joseph, son of David, fear not to take Mary
thy wife, for (though what is born of her is of the Holy Spirit, yet) she
shall bear a son to whom thou shalt give the name Jesus . . . » (« car sans
doute . . . , mais elle . . . »). Thus the virginal conception is not here revealed to Joseph, but presupposed as known to him, indeed as the reason
for his perplexity. Joseph, on account of the divine intervention, would
have renounced his own conjugal rights; but the angel tells him that,
in the divine plan, he must retain them for it is he that must be the child's
foster-father. (LÉON-DUFOUR, *L'annonce à Joseph*, in *Mélanges . . . A.
Robert*, Paris 1957, pp. 390-397; in like sense: *Le juste Joseph*, in *Nouv.
R. Th.* 81 [1959], 225-32)..

CONCLUSION

326   480. I. Errandonea concludes his Epitome grammaticae Graeco-Biblicae with a very useful « Epilogus Syntaxeos ». I may be permitted to
imitate him in this, and quote what he says by way of introduction to
the detailed exposition: « Consideration shows that most of the syntactical differences between Biblical and classical Greek are in the direction
of making the sense of words or phrases more emphatic or explicit, so that
the function and meaning of individual words comes to be more definitely set forth by the use of particles or in other ways, while more direct,
analytic, and simple expressions take the place of more indirect or complex ones. In this we have the combined effect of Hebrew influence and the
evolution of popular Greek speech ».

Since however the laws that govern the evolution of syntax are at
work likewise in lexical and morphological evolution, we will add, in this
summary, some points concerning these also.

One may therefore put under two headings the tendencies which
govern the evolution of popular speech: on the one hand there is a tendency to more explicit expression, and on the other hand a tendency
to greater simplicity and uniformity.

327   481. a) The **tendency to more explicit expression** is a consequence of the weakening, with use, of the force of older expressions. Under
this heading we have, for syntax: εἰς instead of the nominative or accusative in predicates (32, 70); prepositions instead of simple cases (64,
70f, 80, 119f); the frequency of pronouns (196-205, 233); prepositions
improperly so called instead of simple prepositions (83); the frequency
with which the article is prefixed to the infinitive (382-390); emphatic
negative expressions (444-446); reinforcement of verbs by cognate substantives (60-62); the imitation of the Hebrew infinitive absolute by the
cognate dative (60) or the participle (369); « graphic » participles (363);
the frequency of the periphrastic conjugation (360-362); the preference for ἵνα and ὅτι instead of the infinitive (406-410, 380).

328   **482.** Owing to the same tendency the Hellenistic vocabulary prefers fuller and phonetically stronger forms, e. g. καλῶς instead of εὖ, ἀφίημι instead of ἐῶ, ἀκολουθῶ instead of ἕπομαι; and especially where weakening or ambiguity had arisen in the post-archaic pronunciation («itacism»): thus οἷς « sheep » and ὅς « swine » were identical in pronunciation (probably « üs ») and were replaced by πρόβατον and χοῖρος; so too ὕειν (« üin »?) was replaced by βρέχειν which properly meant « moisten ».

483. The same tendency may perhaps account for the use of ὁμοθυμαδόν not necessarily in the sense « unanimously » but instead of ὁμοῦ « together », or for the use of πληροφορῶ for πληρῶ, or (along with « popular etymology ») of ἐρίθεια for ἔρις (?) (CADBURY).

329   **484.** The same tendency to stronger forms led to a preference for compound forms, often used in the sense expressed in classical usage by the simple forms, instead of the one properly denoted by the compound, e. g. ἐπιγινώσκειν, ἀπαρνεῖσθαι, ἐπιδιδόναι, ἐπιζητεῖν, ἐπιδεικνύναι, καταφιλεῖν etc. Words which in classical usage were compounds with one preposition are reinforced by the addition of a second or even a third, e. g. παρείσακτος, παρεπίδημος, ἀπέκδυσις, ἐπενδύομαι, συναναμίγνυμι, συναντιλαμβάνομαι, ὑπερεκπερισσῶς, ὑπεράνω, κατέναντι etc.

485. Later Greek, and especially popular speech, tended to the use of diminutives without diminutive sense. Hence παιδίον is simply equivalent to παῖς, nor can stress be laid in Mark on the diminutive forms 6,22 κοράσιον (for κόρη), 7,27 κυνάριον (for κύων), 7,25 θυγάτριον (for θυγάτηρ).

330   **486. b)** The tendency to greater simplicity and uniformity has led in syntax to the preference for coordination instead of subordination (450-457), to the suspended nominative (25), to the use of the genitive absolute instead of agreement of the participle with an element of the clause (49), to direct instead of indirect speech, and the rapid passage of the latter, where it is used for a longer passage, into direct speech, e. g. Acts 1,4; 17,3. 25,4-5; Finally we may put under this heading all that was said of the confusion of words with affinity of sense, or the neglect of finer distinctions of sense: the accusative instead of the partitive genitive (67), confusion between prepositions (87-110), the loss of the category of duality (147-153), confusion between pronouns (213-221), the levelling of middle-voice forms to active ones (226), the confusion between final and consecutive sense (351-353), the use of ὅτι even after verbs of opinion (380), and the use of ἵνα for almost every kind of infinitive (406-410).

331   **487.** In **morphology**, this tendency has led to the replacing of unusual-seeming forms by new ones formed by analogy, e. g. κλεῖδα for κλεῖν, χάριτα for χάριν, γήρους for γήρως and the like.

332   **488.** Conjugation likewise tends to be rendered uniform, e. g. the plural of οἶδα is formed analogically: οἴδαμεν, οἴδατε, οἴδασιν instead of ἴσμεν, ἴστε, ἴσασι. So too for the aorists ἔδωκα, ἧκα, ἔθηκα, and in the pluperfect: -ειμεν, -ειτε,-εισαν instead of -εμεν,-ετε,-εσαν. Cf. also δύνασαι instead of δύνῃ.

333   **489.** This tendency has in modern demotic Greek made uniform the ending of the past tenses (e. g. active - α, - ες, - ε, - αμεν, - ατε, - αν, for aorist and imperfect alike); in Hellenistic and Biblical Greek it is already operative in this sense for the aorists, i. e. the endings of the « aorist in -α» tend to be used even for aorists in -ov, to a much greater extent than in classical Greek, where this was restricted to certain aorists such as εἶπον and ἤνεγκον (the latter, indeed, is for most of its forms rather an aorist in -α); hence the frequency of such forms as εἶπαν, ἤλθαμεν, ἔλθατε, ἐνέγκαι (one of the forms never found with this ending in classical usage), ἐξενέγκατε (Lk 15,22), προσένεγκον (Mt 8,4), εἰπόν (Mt 18,17; Lk 20,2), εἰλάμην etc.

334   **490.** Not only the « Attic declension » but also the « Attic future » tends to be eliminated; thus the normal Greek ναός is used instead of the Attic νεώς, καλέσω instead of καλῶ, and even verbs in -ίζω tend to form futures in -ίσω instead of the usual -ιῶ.

335   **491.** New and regular forms of aorist (in -α) arise in place of (or alongside) more « difficult » aorists (especially in -ov), e. g. ἔζησα instead of ἔβιων, ἧξα for ἤγαγον, ἡμάρτησα alongside ἥμαρτον, ἐγάμησα for ἔγημα; while on the other hand new futures are found corresponding to aorists in -ov, such as φάγομαι from ἔφαγον, ἐλῶ from εἶλον. In the passive aorist there is a preference for forms without -θ-, e. g. ἐκρύβην is preferred to ἐκρύφθην, ἠνοίγην to ἀνεῴχθην.

336   **492.** Verbs in -αίνω and -αίρω keep the α (i. e. the change ᾱ > η was now inoperative and analogy was stronger for α than for η), e. g. ἐκάθαρα, ἐκέρδανα.

337   **493.** Verbs in -(νυ)μι are much more rarely used, and give place to synonyms or new formations in -ω, e. g. κορέννυμι is replaced by χορτάζω, ἀνοίγνυμι by ἀνοίγω, διασκεδάννυμι by διασκορπίζω. From ἔστηκα a new verb is formed, στήκω.

338   **494.** It remains to sum up the chief points in which **Semitic influence** has been mentioned: the suspended nominative (25-27, 31); εἰς in the predicate instead of nominative or accusative (32,70); nominative for vocative (33); the «Hebrew» genitive (40f); υἱός with the genitive (42-44); the «sociative» and instrumental use of ἐν (116-119); positive for comparative or superlative (144-146); the frequency of pronouns (196); the repetition of a pronoun after a relative (201-203); the proleptic use of pronouns (204); ψυχή for the reflexive (208); the periphrastic conjugation (360-362); «graphic» participles (363-366); ἀποκριθεὶς εἶπεν (366f); λέγων (368); participle for infinitive absolute (369); the temporal use of ἐν τῷ with the infinitive (387-390); πρὸς τό with the infinitive in the sense «... - ing» (391f); εἰ in oaths (400) and in direct questions (401); the ambiguity of the Aramaic particle di (423-429); emphatic negations (445f); the frequency of coordination (450-457).

These are the chief elements which give the gospels their Semitic tinge and thus give us a glimpse as from afar into the world which was that of Our Lord Jesus Christ.

INDEX OF SCRIPTURE TEXTS

Old Testament

New Testament

N. B. - More important texts are given in heavier print

Index of Scripture Texts

Index of Scripture Texts

	NUM.		NUM.		NUM.
5,25	.. 116	9,3	.. 201	14,7	.. 278
5,30	.. 268	9,5	.. 366[n]	14,8	.. 289[n]
5,36	.. 242	9,6	.. 348	14,9	.. 247
5,38[f]	. 97	9,8	.. 235	14,12	.. 363
5,41	.. 34	9,8	.. 470	14,14	.. 343
5,42	.. 62	9,11	.. 222	14,19	.. 10
6,5	.. 470	9,12	.. 459	14,21	... 440[n]
6,7	.. 157	9,19	.. 35	14,28	.. 231
6,9	.. 394	9,28	.. 222	14,31	.. 444[n]
6,9	.. 15[n]	9,35	.. 280	14,36	.. 34
6,14	.. 285	9,37	.. 445	14,36	.. 221
6,16	.. 285	9,42	.. 311	14,39	.. 261
6,17	.. 205	9,45	.. 145	14,40	.. 348
6,17	.. 290	10,3[f]	. 458	14,54	.. 232
6,17	.. 363[n]	10,5	.. 98	14,61	.. 229
6,22	.. 205	10,20	.. 235	15,6D	. 358
6,22	.. 485	10,26	.. 459	15,23	.. 273
6,23[f]	. 234	10,45	.. 91	15,25	.. 455δ
6,26	.. 460	10,51	.. 415	15,44	.. 404
6,31	.. 198	11,1	.. 97	16,6	.. 231
6,36	.. 349	11,12	.. 88	16,9	.. 7
6,39	.. 157	11,13	.. 403	16,13	.. 133
6,41	.. 271	11,14	.. 366[n]	16,14	.. 151
6,45	.. 276	11,19	.. 336	23,3	.. 175
6,55	.. 346[n]	11,19	.. 358	23,37	.. 175
6,56	.. 336	11,24	.. 460	24,25	.. 35
6,56[a]	. 358	11,28	.. 410		
6,56[b]	. 358	11,29	.. 155	Lk 1,3	.. 394
7,13	.. 16	12,12	.. 455β	1,9[f]	. 393
7,19	.. 15	12,14	.. 416	1,13	.. 246
7,25	.. 201	12,15	.. 415	1,13	.. 280
7,25	.. 485	12,19	.. 415	1,15	.. 181[n]
7,27	.. 485	12,28	.. 12	1,15	.. 444
7,37	.. 7[n]	12,35	.. 366[n]	1,15	.. 473
8,1[f]	. 348	12,36[f]	. 205	1,20	.. 92
8,2	.. 54	12,40	.. 15[n]	1,20	.. 219
8,17	.. 447	13,2	.. 444	1,26[f]	. 90
8,18[f]	. 51	13,19	.. 202	1,29	.. 339
8,19	.. 11	13,22	.. 352	1,29	.. 346
8,24	.. 268	13,31	.. 444[n]	1,30	.. 246
8,25	.. 455γ	14,1	.. 3	1,31	.. 280
8,35	.. 336	14,1	.. 5	1,33	.. 124
8,38	.. 205	14,1	.. 117	1,35	.. 181[n]
9,1	.. 268	14,2	.. 344	1,35	.. 283

Index of Scripture Texts

Index of Scripture Texts

Index of Scripture Texts

APPENDIX

selected chapters analysed according to the numbers of this grammar

1) Mt 5-7

5,1 ἰδών 261; τὸ ὄρος 167; καθίσαντος αὐτοῦ 49; 2 ἀνοίξας 363; τὸ στόμα αὐτοῦ 196; ἐδίδασκεν 270; λέγων 368; 3 τῷ πνεύματι 53; 4 αὐτοί 198; 5 τὴν γῆν 67; 6 τὴν δικαιοσύνην 67; χορτασθήσονται 493; 8 τῇ καρδίᾳ 53; 10 δεδιωγμένοι 285; 11 ὅταν 335; πᾶν πονηρόν 188; 13 τὸ ἅλας 487; ἐάν 320; ἐν τίνι 119; 14 τὸ φῶς 172 ss; ἐπάνω 83; 15 καίουσιν 1; αὐτὸν 196; καὶ 455; 16 λαμψάτω 250 s; ἔμπροσθεν 83; 17 μὴ νομίσητε 246; ὅτι 380; ἦλθον καταλῦσαι 381; 18 ἕως ἄν 335; ἐν... οὐ μή 446. 444; ἀπό 80; 19 ὃς ἐάν 335; 20 οὐ μή 444; 21 ἠκούσατε 253; ἐρρέθη 286; οὐ φονεύσεις 443; 22 τῷ ἀδελφῷ αὐτοῦ 196; εἰς τὴν γέενναν 99; γέενναν τοῦ πυρός 40 s; 23 προσφέρῃς 242; σου 208 s; 24 ἔμπροσθεν 83; πρῶτον 151; ἐλθών 365; 25 ἴσθι εὐνοῶν 360; ἕως ὅτου 17; βληθήσῃ 340; 26 οὐ μή 444; ἕως ἄν 335; 27 ἠκούσατε 253; ἐρρέθη 286; οὐ μοιχεύσεις 443; 28 πᾶς ὁ βλέπων 188 ss; πρὸς τὸ ἐπιθυμῆσαι 391; ἐπιθυμῆσαι αὐτήν 67 s; αὐτοῦ 196 s; 29 εἰ 309; σου 208; ἀπό σου 208; ἵνα 408; 31 ὃς ἄν 335; αὐτοῦ 196; 32 παρεκτός 83; ἀπολελυμένην 285; γαμήσῃ 491; 33 ἠκούσατε 253; ἐρρέθη 286; οὐκ ἐπιορκήσεις, ἀποδώσεις δέ 443; σου 208; 34 ἐν τῷ οὐρανῷ 119; 35 εἰς 116 (?); 36 σου 196; μὴ ὀμόσῃς 246; δύνασαι 488; 38 ἀντί 91; 39 ὅστις 25. 215; σου 196; στρέψον 242; τὴν ἄλλην 153; 40 κριθῆναι 229; αὐτῷ 25; 42 τῷ αἰτοῦντι δός 49; 43 cfr. v. 21; 44 ἀγαπᾶτε 242; ὑμῶν 195; 45 ὅτι 424; βρέχει 482; 46 ἐάν 320; ἔχετε 278; 48 ὑμεῖς 198.

6,1 προσέχετε 242. 247; ὑμῶν 196; ποιεῖν 227; ἔμπροσθεν 83; 2 ὅταν 335; ποιῇς 227; μὴ σαλπίσῃς 246 s; ἔμπροσθέν σου 83. 208; 3 ποιοῦντος 48; τί ποιεῖ 346; σου 196; 5 οὐκ ἔσεσθε 443; ὃ τι 424; ἑστῶτες 363; 6 ὅταν προσεύχῃ 335; 7 μὴ βαττολογήσητε 254; ὅτι 380; ἐν τῇ πολυλογίᾳ 119; 8 μὴ ὁμοιωθῆτε 254. 246; ὧν 221; πρὸ τοῦ αἰτῆσαι 382; 9 ὑμεῖς 198; πάτερ 35; ἁγιασθήτω, ἐλθέτω, γενηθήτω etc 255; 10 ἐν οὐρανῷ 182 s; 11 δός 242; 12 ἀφήκαμεν 488; 13 ἀπό 87; 14 ἐάν 320 s; μὴ γίνεσθε 246; 17 ἄλειψαί σου 232 s; νίψαι 232; 19 μὴ θησαυρίζετε 246 s; ὑμῖν 208; ὅπου 215 ss; 20 θησαυρίζετε 242; ἐν οὐρανῷ 183; ὅπου 215 ss; 22 ὁ ὀφθαλμός 172; ἐάν 320; 23 εἰ 309; 24 δυσί 487; τὸν ἕνα 153; 25 μὴ μεριμνᾶτε 246 s; τί φάγητε 348; 26 ἐμβλέψατε 242; ὅτι 424; καὶ 455; μᾶλλον διαφέρετε 481; 27 ἐξ ὑμῶν 68; αὐτοῦ 196; 28 καταμάθετε 242; 29 ἐν 116; περιεβάλετο 232. 253; 30 εἰ δέ 309; 32 ἐπιζητοῦσιν 484; 33 πρῶτον 151; 34 μὴ μεριμνήσητε 246. 254; ἑαυτῆς 208.

181

Appendix

7,1 μὴ κρίνετε 246 s; 2 ἐν ᾧ κρίματι 119; 4 ἐρεῖς 356; 5 ὑποκριτά 35; πρῶτον 151; σου 208; 6 μὴ δῶτε 246, 254; ἔμπροσθεν 83; χοίρων 482; ἐν 119; αὐτῶν 196; στραφέντες 363; 9 τί.ς ἐξ ὑμῶν 68; ἐπιδώσει 484; 11 εἰ οὖν 309; οἴδατε 488; ὑμῶν 196; 12 ὅσα ἐάν 335; ἵνα 406 s; ποιεῖτε αὐτοῖς 52; 13 εἰσέλθατε 489; 15 οἵτινες 215 ss; προβάτων 482; 16 ἐπιγνώσεσθε 484; συλλέγουσιν 1; 24 πᾶς ὅστις 215; ὅστις² 215; ᾠκοδόμησεν 256; 25 προσέπεσαν 489; τεθεμελίωτο 290; 28 ἐγένετο... ἐξεπλήσσοντο 389ⁿ ; 29 ἦν διδάσκων 360.

2) Mk 5-7

5,2 ἐξελθόντος αὐτοῦ 48; ἐν πνεύματι 116 ss; 4 διὰ τὸ αὐτὸν δεδέσθαι 382; 5 ἦν κράζων 360; 6 ἀπὸ μακρόθεν 481; 7 κράξας λέγει 262; μή με βασανίσῃς 246; 8 ἔλεγεν γάρ 290; τὸ πνεῦμα 34; 9 ἐπηρώτα 272 s; 10 παρεκάλει 272 s; ἵνα 408; ἔξω 83; 11 ἦν... βοσκομένη 360; χοίρων 482; 12 παρεκάλεσαν 252; λέγοντες 368; 13 ἐπνίγοντο 270; 14 εἰς 99; ἦλθον ἰδεῖν 282; τί ἐστιν 346; 15 τὸν δαιμονιζόμενον 371; τὸν ἐσχηκότα 289; 16 ἐγένετο 290; 17 ἀπό 87; 18 ἐμβαίνοντος αὐτοῦ 49; παρεκάλει 272; ἵνα 408; 19 ἀφῆκεν 482; σου 196. 208; πεποίηκεν καὶ ἠλέησεν 288; 20 ἐποίησεν 290; ἐθαύμαζον 270; 21 καὶ 457 s; ἐν τῷ πλοίῳ 165. 22 εἷς 155; ὀνόματι 53; 23 λέγων 368; ἵνα 415; ζήσῃ 250; 25 ἐν ῥύσει 116; 26 μηδὲν 440; 28 ἐάν 320 s; 29 ἡ πηγὴ τοῦ αἵματος αὐτῆς 41; ἴαται 285; 30 ἐπιγνούς 484; ἐξ αὐτοῦ 210; 31 ἔλεγον 270; καὶ λέγεις 455 32 περιεβλέπετο 270; 33 γέγονεν 285; 34 θυγάτηρ 34; σέσωκεν 285; εἰς εἰρήνην 99; 36 μὴ φοβοῦ 246; πίστευε 242; ἀφῆκεν 482; μετ' αὐτοῦ 208; 38 εἰς 97; 40 ὅπου 215; ἦν ἀνακαίμενον 360; 41 τὸ κοράσιον 34; 42 περιεπάτει 375; ἐξέστησαν ἐκστάσει 60 s; 43 ἵνα 408 s.

6,1 πατρίδα αὐτοῦ 196; 3 τῆς Μαρίας 165; πρὸς ἡμᾶς 85; ἐσκανδαλίζοντο 270; 4 συγγενεῦσιν 487; 7 δύο δύο 157; ἐδίδου 271; 8 ἵνα 408; εἰς 99; 9 ὑποδεδεμένους 393; σανδάλια 72; μὴ ἐνδύσησθε 246; 10 ὅπου ἐάν 335; ἕως ἄν 335; 11 ὃς ἄν 335; ὑποκάτω 83, ὑμῶν 196; 12 ἵνα 408; ἐκήρυξαν 253 but ἐξέβαλλον, ἤλειφον, ἐθεράπευον 270; 14 ἔλεγον (l, v.) 1; ἐγήγερται 285; αἱ δυνάμεις 165; 16 ἠγέρθη 288; 17 αὐτὸς ὁ Ἡρῴδης 204 s; ἐκράτησεν 250. 290; ἐγάμησεν 491; 20 συνετήρει 270. 484; 21 δεῖπνον ἐποίησεν 227; 22 εἰσελθούσης τῆς θυγατρός 48 s; αὐτῆς τῆς Ἡρῳδιάδος 204 s; αἴτησον 234; ὃ ἐάν 335; 23 ἡμίσους 487; 24 αἰτήσωμαι 234; 25 λέγουσα 368; ἵνα 408; 26 διὰ τοὺς ὅρκους καὶ τοὺς ἀνακειμένους 460; 27 ἐνέγκαι 489; 28 τῇ μητρὶ αὐτῆς 196; 29 ἔθηκαν 488; 30 ἐποίησαν 290; 31 ὑμεῖς αὐτοί 198; 33 ἐπέγνωσαν 484; ἐκεῖ 28; 34 μὴ ἔχοντα 440; 35 προσελθόντες ἔλεγον 363 s; 36 ἀπελθόντες 363; τί 221; φάγωσιν 348; 37 ἀποκριθεὶς εἶπεν 366; ἀπελθόντες 363; δώσωμεν 491; 38 ἰχθύας 487; 39 συμπόσια συμπόσια 157; 40 ἀνέπεσαν 489; 41 ἐδίδου 271; 42 ἐχορτάσθησαν 493; 43 ἀπό 80; 45 ἐμβῆναι καὶ προάγειν 276; 46 τὸ ὄρος 165; ἀπῆλθεν προσεύξασθαι 282; 49 ἔδοξαν ὅτι 380; ἐστιν 346; 50 μὴ φοβεῖσθε 246 s; 51 λίαν ἐκπερισσοῦ 481; 52 συνῆκαν 488; 54 ἐπιγνόντες 484; 55 περιέδραμον 253; ὅτι ἐστίν 346; 56 ὅπου ἂν εἰσεπορεύετο 358; ἵνα 408; ὅσοι ἂν ἥψαντο 358.

7,1 ἀπό 87; 2 τοὺς ἄρτους 165; 10 θανάτῳ τελευτάτω 60 s; 11 ἐάν 320 s; 6 ἐάν

Appendix

335 s; 13 ἤ 16; παρεδώκατε 488; 15 τὰ κοινοῦντα 171 s; 17 εἰς οἶκον 183; ἐπηρώτων 272; 19 καθαρίζων 15; 24 ἀναστὰς ἀπῆλθεν 363; 25 ἧς τὸ θυγάτριον αὐτῆς 201 ss; 26 τῷ γένει 53; ἠρώτα 272; ἵνα 408; αὐτῆς 196; 27 πρῶτον 152; χορτασθῆναι 482. 493; 28 ἀπεκρίθη 229; ὑποκάτω 83; ἀπό 80; 29 ἐξελήλυθεν 285; 30 ἐπὶ τὴν 123; 31 εἰς 97; 32 ἵνα 408; 33 αὐτοῦ¹ 196; 35 ἠνοίγησαν 491; 36 ἵνα 408; μᾶλλον περισσότερον 481; 37 ὑπερπερισσῶς 484; πεποίηκεν 285.

3) Lk 1-2

1,2 παρέδοσαν 488; 3 παρηκολουθηκότι 285; 4 περὶ ὧν κατηχήθης λόγων 18; 5 ὀνόματι 53; 6 ἐναντίον 83; ταῖς 184; 7 προβεβηκότες ἦσαν 360; 8 ἐγένετο... Ἔλαχεν 389¹; ἐν τῷ ἱερατεύειν αὐτόν 387; ἔναντι 83; 9 τοῦ θυμιᾶσαι 382 s; εἰσελθὼν 393; 10 ἦν προσευχόμενον 360; 13 μὴ φοβοῦ 246; 15 ἐνώπιον 83; οὐ μὴ 444; 17 καὶ αὐτὸς 199; ἐνώπιον 83; ἐν 119; πνεύματι καὶ δυνάμει 'Ηλίου 183; ἐν φρονήσει 99 (?); 19 ἀποκριθεὶς 229; 20 ἔσῃ σιωπῶν 360; μὴ δυνάμενος 440; ἄχρι ἧς ἡμέρας 18; ἀνθ' ὧν 92; οἵτινες 215 ss; εἰς 99; 21 ἦν προσδοκῶν 360; ἐν τῷ χρονίζειν 387 (?); 22 ἐπέγνωσαν 484; ἑώρακεν 285; καὶ αὐτὸς 199; ἦν διανεύων 360; 25 πεποίηκεν 285; 26 ἀπό 90; 28 κεχαριτωμένη 285; εὐλογημένη ἐν γυναιξὶν 146; 29 εἴη 357; 30 μὴ φοβοῦ 246; 33 ἐπὶ 124; 35 ἀποκριθεὶς 229·; τὸ γεννώμενον 278; 36 συγγενίς 487; γήρει 487; 37 οὐ... πᾶν 446; 39 ἀναστᾶσα 363; 41 ἐγένετο ἐσκίρτησεν 389¹; 42 εὐλογημένη ἐν γυναιξὶν 146; 43 τοῦτο ἵνα 410; 45 ἡ πιστεύσασα 34; ὅτι 416; λελαλημένοις παρὰ Κυρίου 90; 47 ἠγαλλίασεν 260; 49 καὶ ἅγιον τὸ ὄνομα αὐτοῦ 455 ε; 51 ἐν βραχίονι 119; 54 μνησθῆναι 391 s; 55 τῷ 'Αβραάμ 55 s; 57 αὐτὴν 393; 59 ἦλθον περιτεμεῖν 282; ἐκάλουν 273; 60 ἀποκριθεῖσα 229; 61 εἶπαν 489; 62 τί ἂν θέλοι 356; ἔγραψεν λέγων 368; 73 ὅρκον ὃν 19; τοῦ δοῦναι 383 ss; 76 ἐνώπιον 83; 77 τοῦ δοῦναι 383. 391; ἐν ἀφέσει 99; 78 ἐν οἷς 116; 79 ἐπιφᾶναι 492; τοῦ κατευθῦναι 385.

2,1 ἐγένετο... ἐξῆλθεν 389¹; 2 πρώτη 152; 3 ἐπορεύοντο ἀπογράφεσθαι 282; 4 εἰς πόλιν Δαυὶδ 183; ἥτις 215; διὰ τὸ εἶναι 382; αὐτόν 196; ἐξ οἴκου 183; 6 ἐγένετο... ἐπλήσθησαν 389¹; ἐν τῷ εἶναι αὐτούς 387; 7 αὐτῆς 196; 8 ἦσαν ἀγραυλοῦντες 360; 9 δόξα Κυρίου 183; ἐφοβήθησαν φόβον μέγαν 62, 10 μὴ φοβεῖσθε 246; ἥτις 215 s; 11 πόλει Δαυὶδ 183; 12 τοῦτο 213; 15 ἐγένετο... ἐλάλουν 389¹; ἕως Βηθλεέμ 83; 16 ἦλθον σπεύσαντες 261; 19 συνετήρει 270. 484; αὐτῆς 196; 20 οἷς 16; 21 τοῦ περιτεμεῖν 383; καὶ 457; πρὸ τοῦ 382; 22 ἀνήγαγον παραστῆσαι 282; ἐν νόμῳ Κυρίου 183; 23 διανοῖγον 493; 24 τοῦ δοῦναι 385; 25 παράκλησιν τοῦ 'Ισραήλ 183; 26 ἦν κεχρηματισμένον 360; μὴ 440; πρὶν ἢ ἄν 481; ἐν τῷ πνεύματι 116; 27 ἐν τῷ εἰσαγαγεῖν 390; αὐτούς 196. 393; 31 κατὰ πρόσωπον 83; 33 ἦν... θαυμάζοντες 360; 34 ἀντιλεγόμενον 283; 36 ζήσασα 491; μετ' ἀνδρός 183; 39 ἑαυτῶν 208; 41 ἐπορεύοντο 270; 42 ἀναβαινόντων αὐτῶν 276; 43 ἐν τῷ ὑποστρέφειν 390; 44 ἀνεζήτουν 484; συγγενεῦσιν 487; 45 μὴ 440; 46 ἐγένετο εὗρον 389¹; 47 ἐπὶ τῇ συνέσει καὶ ταῖς ἀποκρίσεσιν 184; 48 τέκνον 35; 49 ᾔδειτε 488; 50 συνῆκαν 488; ἐλάλησεν 290 (?); 51 ἦν ὑποτασσόμενος 360; διετήρει 270. 484; αὐτῆς 196.

Appendix

4) Jo 15

15,1 ἐγώ 196; ἡ ἄμπελος 172; 2 πᾶν κλῆμα... αἴρει αὐτό 25 (?); 3 ὑμεῖς 198; λελάληκα 285; 4 μείνατε 253 s; ἐν 116 (?); ἑαυτοῦ 208; ἐάν 320 s. 325; 6 ἐβλήθη 257; ἔξω 83; ἐξηράνθη 257; συνάγουσιν 1; 7 ἐὰν μείνητε 320; ὃ ἐὰν 335; αἰτήσασθε 242; 8 ἵνα 410; φέρητε καὶ γενήσεσθε 343; 9 ἠγάπησα 253; μείνατε 253; 10 τετήρηκα 285; 12 ἵνα 410; 13 ἵνα 410; αὐτοῦ 196; 15 τί ποιεῖ 346; εἴρηκα 285; 16 ὑμεῖς 198; ὃ τι ἄν 335; 19 εἰ... ἦτε 313 ss; 22 οὐκ εἴχοσαν 319; 25 ἵνα πληρωθῇ 415; 26 ὅταν 335.

5) Acts 17

17, 1 τὴν Ἀμφίπολιν 165; ὅπου 217; 2 ἐπί 70; ἀπό 87; 3 διανοίγων 493; ὁ Χριστός 172; 4 τινὲς ἐξ 68; 5 ἐθορύβουν 270; ἐζήτουν 270; 7 ὑποδέδεχται 285; ἀπέναντι 83; ἕτερον 153; 10 διὰ νυκτός 115; οἵτινες 215 s; 11 οἵτινες 215; εἰ ἔχοι 346; 12 ἐξ αὐτῶν 68; ἐπίστευσαν 250; 13 κατηγγέλη 491; 14 ἕως 83; 16 ἐκδεχομένου 48; παρωξύνετο 270; 18 τί ἂν θέλοι 346; 21 ἕτερον 153; καινότερον 147; 22 σταθείς 229 ss; δεισιδαιμονεστέρους 147; 23 ἐπεγέγραπτο 290; 24 ναοῖς 487; 26 τὲ 466; πᾶν ἔθνος ἀνθρώπων 191; παντὸς προσώπου τῆς γῆς 191; 27 εἰ ψηλαφήσειαν 346 s; 28 τῶν καθ᾽ ὑμᾶς ποιητῶν 130 s; εἰρήκασιν 285; 31 ᾧ ὥρισεν 16; ἐν ἀνδρί 119; παρασχών 261; 32 εἶπαν 489; ἀκουσόμεθα 226; 34 ἐπίστευσαν 250; ὀνόματι 53; ἕτεροι 153.

6) Philippians

1,1 ἐν Χριστῷ 118; 2 ἀπό 90; 4 τὴν (δέησιν) 165; ποιούμενος 227; 5 ἐπί 126; εἰς 107; 6 τοῦτο 213; ἄχρι ἡμέρας 183; 7 ὑπὲρ 96; διὰ τό 382, ἐν τῇ ἀπολογίᾳ καὶ βεβαιώσει 184; 8 ἐν σπλάγχνοις Χριστοῦ 119 (?); 9 τοῦτο 213; ἐπιγνώσει 484; πάσῃ αἰσθήσει 188 s; 10 εἰς τό 382; ὑμᾶς 393; εἰς 107; ἡμέραν Χριστοῦ 183; 12 ἀδελφοί 35; τὰ κατ᾽ ἐμέ 130; ἐλήλυθεν 285; 13 ὥστε 350; ἐν Χριστῷ 118; 14 τοὺς πλείονας 147; περισσοτέρως 147; 15 διὰ φθόνον 112 s; 18 ἐν τούτῳ 119; 19 διὰ τῆς ὑμῶν δεήσεως καὶ ἐπιχορηγίας τοῦ πνεύματος 184 s; 20 ἐν πάσῃ παρρησίᾳ 188 s; 21 τὸ ζῆν 173; 22 εἰ 309; καὶ τί 459; αἱρήσομαι 341; 23 τὴν ἐπιθυμίαν 165; εἰς τό 382; μᾶλλον κρεῖσσον 481; 25 τοῦτο 213; 26 ἐν ἐμοί 119; 27 πολιτεύεσθε 242; στήκετε 493; 28 ἥτις 215; ἀπό 90; 29 τό 382.

2,1 εἴ τις σπλάγχα 9; 2 ἵνα 415 (?); τὸ ἕν 170; 3 τῇ ταπεινοφροσύνῃ 170; ἑαυτῶν 209; 4 ἑτέρων 153; 5 ὃ καὶ ἐν Χριστῷ 463; 6 τὸ εἶναι 382; 7 λαβών 262 (?); σχήματι 53; 8 θανάτου δέ 467; 9 διὸ καὶ 462; 11 εἰς δόξαν 108; 12 ἑαυτῶν 209; 13 ἐνεργῶν τὸ θέλειν 66; 15 ἐν κόσμῳ 183; 16 εἰς ἡμέραν 107 ss; ἔδραμον 253; 17 ἐπὶ τῇ θ.κ.λ. 184; 20 ὅστις 215 ss; 21 οἱ πάντες 188 ss; 22 εἰς τὸ εὐαγγέλιον 107 ss; 23 ὡς ἄν 335; 26 ἐπιποθῶν ἦν 360; 28 σπουδαιοτέρως 147 s; 30 ὅτι 421; τῇ ψυχῇ 53.

3,3 ἡ περιτομή 172 ss; 7 ἅτινα 215; ἥγημαι 285; 9 ἐμὴν δικαιοσύνην 180; 10 τοῦ γνῶναι 383. 386; 11 εἴ πως 403; ἐξανάστασιν 484; 12 εἰ καί 403; ἐφ᾽ ᾧ 126; 13 ἐμαυ-

Appendix

τόν 208; 15 εἴ τι 303 ss; 19 ὁ θεὸς ἡ κοιλία 174; 20 ἐξ οὗ καὶ 463; ἀπεκδεχόμεθα 484; 21 τὸ σῶμα τῆς ταπεινώσεως ἡμῶν 41; τῷ σώματι τῆς δόξης αὐτοῦ 41; αὐτόν 393; αὐτῷ 210.

4,1 στήκετε 493; 3 αἵτινες 215 ss; συνήθλησαν 253; ἐν βίβλῳ ζωῆς 183; 4 ἐρῶ 340 s; 5 πᾶσιν ἀνθρώποις 188 ss; 6 μηδὲν μεριμνᾶτε 246; πρός 97; 7 πάντα νοῦν 188 ss; 9 ἃ καί 463 (?); 10 τό... φρονεῖν 382; ἐφ' ᾧ 126; 12 μεμύημαι 285; 15 οἴδατε 488; ἀπό 87; 17 ἐπιζητῶ 484; 18 πεπλήρωμαι 285; 21 πάντα ἅγιον 188 ss.

7) Iª ad Thessalonicensis

1,2 μνείαν ποιούμενοι 227; 3 ἔμπροσθεν 83; 5 ὅτι 416; εἰς ὑμᾶς 51; ἐν λόγῳ 116 ss; ἐν πνεύματι ἁγίῳ 181; οἴδατε 488; ἐγενήθημεν 230; 8 ἐν τῇ Μακεδονίᾳ καὶ Ἀχαίᾳ 184 s; ἐν παντὶ τόπῳ...ἐξελήλυθεν 99; 10 τὸν ῥυόμενον 371 s.

2,1 οἴδατε 488; γέγονεν 285. 289; 2 ἐπαρρησιασάμεθα 250 s; ἐν πολλῷ ἀγῶνι 116 ss; 3 ἐν δόλῳ 116 ss; 4 δεδοκιμάσμεθα 285; 5 ἐν λόγῳ 116; κολακείας 40; ἐγενήθημεν 230; 8 τὰς ἑαυτῶν ψυχάς 209; 9 πρὸς τό 383; εἰς ὑμᾶς 51; 11 ὡς πατὴρ τέκνα 171; 12 εἰς τὸ περιπατεῖν 382; τοῦ καλοῦντος 371 s; τὴν βασιλείαν καὶ δόξαν 184 s; 13 λόγον ἀκοῆς 183; ὃς καὶ ἐνεργεῖται 66. 463; 15 ἐκδιωξάντων 484; 16 εἰς τό 382; 17 περισσοτέρως 147; ἐν 116; 19 ἔμπροσθεν 83; 20 ἡ δόξα 174;

3,2 εἰς τό 382; ὑπέρ 96; 4 οἴδατε 488; πρὸς ὑμᾶς 99; οἴδατε 488; 5 μή πως ἐπείρασεν... καί... γένηται 344; 6 ἀφ' ὑμῶν 90; 8 ἐὰν στήκετε 331 s. 493; 9 ἀνταποδοῦνται 484; ἔμπροσθεν 83; 10 ὑπερεκπερισσοῦ 484; εἰς τὸ ἰδεῖν 382; 11 κατευθύναι 355; 12 πλεονάσαι 355; 13 εἰς τὸ στηρίξαι 382; ἔμπροσθεν 83;

4,1 ἵνα 408; 2 οἴδατε 488; ἐδώκαμεν 488; 3 τοῦτο 213; ἀπό 80; 4 ἐν ἁγιασμῷ 116; 5 τὰ μὴ εἰδότα 440; 6 προείπαμεν 489; 7 ἐπὶ ἀκαθαρσίᾳ 129; ἐν ἁγιασμῷ 129. 99; 8 τὸν καὶ διδόντα 371; εἰς ὑμᾶς 51; 11 παρηγγείλαμεν 253; 13 μὴ ἔχοντες 440; 14 εἰ 303 ss; 15 ἐν λόγῳ Κυρίου 119. 183; οὐ μή 444; 16 ἐν κελεύσματι 116; πρῶτον 151; 18 ἐν 119.

5,2 οἴδατε 488; 3 ὅταν 335; ἡ ὠδίν 487; οὐ μή 444; 4 ἵνα 409; 5 υἱοὶ φωτός 42 s; 10 περί 96; ζήσωμεν 491; 11 εἰς τὸν ἕνα 156; 12 τοὺς κοπιῶντας καὶ προισταμένους 184 s; 13 ὑπερεκπερισσοῦ 484; ἐν ἑαυτοῖς 209; 22 ἀπό 80; 23 ἁγιάσαι 355; ἐν 99; 24 ὁ καλῶν 371 s; 25 περί 96; 26 ἐν φιλήματι 116; 27 ἐνορκίζω 484.

S̲B̲ SUBSIDIA BIBLICA

40 MONAGHAN Christopher J.
A source critical Edition of the Gospels of Matthew and Luke in Greek and English

2010 • pp. 186+198
ISBN 978-88-7653-652-6 • € 45,00
2 VOLL.

39 ZERWICK Maximilian - GROSVENOR Mary
A Grammatical Analysis of the Greek New Testament

2010 • pp. 796
ISBN 978-88-7653-651-9 • € 40,00
Edizione con nuova introduzione
a cura di James Swetnam, S.J.

38 ZERWICK Maximilian
Il Greco del Nuovo Testamento
Traduzione e adattamento alla lingua italiana
di **Gastone Boscolo**

2010 • pp. 354
ISBN 978-88-7653-648-9 • € 25,00
*In coedizione con
la Facoltà Teologica del Triveneto*

37 ALETTI Jean-Noël
God's Justice in Romans
Keys for interpreting the Epistle to the Romans

2010 • pp. 448
ISBN 978-88-7653-647-2 • € 27,00

Finito di stampare nel mese di maggio 2011
presso Arti Grafiche Srl - Pomezia (Rm)